# BLOOMSBURY
# ESSENTIAL GUIDE FOR
# READING GROUPS

## Susan Osborne

BLOOMSBURY

First published in 2002 by
Bloomsbury Publishing Plc
38 Soho Square
London W1D 3HB

www.bloomsbury.com
Bloomsbury's website offers booklovers the chance to participate
in the literary life online. Its features include advice
for reading groups, a research centre and a writers' area.
Most books mentioned in the *Bloomsbury Essential Guide for Reading Groups,*
where still in print, may be purchased through the website.

A CIP entry for this book is available from the British Library.

ISBN 0 7475 7211 9

10 9 8 7 6 5 4 3 2 1

All papers used by Bloomsbury Publishing are natural,
recyclable products made from wood grown in
well-managed forests. The manufacturing processes
conform to the environmental regulations of the
country of origin.

Typeset by Hewer Text Ltd, Edinburgh
Printed and bound in Great Britain by Clays Ltd, St Ives plc

# CONTENTS

# Introduction

Over the past few years reading groups have found themselves in the limelight. Newspapers have devoted acres of space to them, American publishers waited with bated breath for the announcement of Oprah Winfrey's monthly book club choice (and mourned its passing) and Radio 4 has set up its own monthly book club hosted by broadcasting veteran Jim Naughtie. In a fascinating survey of over 350 groups, Jenny Hartley, author of *Reading Groups*, estimates that there are now over 50,000 reading groups in the UK alone. But as she also points out, such groups are hardly a new phenomenon. Many have been running for decades with one, the Bristol Friendly Reading Society, dating as far back as 1799.

All sorts of people join reading groups, sharing their enjoyment of books in discussions which can add both insight and pleasure to the experience of reading while developing friendships that can last a lifetime. A prospect to fill any avid but sociable reader with enthusiasm. But if you can't find an existing group to join, how do you set about creating your own group and, once established, how do you keep discussions lively and focused? This book is designed to help you achieve both. It offers advice on setting up a new group, resource listings to help you find information on books and reading groups plus readers' guides for fifty of the best books I have read over the last five years, all of which have provoked spirited discussion with friends and family.

The book is divided into six sections.

### Setting up and Running a Reading Group, page 3
This section offers advice on starting your own group, from laying the foundations at the first meeting to leading a discussion.

### Synopses, page 7
The fifty books covered in detail in the Readers' Guides are briefly summarized in this section to help you choose your next book for discussion.

### Themes, page 21
In this section, the fifty books are listed thematically, with a brief introduction to each theme, so that your group can match interests to book choice.

### Readers' Guides, page 27
Central to the book is a set of Readers' Guides for fifty books (forty novels and ten non-fiction), all of which come heartily recommended and all of which provide more than enough meat to stimulate a lively discussion. Each guide includes a detailed summary of the book, a brief author biography, discussion points to spark debate and a set of titles for further reading that pick up on the book's general themes.

### Resources, page 145
This section lists details of books, magazines, websites and other resources which should help you choose books for discussion, track down background information and find out about literary events. Online reading groups are also included in this section.

## Suggested Further Reading, page 149

In addition to the suggestions included in the Readers' Guides, this section includes a further fifty books which I've thoroughly enjoyed and would highly recommend for discussion.

# Setting Up and Running a Reading Group

### What is a reading group?

Reading groups range from a few friends who meet regularly to talk about particular books that they have all read, often sharing a few bottles of wine to ease the discussion along, to more formal meetings, perhaps led by an academic, which explore literature in a more structured manner, rather like a seminar. Over the past few years reading groups have increased in popularity as people meet to share their enjoyment, turning a solitary pleasure into a stimulating social experience. Many reading group members find their reading becomes more rewarding, more focused, and that an exchange of ideas with others can provide a whole new slant on a book. Readers in a rut can find themselves introduced to books they would never have thought of reading, thanks to the recommendations of other group members, while new readers can find a route into what can seem to the uninitiated to be a bewilderingly vast array of books.

### I'd like to join a reading group. How do I go about finding one?

If you're interested in a formal discussion group with a strong element of guidance, you could try your local university. Most universities run extramural studies programmes and they will either send you a prospectus or you should be able to pick one up from your local library.

If you want a more informal approach it's worth putting the word out among friends and colleagues. Reading groups are very much word-of-mouth outfits and you may find that you already know someone involved in a group who would welcome a new member with a fresh point of view. There may even be a reading group where you work. Some companies such as Orange, who sponsor the Orange Prize for Fiction, are particularly sympathetic to workplace reading groups. Many libraries have also begun to set up their own reading groups or keep contact details for local groups. Some bookshops keep information on local groups and a few play host to reading groups on their premises. If you have access to the Internet, try posting a message on a reading group notice board. The publishers Bloomsbury and Penguin, for instance, both have notice boards in the reading groups sections of their websites which are designed to put groups in touch with each other. You could also consider joining an online group. Although many of these are US-based, there are several UK websites, including *The Guardian*, which host reading groups (see page 146 in the Resources section for website details).

If you can't find a group to join, why not set up one of your own? You may find that your enquiries have sparked some interest and you already have the makings of a group.

### How do I start my own group?

The easiest way to start a reading group is to begin with friends and acquaintances, but there are advantages to setting up from scratch with people you don't know. Discussions can be a little predictable among close friends and you are more likely to be introduced to new books by someone from outside your circle. If you do decide to form a new group, community notice boards, particularly in libraries and bookshops, are good places to advertise for members. If you have a staff room at work, perhaps you could put up a notice there. You may be able to negotiate the use of a meeting room. Lunch hours could become much more stimulating than just a sandwich and a rehash of last night's soaps.

Depending on the response, you'll need to decide how many members you want. Around six to ten seems to work well. Too many people and not everyone gets a say, particularly bashful types; too few, and it's hard to get a range of views on which to base an interesting discussion.

## The first meeting – laying the foundations
*Planning the meeting*
As you're the one taking the initiative, you'll also be the one who organizes the group's first meeting. If you don't know each other, you may feel more comfortable holding the meeting in a public place rather than your own home. Wherever you choose will need to be reasonably quiet so that you can have a relaxed discussion without shouting to make yourself heard. Ask people to bring their diaries so that you can get some idea of what sort of schedule to set up. You'll need to plan what needs to be discussed, allowing enough time so that you can cover everything and give everyone a chance to speak.

*What do you all want to get out of the group?*
This is a good starting point for the first meeting and a quick canvassing of opinion round the table should get everyone talking. Do you want an in-depth analysis of the text or do you just want to exchange opinions about the story? Is everyone happy for members to attend if they have not had time to read the book? You may want to stress that this should only happen occasionally, otherwise you could find you have lots of spectators and not much discussion. Many of us read hurriedly when we can find the time, but a book to be discussed needs more attention and you might want to agree some guidelines for preparation. Members might find it helpful to make a few notes as they read, for instance, jotting down themes that they want to discuss or particular passages in the book that catch their imagination. You may also want to back up your discussions with a bit of research. Some groups use the Internet or the library to find out about the author or the context of the book before they discuss it.

*Who should lead discussions?*
Most reading groups appoint a member to lead meetings to give the discussion a structure and to make sure that everyone who wants to speak gets the opportunity. You may want to avoid one person bearing sole responsibility for running the group. One solution, if you're meeting in each other's homes, is for the host to run the session. Another might be for the member who chose the book to lead the discussion. Whatever you decide, the leader will need to know well in advance of the meeting so that he or she can prepare.

*Where will you meet?*
Lots of groups take it in turns to meet in each other's homes, or you could hire a room at your local university, village hall or even a pub. Some groups like the idea of meeting on neutral ground, which gets around any pressure that hosts might feel in their own homes.

*How often should you meet?*
You will want to make sure that everyone's schedule is catered for as far as possible. Monthly meetings will probably suit most people's available free time

and will also mean they have time to prepare. It's a good idea to make sure that there's a list of everyone's names and phone numbers so that members can be informed of any changes to arrangements. Make sure that people are aware that they should let the discussion leader know if they can't make it; if you have a small group, two missing members might mean you want to reschedule.

### How long should meetings last?

Two hours should probably be enough for a lively discussion but if you all know each other well, you might think about setting aside some time for socializing. Gossip is deliciously seductive, so much so that if you don't set a time limit, you may never get around to discussing the book.

### Refreshments

Do you want to have food and drink and, if so, how will this be organized? You may want a simple bring-a-bottle-and-a-little-something-to-eat policy, or arrange a kitty. For some groups, food and drink are essential elements, almost as important as discussing the book – and sometimes more so. Many American reading group websites even include a monthly recipe. Some members, however, may feel pressured by having to provide an enticing spread when it's their turn to host the group. Deciding a policy from the outset will avoid any embarrassment and establish the group's priorities.

## Choosing books

Perhaps the easiest way to decide which book to discuss next is for each member to take a turn in nominating a title. Some people will already have favourites in mind. Other sources of information include paperback sections of the weekend papers; booksellers and librarians, who are usually happy to recommend books; Radio 4's excellent book coverage which includes its own book club; and the legions of book-related sites on the Internet. Listed in the Resources section, you'll find details of magazines, websites and books that offer lots of information and recommendations for books to discuss.

It's worth making your choice some time in advance of the discussion. Books can go out of print which means bookshops will not be able to order them from the publishers, or it may simply be that your local bookshop doesn't usually keep more than one or two copies of the book you've chosen. Although bookshops will order in extra copies for you, it can take up to two or three weeks for the book to arrive.

As a starting point, this book contains fifty Readers' Guides for books which contain lots of meat for a lively discussion. Each guide includes a detailed synopsis together with a list of suggested further reading on a similar theme. All the books are available in paperback and should be reasonably easy to obtain. To help you choose, each book has been briefly summarized in the Synopses section and you'll find a thematic listing of the books beginning on page 21. A further set of fifty highly recommended books can be found in the Suggested Further Reading section at the back of the book.

## Leading a discussion

This may seem a bit daunting but it's really a case of getting the discussion going and making sure that everyone gets a chance to have their say if they want to. You may feel more comfortable leading the discussion if you have prepared a list of points as you read the book, noting its main themes, points at which particular characters change or significant passages. Each of the fifty Readers' Guides in this book lists a set of questions designed to get a discussion off the ground. This should help in the group's early days when members may be a little shy with each other.

You could start the ball rolling by asking the person who nominated the book to summarize it briefly and state its main themes, then ask each of the other members what they thought. Try to make sure that any questions you ask the group are open-ended. 'Did you like the book?' could result in 'Yes' or 'No' followed by silence, but 'What did you think of the book?' is an opening for discussion. Try to get people to explain their reactions. If they didn't like the book, what was it that didn't work for them? Was it a particular character? The writer's style? Equally, if they liked the book, what worked for them? Look out for anyone who seems to be bursting with something to say but having trouble finding a gap in the conversation. Try to avoid pushing more bashful members into the full glare of the spotlight. Round-the-table questions are one way to give quieter members a chance to have a say if they want it.

Opinions may differ radically but there aren't any rights and wrongs in the interpretation of a book. We all bring our own experience to reading. Everyone's opinion is valid, as long as it's expressed tactfully, but you probably want people to explain their conclusions and compare them with other members' ideas. Don't worry if the discussion gets a little heated; it's a good sign that people are thoroughly involved. As long as everyone's opinion is taken seriously, you should all part as friends.

Before you go home, check that everyone knows when and where the next meeting will be and what the next book choice is. If you're rotating the leadership, make sure that the next leader knows.

### Some discussion points
- What were your reactions to the book and why?
- What were the book's main themes? What message is the author trying to get across?
- Does the book tackle any contemporary or universal issues such as racism, war or the environment and, if so, how did it change or clarify your views?
- Who are the main characters? How much do they change over the course of the book and why?
- Did particular characters engage your sympathy? Were there others that you couldn't stand? What are your reasons?
- Did the book have any relevance to your own experience and, if so, in what way?
- Are aspects of the author's life reflected in the book and, if so, what are they?
- Did the book remind you of anything else you've read?
- How important is the author's use of language? Were there particular passages that caught your imagination and, if so, why?
- Was there anything unusual about the structure of the book and, if so, was it effective? Perhaps the book was in letter form or composed mainly of flashbacks.
- If you nominated the book, have your feelings about it been changed by exchanging views with others?

# Synopses

This section is designed to help you choose a book for discussion from the fifty Readers' Guides. Split into fiction and non-fiction then listed A–Z by author, each books has a brief synopsis together with a page reference to the Readers' Guide. If you would prefer to choose a book by theme, see page 21.

## FICTION

### *The Romance Reader* by Pearl Abraham, page 31

As the eldest daughter of a rabbi struggling to establish his first synagogue, Rachel is expected to observe and exemplify the many exacting standards of the Hasidic community to which she belongs. As she enters adolescence, she finds herself chafing at these strictures. She loves to swim but is forbidden to wear a bathing suit in public; she wants to dress attractively but must conform to a strict dress code designed to hide her body; most of all, she loves the trashy romantic novels which give her a fascinating, if misleading, glimpse of a world which is forbidden to her. She would dearly love to escape but does not know how. As she faces the prospect of an arranged marriage she realizes that, perverse as it might seem, marriage may be the only way to attain the freedom she craves.

### *Behind the Scenes at the Museum* by Kate Atkinson, page 32

This is the story of Ruby Lennox told in her own voice from the moment of her conception, heralded by a few grunts and groans from her father while her mother feigns sleep. Ruby and her family live above their pet shop in the shadow of York Minster. Theirs is a story of humdrum family life in the 50s – endless housework, minor peccadilloes on the part of Ruby's father, homework, weddings and funerals. Interwoven with Ruby's story is that of her great-grandmother, her grandmother, uncles, aunts and cousins as they struggle through two world wars. But there are small gaps in the narrative, hints of something amiss. Family secrets, long hidden, begin to surface – one so devastating that it overwhelms Ruby even as it explains so much that has been puzzling in her life.

### *Alias Grace* by Margaret Atwood, page 34

*Alias Grace* is a fictionalized account of a celebrated Canadian murder case. Two immigrant servants, James McDermott and sixteen-year-old Grace Marks, were accused of the brutal slayings of their employer and his mistress in 1843. Both of the accused were found guilty and sentenced to death but Grace's sentence was commuted. She was confined to Kingston Penitentiary, spending some time in the Toronto mental asylum. In Margaret Atwood's novel, Simon Jordan, a young psychologist, is asked to assess Grace's mental state so that an application for pardon may be made on the grounds of insanity. Dr Jordan listens to Grace's story with a mixture of disbelief and sympathy. As he draws her towards the day of the murders, an event which she claims not to remember, he grapples with the question that haunts the novel – is Grace an innocent victim of circumstance or a vicious murderer?

### *Eucalyptus* by Murray Bail, page 37

With his wife dead, his daughter Ellen away at school and no apparent need to make a living, Holland perfects his eucalyptus collection until he has over five hundred trees on his isolated New South Wales estate. When Ellen joins him, she passes her days walking, listening to her father's stories, occasionally yearning for city life. As she reaches marriageable age, Holland sets up a competition with Ellen's apparent acquiescence – the first man who names all his eucalypts will marry her. So begins a long parade of suitors beating a path to Holland's door, their imagination captured by stories of Ellen's beauty. Finally, one remains – Roy Cave, steeped in knowledge of eucalypts and little else. But Ellen has another suitor who appears on her daily walks, beguiling her with his storytelling. When it seems that Cave cannot fail, Ellen takes to her bed and it is left to the young storyteller to revive her with one last tale.

### *The Crow Road* by Iain Banks, page 39

When Prentice McHoan comes home from Glasgow University to attend his grandmother's funeral, he has more than the usual family troubles to confront or, preferably, avoid. There is the widening rift between him and his father, the unsolved mystery of his uncle Rory's disappearance, his infatuation with the lovely Verity, not to mention a burgeoning sibling rivalry with his brother, Lewis. When his father dies in a freak accident, their differences still unresolved, Prentice knows it's time to shape up. He learns to deal graciously, if painfully, with Lewis's successful career and the happiness he has found with Verity. But when his old friend Ashley uncovers some leads about his uncle Rory, Prentice cannot resist following them no matter how shocking the outcome or how dangerous the path.

### *The Voyage of the Narwhal* by Andrea Barrett, page 42

In 1855 Zeke Voorhees sets off on an ill-judged voyage in search of the remains of the great Franklin expedition to the Arctic. Accompanying him is his future brother-in-law Erasmus Darwin Wells, an amateur naturalist. As Zeke's enthusiasm transforms itself into a lonely despotic command of the voyage, Erasmus becomes more and more uneasy about the outcome of the adventure. When Zeke strikes out on his own, Erasmus has no option but to try to guide the crew of the *Narwhal*, much depleted by the hardships of facing a winter ill prepared, to safety. On his return, he finds himself estranged from his sister who blames him for leaving Zeke behind, and derided by the public for the failure of his mission. When Zeke returns with two Eskimos Erasmus is at first delighted and then appalled by his plan to stage a lecture tour featuring the Eskimos as exhibits.

### *Island Madness* by Tim Binding, page 44

It is 1943 and the Germans have suffered their first crushing defeat at Stalingrad. Far away in Nazi-occupied Guernsey, life goes on with its parties, love affairs and amateur dramatics. But when Isobel van Dielen, daughter of a wealthy construction magnate, is found murdered, the powder keg of resentment and suspicion that has been contained during the three years of Occupation is on the point of blowing. The Germans have taken up Occupation in every possible way – requisitioning houses, redeploying servants and, not least, monopolizing the sexual favours of every young woman with an eye to the main chance. As he goes about the unenviable task of solving the murder, Ned Luscombe, head of the local police force, begins to uncover the decadence and corruption of both occupying power and islanders alike.

### *Visible Worlds* by Marilyn Bowering, page 46

In 1960 Nate Bone, national football star and local hero, dies in a freak accident playing football in his hometown of Winnipeg. Nate held the key to the story which links three neighbouring families with Fika, a young woman who is using the full force of her will and endurance to cross the Arctic snows from Russia to Canada. When Albrecht finds a map of Siberia, dated 1951, in Nate's boot he immediately recognizes it as his twin brother's work. But Gerhard has been missing since 1945. Albrecht tells the story of the three families whose lives have become so entwined over two wars and a multitude of misfortunes that each has become a part of the other. Fighting for survival as she crosses the Polar ice cap, Fika tells her own story. As each narrative unfolds, small details coincide, family links become clear until, finally, Fika finds her way to safety and the two stories become one.

### *Wise Children* by Angela Carter, page 48

On her seventy-fifth birthday, Dora Chance sits down to write her memoirs. She and her twin are the illegitimate daughters of the renowned Shakespearean actor Sir Melchior Hazard, whose one-hundredth birthday is to be honoured at a magnificent party that evening. Both the Chances and the Hazards are show business to the core but while the Hazards are members of the theatrical aristocracy, the Chances were chorus girls. As Dora looks back over her life a tale unfolds of unacknowledged paternity, mistaken identities, twins at every turn, Shakespeare, Hollywood, music hall, discarded wives, glorious love and rollicking good times. Despite the social gulf that divides them and the refusal of Melchior to acknowledge the twins as his daughters, the paths of the Hazards and the Chances criss-cross throughout their lives until the glorious finale, worthy of a Shakespearean comedy, when all the players are assembled, identities revealed and more than a few home truths told.

### *The House of Sleep* by Jonathan Coe, page 50

In Ashdown, a university hall of residence, Sarah is about to break up with Gregory, fed up with being treated like his research subject rather than his lover. He is fascinated by her narcolepsy, a sleep disorder which occasionally results in dreams so vivid that she is convinced that they are real. Among the other residents, Robert, hopelessly in love with Sarah, looks on in mute despair as she becomes drawn into a relationship with a woman, while Terry is immersed in his obsession with cinema and his spectacular, fourteen-hour, Technicolor dreams. Twelve years later Terry, now chronically insomniac, hears that Ashdown has become a sleep disorder clinic. He books himself in and through a number of strange coincidences, finds himself reacquainted with his old housemates. With more than a touch of comedy, the intricately plotted narrative loops backwards and forwards through twelve years, spilling a multitude of clues at every turn, and neatly resolving every one of them.

### *Being Dead* by Jim Crace, page 52

On a beautiful afternoon a couple lies dead on a beach, their bodies bloody and battered. They have been married for almost thirty years and even in the throes of a violent death they appear devoted, as Joseph's hand is curved around Celice's shin. In acknowledgement of their death, Crace tells us that the novel is to be a 'quivering', a retelling of their lives in an expiation of grief in accordance with an ancient custom. So begins the narrative of Joseph and Celice's life from their first meeting and when they had made love for the first time on that same beach, to their brutal murders. Woven into their story are the details of what happens to their bodies as they lie undiscovered for six days on the deserted beach. Written in language that is graphic yet poetic, Crace makes the unbearable and the inevitable into something to be looked in the face.

### *A Home at the End of the World* by Michael Cunningham, page 54

When Jonathan Glover meets Bobby Morrow at high school, he is desperate to impress and falls more than a little in love. But what seems to be the essence of cool to Jonathan, is really the stunned, trance-like state of a young boy in deep shock, the result of an appalling tragedy. Bobby watched his brother die in his mother's arms after a freak accident and his mother died of an overdose shortly after. While the two boys experiment with sex and drugs, Jonathan's mother, Alice, realizes that Bobby desperately needs a family, and when Jonathan goes to university, Bobby stays behind with the Glovers. In New York, Jonathan meets Clare, spiky and eccentric, with whom he shares an apartment and fantasies of family life. When Bobby joins them, the family is almost complete and the birth of Rebecca makes it so. But the country idyll that they build for themselves in upstate New York is at best precarious and, finally, blown off course.

### *Talking to the Dead* by Helen Dunmore, page 56

Nina, going to help her sister Isabel after the difficult birth of her first child, finds Isabel, weak from the birth, caught up in a fearful love for her new son and in retreat from the rest of the world. Both Nina and Isabel's husband Richard are deeply concerned for her mental and physical welfare but eventually find themselves drawn into an obsessive affair. As the heat of the summer intensifies so do relationships within the household. Nina begins to remember scenes from her childhood with Isabel, in particular disturbing memories of their brother Colin, who died at three months supposedly of cot death. The pace of the narrative quickens as it works towards its shocking climax when Isabel goes missing.

### *Birdsong* by Sebastian Faulks, page 59

When Stephen Wraysford is sent to Amiens in 1910 to learn what he can of the French textile business, he finds himself obsessed with his host's wife. The couple begin an affair so passionate that it rocks both their lives. Six years later, Stephen is again in Picardy, fighting as an officer in the British army. Possessed by a seemingly invincible will to survive, he lives through some of the fiercest battles of the Western Front. Sixty years after the war, his granddaughter Elizabeth begins a journey into the past as she tries to understand both the grandfather she never knew and the terrible events which shaped his life. *Birdsong* tells the harrowing story of men who lived in conditions which are barely imaginable, witnessing the gruesome deaths of friends and enemies alike, trying to find ways to survive in a world fractured by one of the bloodiest wars of the twentieth century.

### *Cold Mountain* by Charles Frazier, page 61

Set in North Carolina during the American Civil War, *Cold Mountain* tells the story of Inman and Ada, separated at the beginning of a tentative love when Inman enlists in the Confederate army. Four years later, weary of a war whose brutality and bitterness have left him so changed that he hardly knows himself, Inman decides to leave his hospital bed and walk home to Cold Mountain where he hopes to find his sweetheart. His journey takes him through a country as changed as he is: farms in ruins, terrible poverty, lawlessness and degradation. At home, Ada's ladylike education has left her ill-equipped to run a farm or deal with the depredations of war. Her relationship with Ruby, a young woman well versed in the practicalities of life, has literally saved her from starvation. As Ada learns to master the skills she needs to survive so she, too, is irrevocably changed by the war.

### Sheer Blue Bliss by Lesley Glaister, page 63

Connie Benson is plucked from the isolation of her Norfolk home when a retrospective exhibition of her work is mounted at the National Portrait Gallery in London. The centrepiece of the exhibition is the final portrait of her lover, Patrick Mount, who mysteriously disappeared in 1965. Mount was an eccentric whose theory of the Seven Steps to Bliss has sunk into obscurity. But for Tony, a disturbed and beautiful young man who stalks Connie in the hope of finding the key to the elixir of bliss, Mount is still a heroic figure. Tony is haunted by his obsession, desperately trying to suppress his dark and fearful childhood memories, which are in stark contrast to the startlingly vivid memories which Connie summons of her own youth. Their narratives are interwoven as each draws inexorably towards the other until the two merge in a gripping dénouement.

### Disobedience by Jane Hamilton, page 65

When seventeen-year-old Henry Shaw stumbles upon an email correspondence that reveals his mother's passionate affair, all the certainties of his life are thrown into question. Unable to resist his electronic eavesdropping, Henry's emotional confusion spills over into his own first love affair and continues to haunt the adult Henry as he looks back, a decade later, over the year of his mother's infidelity. Meanwhile, Elvira, Henry's sister, strides around wearing the regimental uniform of a nineteenth-century drummer boy, obsessed with re-enacting Civil War battles – much to her mother's horror and her father's delight. Elvira's ambitions to take part in a re-enactment at the historic site of Shiloh are shattered when she is violently unmasked and her gender revealed. It is this traumatic event that pulls the family back together as both parents, each in their own way, come to the defence of their beleaguered daughter.

### Stones From the River by Ursula Hegi, page 67

Trudi Montag is a *zwerg*, a dwarf, living in the small German town of Burgdorf and struggling to bridge the gulf between the way she sees herself and the way others see her. Burgdorf is engaged in its own struggle as it tries to deal with the crushing defeat of the First World War and ever-worsening economic conditions. As Trudi becomes an adult, a target for the insecurities and prejudices of those around her, she empathizes with the humiliations inflicted upon her Jewish neighbours when the newly established Nazi regime begins to flex its muscles. At great risk to themselves, Trudi and her father provide a hiding place for Jews, friends and strangers alike. When the war is finally over, the people of Burgdorf are faced with the shame and guilt, not only of a second defeat, but also of the atrocities of the Holocaust and the implications of their own part in it.

### Empress of the Splendid Season by Oscar Hijuelos, page 70

Lydia is a Cuban cleaning lady living in New York with her family, just about getting by. Anyone who passes her on the street might think of her, if they notice her at all, as just another dowdy drudge. But Lydia has a very different view of herself. After a terrible quarrel with her father when she was sixteen, she left the trappings of a well-to-do family in Cuba but has never relinquished her sense of superiority. Married to Raul, a waiter struck down by a heart attack at the age of forty-one, Lydia has had to go back to work. From her ambitions for her children, her cherished memories of her youthful beauty and vibrant sexuality, to her tentative feelings of friendship for one of her kindly employers, and the uncovering of the secrets of others, Oscar Hijuelos tells Lydia's story through a series of closely linked vignettes.

### Animal Dreams by Barbara Kingsolver, page 72

Adrift in her own life, Codi Noline returns to the small community of Grace, Arizona, to take care of her father with his worsening dementia. She feels an outsider in Grace, yet everyone seems to know and welcome her. Lonely and missing her sister who has gone to help the struggling farmers of Nicaragua, Codi finds solace with her old high school friend, Emelina, and in her job as a science teacher. Her relationship with Loyd Peregrina, a Native American, awakens her to a new way of looking at the natural world. When she and her students discover the extent to which the local mining company has contaminated the river, she is shocked into action, enlisting the help of the matriarchs of the Stitch and Bitch Club to raise funds to combat the company. As Codi opens up to the community she comes to a hard-won realization both of her own place in the world and of the things which are ultimately important in her life.

### The Vintner's Luck by Elizabeth Knox, page 74

This is the tale of Sobran Jodeau and Xas, the angel into whose arms he quite literally falls one midsummer night. When the two decide to share a bottle of wine and exchange news on the anniversary of their first meeting, a relationship begins that will span fifty-five years, intensifying as each year passes. Life in Sobran's village in Burgundy goes on, its small tragedies, marriages and affairs punctuated by the turbulent years of the Napoleonic Wars. The murders of two young girls remain unsolved for many years until Sobran thinks he has found the key to the crimes. His family continues to burgeon and his wine to improve. His friendship with the mistress of the neighbouring château provides the villagers with fuel for speculation, as does his strange behaviour on a certain midsummer evening every year. But when one day Xas arrives unannounced and terribly injured, the relationship between angel and man changes irrevocably.

### Charming Billy by Alice McDermott, page 76

When Billy Lynch's family and friends adjourn to a bar in the Bronx after his funeral it's a time for affectionate reminiscing. Billy was someone that everyone loved; a romantic and poetic figure who left an impression on all who met him. But Billy's death was far from romantic. He died an alcoholic – passed out on the street like a tramp. His life had been marked by heartbreak and many who knew him were convinced that he drank to ease the pain of the loss of his sweetheart many years ago. His devoted cousin, Dennis, came to his aid at any time of the day or night. But it is only after Billy's funeral that Dennis tells his daughter the truth behind the legend of Billy's sweetheart and the lie that was at the heart of his friendship with Billy.

### *Brightness Falls* by Jay McInerney, page 78

Corrine and Russell are a glittering New York couple, in love with each other and pursuing successful careers in a world where anything seems possible if you are young, bright and fearless. To their friends, they epitomize the perfect marriage but when Russell becomes caught up in an audacious plan to take over the publishing company in which he is the rising editorial star, things begin to fall apart. The adrenaline-fuelled atmosphere of the deal begins to take its toll on both Russell and Corrine, just as the excesses of the 1980s have taken their toll on many others in New York City, from their close friend Jeff, now in detox, to the homeless crack addicts on every street corner. With the knowledge gained from her job as a stockbroker, Corrine begins to realize that the heady days of the rising Dow must surely come to an end. The reckoning finally comes on 19 October 1987 when the bubble bursts with the Wall Street crash.

### *The Orchard on Fire* by Shena Mackay, page 80

In 1953 eight-year-old April Harlency's parents escape from their gloomy Streatham pub to take over the running of the Copper Kettle tea rooms in a small village in Kent. When April meets Ruby, they become best friends, forming an exclusive alliance against the rest of the world. Ruby, a little too in love with adventure, valiantly contends with her bullying parents while fiercely protecting April against the inevitable teasing which any newcomer suffers. While her parents struggle with their new business, April tries to cope with the unwelcome and unhealthy attentions of the seemingly respectable Mr Greenidge. Seeking refuge in their camp, writing letters in invisible ink and calling to each other with their secret signal, April and Ruby cement a friendship that seems unassailable. Told through April's voice, *The Orchard on Fire* vividly evokes a rural childhood in the 1950s.

### *Remembering Babylon* by David Malouf, page 82

On a sweltering day in the mid-nineteenth century, a strange and ragged figure dances out of the Australian bush and into the lives of a small group of white settlers. Gemmy Fairley has spent almost sixteen years living with aborigines. At first his eccentricities are greeted with the amusement of novelty but in time the settlement becomes riven with suspicion. As the settlers attempt to impose their own kind of order on an environment which they perceive as hostile, many of them find Gemmy's presence both unsettling and threatening. Where do the loyalties of this man, who is white like them but seems to have more in common with aborigines, lie? As Gemmy tries to find a place for himself in the community, friendships are strained to breaking point, brutality begins to surface but one family finds a new way to look at the world.

### *Fugitive Pieces* by Anne Michaels, page 85

Athos Roussos discovers a mud-covered boy while excavating an archaeological site in Poland, and takes the child home to the Greek island of Zakynthos. Seven-year-old Jakob Beer has escaped the Nazis, forced to listen to the cries of his parents as they were murdered while he lay hidden in a closet. Athos nourishes Jakob with knowledge and words, applying balm to the wounds inflicted by such devastating loss. After the war they move to Toronto but when his beloved mentor dies and his brief marriage fails, Jakob returns to Greece to work as a translator and write poetry. When he meets Michaela, the possibility of happiness finally becomes a reality only to be snuffed out by a traffic accident. After Jakob's death

Ben, the child of concentration camp survivors, sets out in search of Jakob's journals. Written in richly poetic language and studded with striking images, *Fugitive Pieces* is profound meditation upon the nature of loss, love and the healing power of words.

### *Ingenious Pain* by Andrew Miller, page 87

Conceived on an icy night in the middle of the eighteenth century, the result of an adulterous coupling with a stranger, James Dyer is a strange child whose inability to feel physical or emotional pain marks him out. When his family are all but wiped out by smallpox his adventures begin. He attaches himself to a quack show, is abducted and kept in a rich man's house as a curiosity, acts as an assistant to a ship's physician and, later, becomes a brilliant but supremely arrogant surgeon in fashionable Bath. When scandal ruins his practice he joins the race to St Petersburg to inoculate the Empress of Russia against smallpox. En route he meets his nemesis – a strange woman whose miraculous powers give him the gift of pain. From here the road to redemption leads through madness and eventually to a modicum of peace before he dies, aged thirty-three, in a small West Country village.

### *The World Below* by Sue Miller, page 89

Fifty-two years old, twice divorced, the mother of three grown-up children and holding down the kind of humdrum teaching job that she could do in her sleep, Catherine Hubbard has reached a stage in her life when it's time to take stock. When she learns that her aunt has bequeathed the old family home to her and her brother, she negotiates a sabbatical, rents out her San Francisco house, packs up and sets off east. After she stumbles upon her grandmother's diaries in the attic of the old Vermont house, Catherine begins to understand that the bedrock of security and love she had taken for granted in her grandparents' home was not as easily won as she had assumed. Woven through Catherine's reflections on her own life and tentative beginnings of something new, is her grandmother's story of sexual awakening, misunderstandings and the eventual negotiation of a marriage based on partnership.

### *The Boy in the Moon* by Kate O'Riordan, page 92

Julia and Brian have been married for ten years. Their marriage is full of cracks, papered over and held together by the presence of their seven-year-old son, Sam. On a visit to Brian's family in Ireland, tragedy strikes when Sam is killed in an accident while playing with his father. Stunned with grief, Julia leaves Brian to try to deal with his terrible guilt, made worse by childhood memories of the accidental death of his twin brother. When Julia decides to go to Ireland to stay with Brian's tyrannical father, Jeremiah, the decision seems perverse. At first, she finds an escape in routine and hard work, inching her way back to some sort of normality. But when she discovers a diary that unlocks the secrets of Brian's childhood fears, Julia begins to understand that Jeremiah has inflicted terrible pain on his children. When, eventually, Brian and Julia come together again, they share a new understanding and the beginnings of a hard-won peace.

### *The Magician's Assistant* by Ann Patchett, page 94

Sabine has loved her husband for over twenty years but this is no ordinary love story, for Parsifal is gay and Sabine has always known it. When Parsifal dies suddenly, she is devastated. Swaddling herself in her duvet in an attempt to hide from her grief, she is shocked out of it by her lawyer, who tells her that Parsifal's family want to get in touch with her. This would hardly be surprising except that he had long ago told Sabine that they had been killed in a car crash. Her suspicions are aroused but when she meets Dot and Bertie Fetters, they want nothing more than to envelop her in love and affection. At first unwillingly and then wholeheartedly, she is drawn into their world agreeing to leave her beloved Los Angeles for the snowy wastes of Nebraska. There she learns the shocking truth behind Parsifal's break with his family and finds love where she least expects it.

### In a Land of Plenty by Tim Pears, page 96

Charles Freeman is an ebullient, ambitious industrialist who knows exactly what he wants and generally achieves it. It's the early 1950s and although Britain is still experiencing post-war austerity, Charles's optimism is in tune with the times. He buys a mansion overlooking the small middle England town where he was born, marries his beautiful fiancée and transforms the family firm into a thriving business empire, fathering four children and acquiring an extended family along the way. But life is far from easy. He becomes estranged from one of his sons, his wife dies tragically, industrial relations are strained to breaking point and finally, out of step with the modern technological world, he is overtaken by a son-in-law whose ambition equals his own. From the early 1950s to the early 1990s, *In a Land of Plenty* documents a period of enormous social upheaval through the changing fortunes of the Freeman family and the small town they overlook.

### The Shipping News by Annie Proulx, page 98

Quoyle loses his wife in the most dreadful circumstances. For one thing she has already left him, having spent much of their married life in the arms of other men. She has also 'sold' their two daughters to a man whose intentions are all too clear. When the wreckage of her car is discovered, the address of their 'purchaser' is found on a receipt in her bag. Yet Quoyle continues to love her. When his long-lost aunt turns up, he finds himself accompanying her back to Newfoundland with his rescued daughters. Together they begin a new life back in the old family home, rubbing along as best they can. Battling with dreadful weather, his own demons and the eccentricities of the people around him, Quoyle manages to turn his life around until he has a new home, a new love and a measure of unexpected happiness.

### Promised Lands by Jane Rogers, page 100

On 2 January 1788 those aboard the First Fleet, laden with a cargo of convicts, catch their first glimpse of Australia. On board the *Supply*, William Dawes has the astronomical instruments with which he has been entrusted by the Board of Longitude to observe the Australian sky. This is the story of the settling of Sydney, built with the blood, sweat and tears of convicts. As Governor Phillip struggles to keep his unruly labour force under control, the seeds of a tragedy that will reverberate through the centuries are sown. Woven through this account are two twentieth-century narratives. Stephen is an idealist but his attempts to build an egalitarian school have ended in disaster and his marriage is in tatters. His wife, Olla, is convinced that their severely brain-damaged son has messianic powers, which he will reveal to the world when the time is right. These three narratives loop in and out of each other, reflecting and refracting history as each story unfolds.

### *The Reader* by Bernhard Schlink, page 102

At the age of fifteen, Michael Berg begins a passionate affair with Hanna, a thirty-six-year-old woman. At first the affair is purely physical but when Michael starts to read to his lover, it becomes an essential part of their lovemaking ritual. One day Hanna disappears from Michael's life. When he next sees her, he is a law student and she is on trial as an SS camp guard. Michael becomes obsessed by the trial, convinced that in loving Hanna he is also guilty. When she is convicted, he remains haunted by the unanswered questions that the trial has posed for him. His marriage fails after five years and he struggles to find some sort of meaning in his work. Eventually, he begins to record his favourite books for Hanna. When the prison governor writes to tell him that Hanna will soon be leaving prison, he visits her for the first, and last, time.

### *Larry's Party* by Carol Shields, page 105

Larry Weller's story unfolds year by year, starting in 1977 when he is twenty-seven and culminating twenty years later at the eponymous party. Larry is an average kind of guy; the only thing that really marks him out is his passion for mazes, a passion conceived at Hampton Court on honeymoon with his first wife, Dorrie. But despite his ordinariness he is never dull. As each year is recounted we are privy to the shifts in Larry's relationships with his family and friends, the amazed joyfulness of his love for both his wives, the pain of divorce and the changes in his work from florist to acclaimed maze maker. The centrepiece of the concluding year is the dinner party at which the many threads of Larry's life are satisfyingly pulled together.

### *The Last Time They Met* by Anita Shreve, page 107

When Linda Fallon and Thomas Janes meet at a literary festival in Toronto, it is the first time they have seen each other since the end of their affair in Nairobi, twenty-six years ago. Each had been in the kind of marriage that, although companionable enough, lacked the irresistible passion that drove Linda and Thomas to deception, betrayal and the brink of tragedy. But even this had not been the beginning. They had first met when they were seventeen-year-old students at a Massachusetts high school, their tentative relationship blown apart by a car crash. Using the unusual structure of telling their story in reverse chronological order, Anita Shreve peels back the layers of Linda's and Thomas's lives. Beginning in their fifties, the novel traces the intervening years, marked by the tragic loss of Thomas's child and the early death of Linda's husband, back to their heady days in Kenya and then to their high school years in the 1960s, edging towards a startling finale which turns the story upon its head.

### *The Death of Vishnu* by Manil Suri, page 109

Vishnu, the odd-job man in a Bombay apartment block, lies dying on the stairs of the building where he both lives and works. Tenants tiptoe around him, wondering whether he still needs his daily cup of tea and arguing about who should pay for the ambulance to take him to hospital, swatting away the nagging buzz of conscience as if it were an especially irritating fly. Meanwhile, life goes on. Food is prepared, card parties are disrupted amid accusations of cheating, elopements planned and a terrible violence ignited. Manil Suri weaves a bright thread of Hindu mythology through this tale of life in Bombay, as Vishnu's soul begins its ascent of the stairs, observing the lives of the tenants while sights, sounds and smells vividly evoke memories of his own life.

### *Anita and Me* by Meera Syal, page 112

When the local bad girl, Anita, suggests that she and nine-year-old Meena get together and form their own gang, Meena can hardly believe her luck. Daughter of the only Sikh family in the village of Tollington, she is more used to living in her own imagined world than being part of a gang. Soon she is adopting a Wolverhampton accent and doing everything else she can to fit in, while her parents and her legions of aunties fret over her misdemeanours. But Anita blows hot and cold, playing one friend off against another, flexing her popularity by manipulating others. When her mother gives birth to a little boy, Meena's grandmother comes over from India to help and Meena's view of her Punjabi roots begins to change. When the racism bubbling away below the community's surface boils over, Meena finally realizes that her friendship with Anita is not what she had hoped.

### *The Hundred Secret Senses* by Amy Tan, page 114

Just before Olivia Yee's father dies in a San Francisco hospital he drops a bombshell. He asks his American wife to send for the daughter he left behind in China many years ago. True to her fondness for lost causes, Olivia's mother does just that and five-year-old Olivia finds herself sharing her room with her adoring new sister, Kwan. Olivia grows up with Kwan's stories of ghosts, past lives, missionaries and mercenaries, which intrigue yet irritate her with their strangeness. Thirty years later, when Olivia's marriage falters, Kwan does all she can to get the couple back together again. When the three of them agree to visit China together, Olivia finds her mind opened to all sorts of Kwan's ideas to which she had kept it firmly closed for so many years.

### *Morality Play* by Barry Unsworth, page 116

In the late fourteenth century, the country stricken with plague, famine and the consequences of war with France, a priest joins a group of impoverished travelling players as they take the body of their dear friend to the nearest town for burial. To pay the burial fees they decide to put on a play. On hearing that a young woman is to be hanged for the murder of a twelve-year-old boy the company leader, desperate to augment their depleted funds, persuades the players to re-enact the murder. But as the players investigate the circumstances of the boy's death doubt is thrown on the young woman's guilt. Over the two days that they perform their play, digging deeper into the murky circumstances that surround the murder, they come close to revealing a shocking truth that puts them all in mortal danger.

## NON-FICTION
### *Paula* by Isabel Allende, page 121

In December 1991 Isabel Allende's daughter collapsed with an attack of porphyria, an inherited metabolic disorder. Shortly after her collapse, Paula fell into a coma from which she was to emerge, after many months, severely brain damaged. *Paula* is Isabel Allende's long, moving letter to her daughter, in which she sets out to tell her the story of their extraordinary family, starting with Paula's great-grandparents. In the telling, the book becomes a meditation on life and death, the chronicle of a mother's pain and her eventual acceptance of the death of her child, and a memorial to a beloved daughter. It also offers those who are already acquainted with Allende's fiction an insight into the events which both inspire and inform her novels.

### Midnight in the Garden of Good and Evil by John Berendt, page 123

John Berendt began taking regular weekend trips when he discovered that for the price of a good meal in New York he could spend three days exploring a new city. In 1982 he visited Savannah, Georgia, and was so taken with it that he spent the next eight years dividing his time between Savannah and New York. *Midnight in the Garden of Good and Evil* began as an account of a beautiful city, with a cast of characters ranging from mildly eccentric to downright bizarre, packed with amusing and interesting anecdotes. It took a rather different turn when, in May 1991, Jim Williams, a prominent figure in Savannah society, was accused of murdering his homosexual lover. Williams stood trial for murder four times, a record in the state of Georgia.

### Skating to Antarctica by Jenny Diski, page 125

*Skating to Antarctica* is Jenny Diski's account of her journey into the landscape of those legendary explorers Shackleton and Scott. It is coupled with her own exploration, perhaps equally brave, of a childhood which hardly bears contemplation, littered as it is with suicide attempts by both parents, sudden departures, the arrival of the bailiffs and the threat of eviction – all set against a continuous soundtrack of almost melodramatic histrionics. Diski sets off to Antarctica in search of oblivion, a pristine whiteout, but she finds a landscape which is often bleak, sometimes luminously beautiful, but rarely, if ever, monochrome. Leavened with a wry humour and astute observation, *Skating to Antarctica* is the story of two adventures – one into the Antarctic and one into a troubled past.

### Hidden Lives by Margaret Forster, page 127

Shortly after the death of Margaret Forster's grandmother, a mysterious woman knocked at the door claiming to be her daughter. No one in the family had ever heard of such a person. The woman was sent on her way and a discreet veil was drawn over the incident. When Forster's mother died it was as if a taboo had been lifted and Forster set about investigating who the unknown woman might be. She found a common enough answer; the woman was her grandmother's illegitimate child, a secret successfully hidden to preserve the family's respectability. But while *Hidden Lives* begins as an account of Forster's investigations, it soon becomes a searching portrait of a family during a period of great social change and, in particular, an account of Forster's relationship with her mother.

### Lost in Translation by Eva Hoffman, page 129

At the age of thirteen, when most of us are beginning to forge an identity for ourselves, Eva Hoffman was uprooted from her beloved Poland to emigrate with her family to Canada. Born in 1945, her early years had been spent in Cracow, surrounded by friends, thoroughly immersed in a way of life she knew and loved. When she arrived in Vancouver, she had not only to learn a new language but also a completely different set of cultural references, a long, slow process which set her at a distance from other young people. When she won a scholarship to a university in the United States, she began to find ways of belonging in her new world without rejecting the old. *Lost in Translation* is an eloquent account of Hoffman's experience of the dislocation of being caught between two cultures.

### An Unquiet Mind by Kay Redfield Jamison, page 131

*An Unquiet Mind* is Kay Redfield Jamison's courageous account of her experience of manic depression, an illness which afflicted her as a young student and has continued to do so for most of her adult life. She recalls the many and varied passions that overtook her as a child, echoing the manic enthusiasms that seized her father and eventually led to him losing his job. Drawn to medicine, Jamison became interested in psychology and eventually qualified as a psychiatrist. After years of struggling with vivid but destructive manic episodes followed by paralysing depressions, Jamison faced up to the truth of her illness and sought treatment. With the help of friends, family and lovers she came to accept the fading of her vibrant moods into a steadier life. Her insight into manic-depressive illness has led her to become one of the foremost American practitioners in its treatment.

### *The Drowned and the Saved* by Primo Levi, page 134

In *The Drowned and the Saved* Primo Levi attempts to understand the rationale behind the systematic atrocities committed by the Nazis at concentration camps such as Auschwitz and Treblinka. Drawing on his experiences in Auschwitz, where he was held for a year from January 1944 until the liberation of the camp by the Russians, Levi explores the painful issues of collaboration between prisoners and their guards, the shame felt by survivors and explains his premise that those who survived were not the true witnesses. Clearly, lucidly and without resorting to stereotypes, Levi discusses the ways in which prisoners were treated by their SS guards in an attempt to understand how such horrors could be perpetrated. *The Drowned and the Saved* was Primo Levi's final book before his death in 1987.

### *And When Did You Last See Your Father?* by Blake Morrison, page 137

Blake Morrison's moving and candid memoir of his father covers the few short weeks between his diagnosis with terminal cancer and his death. Morrison travelled to Yorkshire to stay with his mother in the village where he grew up, visiting his father at the hospital where he had spent so much time with his own patients as a GP. As his father's condition worsens Morrison contemplates their shared experiences, the intimacies and the irritations of their relationship. After his father's death Morrison questions the nature of the bond between them, articulately expressing the contradictions, frustrations, love and loss bound into the complicated relationships which many of us have with our parents when we become adults.

### *The Hacienda* by Lisa St Aubin de Terán, page 139

Married at the age of seventeen to a Venezuelan aristocrat turned bank robber who pursued her mercilessly, Lisa St Aubin de Terán spent the next two years travelling around Europe with her husband and his two compadres. When the Venezuelan government pardoned Don Jaime, St Aubin de Terán returned with him to his beloved but dilapidated *hacienda* where she was left to fend for herself with only two beagles, a vulture and a servant girl for company. As her husband became increasingly withdrawn, hardly ever present and often violent when he was, St Aubin de Terán began to doubt his sanity. With the help and support of the farm workers, she succeeded in taking control of the estate, getting it back on its feet and providing a home for her baby daughter. She remained in Venezuela for seven years until it became apparent that the lives of both her daughter and herself were in great danger as Jaime Terán lost his tenuous grip on his sanity.

### *Girlitude* by Emma Tennant, page 141

*Girlitude* covers the early years of Emma Tennant's life from 1955 when she became a debutante, to the birth of her second child in 1969. Taking the traditional route for both her generation and her class by entering the 'marriage market', Tennant departed from the straight and narrow with a turbulent and dangerous love affair, briefly getting back on track with her marriage to the novelist Henry Green's son, Sebastian Yorke, with whom she had a son. When that marriage ended, Tennant took up a semi-nomadic life, spending time in Paris, Rome, Greece and New York, frequently attracted to unsuitable men. A second hasty marriage to the satirist Christopher Booker ended in divorce. By this time the 1960s were in full swing and Tennant, now attached to the literary and artistic avant-garde, joined the 'revolution'. The book ends with a third marriage and the birth of her second child, a daughter.

# Themes

This section has been arranged thematically to help you choose a book which suits your particular interests. Each of the headings identifies a major theme which should provoke an interesting discussion. Books relevant to that theme are then listed, but because each book may have more than one theme, some titles appear under several different headings. The page number beside each title refers to the full Readers' Guide. You'll also find a brief summary of the book in the Synopses section.

## Childhood

Traditionally portrayed as a time of blissful innocence, childhood can often be beset by anxiety and puzzlement at the way in which adults behave. Several of the books listed here explore this theme. Shena Mackay's *The Orchard on Fire*, for example, is told through the voice of an eight-year-old, while Jenny Diski's autobiographical *Skating to Antarctica* explores the effects of a difficult childhood on adult life.

*Behind the Scenes at the Museum* by Kate Atkinson, page 32
*Skating to Antarctica* by Jenny Diski, page 125
*Talking to the Dead* by Helen Dunmore, page 56
*Stones From the River* by Ursula Hegi, page 67
*The Orchard on Fire* by Shena Mackay, page 80
*Anita and Me* by Meera Syal, page 112

## Growing up

For most of us, struggling through adolescence is an uncomfortable experience marked by embarrassment, awkwardness and an excruciating hypersensitivity. Some of the books listed below, such as Eva Hoffman's account of her painful uprooting from one culture to another and Pearl Abraham's tale of a young Hasidic girl's battle for independence, examine what it is to cope with this experience in the most straitening of circumstances. Others, such as Iain Banks's *The Crow Road* and Emma Tennant's *Girlitude*, explore a process of growing up that continues well past adolescence.

*The Romance Reader* by Pearl Abraham, page 31
*The Crow Road* by Iain Banks, page 39
*Disobedience* by Jane Hamilton, page 65
*Lost in Translation* by Eva Hoffman, page 129
*The World Below* by Sue Miller, page 89
*In a Land of Plenty* by Tim Pears, page 96
*The Hacienda* by Lisa St Aubin de Terán, page 139
*Girlitude* by Emma Tennant, page 141

## Growing older

Ageing has become something of a thorny issue in our youth-obsessed society. Angela Carter's feisty septuagenarian twins and Lesley Glaister's eccentric elderly artist are vivid depictions of characters who refuse to lie down and be quiet. In contrast, Oscar Hijuelos offers a tender portrayal of a vibrantly sexual woman gradually accepting fewer turned heads as she walks down the street.

*Wise Children* by Angela Carter, page 48
*Sheer Blue Bliss* by Lesley Glaister, page 63
*Empress of the Splendid Season* by Oscar Hijuelos, page 70
*Larry's Party* by Carol Shields, page 105
*The Last Time They Met* by Anita Shreve, page 107

## Death and how we cope with it

In a society where youth is prized and life expectancy seems constantly to be extended, death has become the great unmentionable – and yet we all have to face both our own death and the death of those we love. These books explore the ways in which we cope with death and bereavement, from Isabel Allende's family history written for a much-loved daughter struck down by a rare disease, to Blake Morrison's unflinching account of his father's last weeks.

*Paula* by Isabel Allende, page 121
*Being Dead* by Jim Crace, page 52
*And When Did You Last See Your Father?* by Blake Morrison, page 137
*The Boy in the Moon* by Kate O'Riordan, page 92
*The Magician's Assistant* by Ann Patchett, page 94

## Family life and the ties that bind

Our families, dysfunctional or otherwise, shape us all to some extent, and this theme is endlessly explored in fiction. The books listed below range from explorations of the effects of war, social upheaval and deception on family life to an attempt to create a family out of a group of friends in Michael Cunningham's *A Home at the End of the World*.

*Behind the Scenes at the Museum* by Kate Atkinson, page 32
*The Crow Road* by Iain Banks, page 39
*Visible Worlds* by Marilyn Bowering, page 46
*A Home at the End of the World* by Michael Cunningham, page 54
*Hidden Lives* by Margaret Forster, page 127
*Disobedience* by Jane Hamilton, page 65
*The World Below* by Sue Miller, page 89
*In a Land of Plenty* by Tim Pears, page 96
*Anita and Me* by Meera Syal, page 112
*The Hundred Secret Senses* by Amy Tan, page 114

## Friendship

From the vivid intensity of childhood friendship, exemplified by the 'us against the rest of the world' alliance between Ruby and April in *The Orchard on Fire*, to the curious, unearthly friendship that grows between man and angel in *The Vintner's Luck*, these novels explore the importance of relationships which can often be as strong as family ties.

*The Crow Road* by Iain Banks, page 39
*The Voyage of the Narwhal* by Andrea Barrett, page 42
*A Home at the End of the World* by Michael Cunningham, page 54
*The Vintner's Luck* by Elizabeth Knox, page 74
*Charming Billy* by Alice McDermott, page 76
*Brightness Falls* by Jay McInerney, page 78
*The Orchard on Fire* by Shena Mackay, page 80
*Anita and Me* by Meera Syal, page 112

## Love, marriage and infidelity

Although Anita Shreve's *The Last Time They Met* is perhaps the only book included here that could be described primarily as a love story, these novels all explore the complexities of love and marriage, while several, in particular Jane Hamilton's *Disobedience*, examine the painful effects of betrayal.

## Secrets

The revelation of a secret that has haunted a book since the first page makes for an immensely satisfying read, particularly in tightly plotted novels. Clues and hints are strewn through several of the books listed here, including Kate Atkinson's *Behind the Scenes at the Museum* and Jonathan Coe's *The House of Sleep*, so that you want to go back and read the book again, fitting each piece of the puzzle into place. Other books, such as Alice McDermott's *Charming Billy* and Margaret Forster's family history, *Hidden Lives*, explore the effect of long-concealed secrets.

## Historical

The books listed here are all set at a time far removed from our own, from the eighteenth century *Ingenious Pain*, teetering on the brink of the modern age, to Barry Unsworth's *Morality Play*, performed against the backdrop of a fourteenth-century England battle-scarred from the long wars with France and stricken with plague and famine.

## Colonialism and exploration

From the nineteenth-century Arctic explorers in *The Voyage of the Narwhal* to the settling of Sydney in *Promised Lands*, these four novels explore the repercussions of colonialism and exploration on both the indigenous peoples and those who set out to colonize their land.

## Different cultures

Each of these books is set against a different cultural backdrop, ranging from an Indian apartment block in Manil Suri's *The Death of Vishnu* to Barbara Kingsolver's *Animal Dreams,* which includes a depiction of a Native American community in Arizona. Some, such as *Anita and Me* and *The Hundred Secret Senses*, explore the conflict that can arise between different cultures and the feelings of dislocation that can result from being caught between two very different worlds.

## War and its aftermath

Each of these books is set against the backdrop of a very different war. Tim Binding explores the occupation of Guernsey in the Second World War, while Sebastian Faulks graphically describes the bloody struggles at the Western Front during the First World War and Charles Frazier charts two journeys during the American Civil War.

## The Holocaust and its aftermath

In different ways, these four books explore the effects of the cataclysmic events that helped to shape the second half of the twentieth century. They range from Primo Levi, himself a concentration camp survivor, attempting to understand how such atrocities came to be committed, to Ursula Hegi's novel, which depicts a small German town during the first half of the twentieth century, and traces its justification and shame at the horrors perpetrated by the Hitler regime.

## Crime

Strictly speaking, there are no crime novels in the traditional whodunit sense among the Readers' Guides included in this book. That said, all of the books listed below deal with a serious crime and its repercussions, and all include the attendant elements of mystery, suspense and plot.

## Disturbed mental states

Each of these books explores the effect of altered mental states, from Jonathan Coe's comic yet humane depiction of narcolepsy to Kay Redfield Jamison's brave account of her own experiences of manic depression.

## Eccentricity and the unusual

This list encompasses both Murray Bail's *Eucalyptus,* which adopts the traditional fairytale device in which a father sets an impossible task to be achieved by his daughter's suitors, and the intense friendship which develops between a man and an angel in Elizabeth Knox's *The Vintner's Luck*. Other books include a range of eccentric characters, from Amy Tan's Kwan, who sees the spirit world through her 'yin' eyes, to the cast of bizarre individuals that people the town of Savannah, Georgia, in *Midnight in the Garden of Good and Evil*.

## Humour

If you're in need of a little light relief, humour is a strong element running through all five of these books.

## The natural world
From Jim Crace's depiction of physical decay to Barbara Kingsolver's exploration of the gulf between those who have lived harmoniously with nature for centuries and those determined to profit from it, these four novels examine the relationship between human beings and the natural world.

## The role of women
Although this book includes no novels traditionally perceived as feminist, in the vein of Charlotte Perkins Gilman's *The Yellow Wallpaper* or Doris Lessing's *The Golden Notebook,* all the books listed below consider women's role in society, with some, such as Margaret Forster's family history, offering a clear insight into the way in which that role has changed over the years.

# Readers' Guides

The books for the fifty Readers' Guides in this section have been chosen with a lively discussion in mind. They range from novels such as Ursula Hegi's *Stones From the River,* a humane and profound attempt to understand how ordinary Germans dealt with the horrors of Hitler's regime, to Anita Shreve's *The Last Time They Met*, a delicately drawn love story with a twist. In the non-fiction section you'll find John Berendt's colourful travelogue and true crime story, *Midnight in the Garden of Good and Evil*, alongside Kay Redfield Jamison's moving and brave account of her experiences of manic depression, *An Unquiet Mind*.

Each of the guides includes a detailed synopsis, designed to act as an *aide-mémoire*, which also identifies the book's major themes. The synopsis is followed by a brief biography of the author, which, in some cases, may shed light on the writing of the book. The discussion points that follow the author biography are designed to get a discussion going rather than to be followed to the letter. Finally, the list of suggested further reading includes books by the same author, books by other authors that may share the same major themes or elements of the book's style, and books that may provide a useful context for the book should you want to research it further. Titles in **bold type** have their own entry in this book.

# FICTION

# The Romance Reader (1995)
## Pearl Abraham

### ABOUT THE BOOK

*The Romance Reader* is rich in cultural references, offering an insight into a way of life far removed from the Western mainstream, for the Benjamins are members of the minority Jewish sect known as Hasids (or *Chassids* in Yiddish). The central theme of the novel is Rachel's struggle for independence in a community depicted by Pearl Abraham as insular, inward-looking and regulated by strict rules. Reading books in English is forbidden but Rachel and her sister Leah have a passion for romantic novels which they devour in bed, late at night, and at any other opportunity they can snatch.

*The Romance Reader* spans the years of Rachel's adolescence, beginning with her mother's return from hospital after giving birth to her seventh child. Mrs Benjamin seems to be engaged in a perpetual battle for survival, managing on small amounts of money, caring for a large family, constantly aware that all eyes are upon them, while her husband, an idealist fired by faith and dreams, tries to establish a synagogue. The Benjamins live all year round on a summer estate in New York State. Their isolation as the family of a rabbi is exacerbated by the loneliness of the winter months when the summer residents return to the city.

A trip to Williamsburg, a Hasidic centre, shakes the family out of their isolation. Rachel's mother blossoms in the warmth of friendship and acceptance, her father's confidence is boosted by the respect he has won for his book and Rachel finds that she can almost leave her romances behind. There's so much to do in the city and for once she does not have to endure the stares and snide comments of outsiders.

The visit to Williamsburg marks a turning point for Mrs Benjamin and she insists that she be allowed to visit her family in Jerusalem. In her absence, Mr Benjamin takes to the road selling copies of his book to raise funds for his beloved synagogue, leaving Rachel in charge of the family. She and Leah seize the opportunity to grasp a sliver of independence. They train as lifeguards and find jobs for the summer. When Mrs Benjamin returns, Rachel's world begins to close in again. She is faced with her mother's shame at her wearing a swimming costume in public, but when Rachel saves a child's life, a small victory is secured.

As Rachel nears adulthood she knows that her parents will arrange a marriage for her. Her friend Elke's marriage becomes a love match almost in keeping with the romantic expectations raised by Rachel's novels. But another thought appears on Rachel's horizon: if she can be married, she can also be divorced and this might offer a means of escape. Her marriage to Israel Mittelman, dominated by Mr Benjamin's influence, can be seen as either a disaster or a triumph, for Rachel does indeed get divorced. She returns to her family home and we are left to ponder the central question of the book – can Rachel turn her back on her family and leave?

### ABOUT THE AUTHOR

Pearl Abraham grew up in a Hasidic community where Yiddish was the first language. She teaches creative writing at New York University and lives in New York City. *The Romance Reader* is her first novel.

**FOR DISCUSSION**

▷ Why do you think Pearl Abraham chose *The Romance Reader* as the title for the novel? Why is reading so important to Rachel? Why does she not read so much in Williamsburg? Rachel reads a very particular sort of book. How do you think this shapes her view of the world outside her community? She says: 'Novels are lies, lies upon lies.' What has brought her to this conclusion?

▷ What do you notice about the ways that men and women behave in the community? What are the differences? Do you think men or women have the harder life? Can you find examples to back up your ideas?

▷ What is your view of Rachel's mother? What made you come to these conclusions? What do you make of the relationship between Rachel's mother and her father? Why do you think their relationship is like this?

▷ Both Rachel and Leah have to be constantly on their guard against being found out – about reading books in English, about their lifeguard training. How do you think this affects them?

▷ Why is it so hard for Rachel to gain her independence? Do you think she should just turn her back on her family and leave? If not, why not? If so, why do you think she doesn't? She says: 'I won't be here, on their hands, for long.' Do you think she will leave? The last sentence reads: 'I wonder how high I will get before I fall.' What do you think she means by this?

▷ When Rachel and Elke talk about marriage. Elke has no qualms about her arranged marriage. What do you think of the position she takes? Rachel says: 'I think it's easier for Elke because she doesn't think about love in novels.' What questions do you think might be raised about the Western idea of romantic love as opposed to arranged marriages? Why do you think Rachel decides to marry Israel?

▷ Has anyone in the group any experience as part of a minority group? If so, how do you feel about Pearl Abraham's descriptions of the response of the outside world to the Hasids? Do Rachel's struggles ring any bells?

**SUGGESTED FURTHER READING**

FICTION

▶ *Oscar and Lucinda* by Peter Carey (1998)
▶ *My Name is Asher Lev* by Chaim Potok (1972)
▶ **Anita and Me by Meera Syal (1996)**
▶ *Oranges are Not the Only Fruit* by Jeanette Winterson (1985)

NON-FICTION

▶ **Lost in Translation by Eva Hoffman (1989)**
▶ *The Joys of Yiddish* by Leo Rosten (1970)
▶ *Boychiks in the Hood* by Robert Eisenberg (1995)

**OTHER BOOKS BY PEARL ABRAHAM**

▶ *Giving Up on America* (1998)

# Behind the Scenes at the Museum (1995)
## Kate Atkinson

**ABOUT THE BOOK**

*Behind the Scenes at the Museum* is a domestic novel with a twist. Its complicated structure draws together the many threads running through the lives of four generations of women, spilling clues and rattling skeletons kept firmly shut away in the closet. The novel requires close attention to appreciate the many hints dropped and turns taken but every loose end is satisfyingly tied in.

The novel opens in 1952. George arrives home from the pub, drunk but not incapable. His wife, Bunty, appears to be asleep but George is undeterred. Ruby is conceived and her narrative begins.

Bunty's ceaseless routine of shopping, housework, looking after Ruby's sisters and visiting her mother, is accompanied by an internal litany of complaint. Her well-founded suspicion about George's infidelity heads her agenda. Ruby grows up in the flat above the family pet shop with her sisters, the rebellious Patricia and pretty, over-indulged Gillian. From the start it's made clear that Gillian is not long for this world.

In 1956 Ruby is whisked away to stay with her Auntie Babs. She has no idea why, although she's sure that it's not a holiday. She has nightmares and begins to sleepwalk. When she returns, no explanation is offered but her mother seems even more unhappy. Eventually, having 'had enough' of the endless grind, Bunty takes off for a few weeks just before the family holiday. George arranges for the children to be taken to Whitby by 'Auntie' Doreen, warm, loving and one of his many girlfriends.

In 1959 Gillian is killed in a car accident. In her grief Bunty becomes increasingly dependent on tranquillizers. This catastrophe is followed by the Great Pet Shop Fire which results in a new home and a new business.

When Ruby is eleven, she discovers that her mother is having an affair with the next-door neighbour. The following year the two families have a disastrous holiday where both the affair and Patricia's pregnancy are revealed. Patricia disappears to have the baby and returns without it. Soon she will disappear on a more permanent basis.

Uncle Ted's wedding day in 1966 marks George's undoing. Caught in a disgraceful position with a waitress, he has a fatal heart attack. Bunty later takes up with Mr Belling who tells Ruby a devastating secret.

Each chapter of Ruby's narrative has a footnote telling the story of the previous two generations, beginning with Ruby's great-grandmother Alice, who supposedly died while giving birth to Bunty's mother, Nell.

When the First World War breaks out Albert, the beloved eldest brother, enlists. Nell, who has already lost one fiancé to a burst appendix, finds herself bereft once again when Albert is also lost. Nell marries Frank, one of his friends. Her sister Lillian eventually emigrates to Canada with her child whose paternity is a closely guarded secret.

Nell and Frank raise their family in York. Bunty is the middle child, dreamy and overlooked. By the outbreak of the Second World War she is grown up but still a dreamer. She meets George who fails to live up to her hopes but suffices. And so begins the story of Bunty, George, Ruby and her sisters.

## ABOUT THE AUTHOR

Kate Atkinson was born in York in 1951. She took a master's degree in English Literature at Dundee University and went on to do further post-graduate work in American literature. While raising her two daughters she did a wide variety of jobs, from university tutor to home help. Her short stories have been published in several British magazines. *Behind the Scenes at the Museum* was her first novel. It was greeted with a storm of critical acclaim culminating in the Whitbread Book of the Year award.

## FOR DISCUSSION

▷ Atkinson's structure is extremely complex, weaving backward and forward through the years, dropping clues and hints along the way. How does she mesh the two narratives together? How successful is her technique?

▷ How successful is Atkinson at capturing both time and place in the novel? What techniques does she use to achieve this?

▷ Ruby Lennox narrates half of the novel. How would you describe her voice? How does the tone of her narrative differ from the footnotes? What effect does this achieve?

▷ There are four generations of women in the book. How do their lives and circumstances differ? What are the biggest changes? What do they have in common? Many of the women have 'had enough'. What do you think they mean by this and why is the phrase never associated with the male characters?

▷ Bunty can hardly be described as the best of mothers. Do you have any sympathy with her constant irritation and if so why?

▷ What is Ruby's Lost Property Cupboard Theory of Life? How does it apply to her own life?

▷ Many secrets are revealed over the course of the book. How does this affect individual characters? How typical do you think this is of family life?

▷ Would you describe the novel as a comedy or a tragedy, and why?

## SUGGESTED FURTHER READING
### FICTION
▶ *Wise Children* by Angela Carter (1991)
▶ *The House of Sleep* by Jonathan Coe (1997)
▶ *Crocodile Soup* by Julia Darling (1998)
▶ *David Copperfield* by Charles Dickens (1849–50)
▶ *The Ten O'Clock Horses* by Laurie Graham (1996)
▶ *War Crimes for the Home* by Liz Jensen (2002)
▶ *The Orchard on Fire* by Shena Mackay (1995)
▶ *Tristram Shandy* by Laurence Sterne (1760)
▶ *Anita and Me* by Meera Syal (1996)
### NON-FICTION
▶ *Hidden Lives* by Margaret Forster (1995)

## OTHER BOOKS BY KATE ATKINSON
### NOVELS
▶ *Human Croquet* (1997)
▶ *Emotionally Weird* (2000)
▶ *Not the End of the World* (2002)
### DRAMA
▶ *Abandonment* (2000)

# Alias Grace (1996)
Margaret Atwood

## ABOUT THE BOOK
This novel is the product of Margaret Atwood's long fascination with Grace Marks, who, along with her fellow servant, James McDermott, was accused of the

murders of both her employer and his mistress in 1843. This fascination was sparked off by Susanna Moodie's account of the murders in *Life in the Clearings* (1853). In the 1970s, Atwood wrote a television drama based on the notorious case. Twenty years later, *Alias Grace* takes her interpretation of Grace's story several steps further, filling in the many gaps that were undocumented but leaving known facts unchanged. The novel touches on many themes contemporary to the period, from the Victorian ambivalence towards women and the tensions between servants and employers, to the insatiable public appetite for scandal and the enthusiasm for spiritualism which swept Canada in the mid-nineteenth century.

In the main, the novel is told from Grace's point of view with occasional chapters narrated by a young psychologist, Simon Jordan.

Since she and her fellow servant were found guilty of Thomas Kinnear's murder, eight years before, Grace has been confined either to Kingston Penitentiary or to the Toronto asylum where she was exhibited to anyone who cared to ask. Both defendants were sentenced to death but, because of her age and sex, Grace's sentence was commuted to life imprisonment. The newspapers were filled with contradictory and sensational reports about the murders. At the time of her trial Grace gave three different versions of events.

Grace is now sufficiently trusted to act as a servant to the Governor's wife. A committee, set up to petition for her pardon, has engaged Dr Simon Jordan, a young enthusiast in the newly born practice of psychology, to assess the likely state of Grace's sanity at the time of the murders.

This is the story that Grace tells Dr Jordan.

After her mother's death during the long voyage from Ireland, her drunken father proved incapable of supporting his family. Grace found work as a servant and forged a close friendship with Mary Whitney in the Parkinson household. When Mary died after a botched abortion, Grace was left alone in the world. Hoping that Nancy Montgomery would provide the friendship she so badly missed, Grace accepted her offer of work at Richmond Hill, not realizing that Nancy was the mistress of Thomas Kinnear, the owner of the house. James McDermott, Grace's fellow servant, was sullen, irascible and resentful of Nancy. When the master absented himself, the atmosphere brightened and Grace enjoyed small intimacies with Nancy but when Kinnear began to pay Grace attention, Nancy decided to rid herself of both servants. Furious at being turned out, McDermott told Grace of his plan to kill Nancy. Her attempts to dissuade him failed and when Kinnear returned looking for his lover, McDermott shot him.

In McDermott's version, the murders were at Grace's instigation but she claims to have no memory of the killings.

Throughout the interviews, Dr Jordan has been troubled by his own problems. His loneliness, his increasing sexual frustration and his puzzlement over the enigmatic Grace begin to overwhelm him. He finds himself involved in a sexual entanglement with his landlady and flees to avoid scandal, leaving the puzzle of Grace unsolved.

## ABOUT THE AUTHOR

Margaret Atwood was born in Ottawa, Ontario, in 1939. She was educated at the University of Toronto, Radcliffe College and Harvard. She has since lived in the United States, England, France, Italy and Germany but currently lives in her native Canada. Atwood has held a wide variety of teaching positions and has been granted many honorary degrees and literary awards. She is both a prolific and internationally acclaimed writer in a wide range of areas including fiction, poetry and children's literature. *Alias Grace*, her ninth novel, was published in 1996. It won the prestigious Canadian Giller award and was shortlisted for the Orange Prize. Often tipped as a favourite for the Booker Prize, Atwood finally won it in 2000 with her novel, *The Blind Assassin*.

## FOR DISCUSSION

▷ *Alias Grace* is a fictionalized account of an historical event. To what extent did this affect your reading of it? What light did the extracts from the various records of the events at the time shed on the book for you? Did the Afterword change your interpretation of the novel in any way?

▷ How would you interpret the title of the book?

▷ Atwood uses the interviews with Simon Jordan as a means of telling some of Grace's story rather than having Grace speak directly to us at all times. What effect does this achieve?

▷ Mary Whitney is mentioned almost from the beginning of the novel although we do not meet her for some time. How important an influence on Grace was Mary? What do you make of her final 'appearance'?

▷ Both Simon's and Grace's dreams are recounted in great detail. To what extent did you find that their dreams illuminated the rest of the novel?

▷ Grace gives three different versions of the events surrounding the murders at the time of her trial. She continued to deny the memory of the murder. Did your opinion about Grace's guilt or innocence change during the course of the novel? What factors influenced your opinion? What conclusion did you reach by the end of the book, and why?

▷ As Margaret Atwood says in her Afterword, there was a good deal of fascination with Grace's part in the murder. Attitudes towards her reflected the Victorian ambivalence towards the nature of women. What were those attitudes? Are there other female characters that illustrate this ambivalence?

▷ How do their employers, particularly men, treat servants? In what ways do the worlds of servants and employers overlap? How do servants see their employers and vice versa?

## SUGGESTED FURTHER READING

▶ *Hawksmoor* by Peter Ackroyd (1985)
▶ *The Alienist* by Caleb Carr (1994)
▶ *The French Lieutenant's Woman* by John Fowles (1965)
▶ *Electricity* by Victoria Glendinning (1995)
▶ *The Conversations at Curlow Creek* by David Malouf (1996)
▶ *Fortune's Rocks* by Anita Shreve (1999)
▶ **Morality Play by Barry Unsworth (1995)**

## OTHER BOOKS BY MARGARET ATWOOD
NOVELS

▶ *The Edible Woman* (1969)
▶ *Surfacing* (1972)
▶ *Lady Oracle* (1976)
▶ *Life Before Man* (1979)
▶ *Bodily Harm* (1981)
▶ *The Handmaid's Tale* (1985)
▶ *Cat's Eye* (1988)

▶ *The Robber Bride* (1993)
▶ *The Blind Assassin* (2000)

**SHORT STORIES**
▶ *Dancing Girls* (1977)
▶ *Bluebeard's Egg* (1983)
▶ *Murder in the Dark* (1983)
▶ *Wilderness Tips* (1991)
▶ *Good Bones* (1992)

**FOR CHILDREN**
▶ *Up the Tree* (1978)
▶ *Anna's Pet* (with Joyce Barkhouse) (1980)
▶ *For the Birds* (1990)
▶ *Princess Prunella and the Purple Peanut* (1995)

**POETRY**
▶ *Double Persephone* (1961)
▶ *The Circle Game* (1966)
▶ *The Animals in That Country* (1968)
▶ *The Journals of Susanna Moodie* (1970)
▶ *Procedures for Underground* (1970)
▶ *Power Politics* (1971)
▶ *You Are Happy* (1974)
▶ *Selected Poems* (1976)
▶ *Two-Headed Poems* (1978)
▶ *True Stories* (1981)
▶ *Interlunar* (1984)
▶ *Selected Poems II: Poems Selected and New 1976–1986* (1986)
▶ *Morning in the Burned House* (1995)

**NON-FICTION**
▶ *Survival: A Thematic Guide to Canadian Literature* (1972)
▶ *Days of the Rebels 1815–1840* (1977)
▶ *Second Words* (1982)
▶ *Strange Things: The Malevolent North in Canadian Literature* (1996)
▶ *Two Solicitudes: Conversations* (with Victor-Lévy Beaulieu) (1998)

# Eucalyptus (1998)
## Murray Bail

### ABOUT THE BOOK

*Eucalyptus* is about storytelling. Holland tells stories to his daughter, Ellen is enthralled by a young storyteller, the narrator tells us stories about eucalypts, even Cave, the dullest of suitors, has his story to tell, albeit brief and uneventful. The novel employs a classic device of the traditional fairytale – a father offers the hand of his daughter in marriage to the man who can complete a seemingly impossible task. Bail's language is rich in fabulous imagery and it is only the occasional mention of motorcycles or hairdryers that reminds us that this tale is set in contemporary Australia.

When the novel opens, Holland is living alone in rural New South Wales. His wife has died of a broken heart after the loss of one of her twin babies. Comfortably off from the proceeds of an insurance policy, Holland has bought some land and indulged his passion for eucalypts by planting them all over it. When his daughter, Ellen, comes home from her convent school in Sydney, she slips into a dream-like life of listening to her father's stories, wandering the estate and thinking of her mother.

But tales of Ellen's 'speckled beauty' spread. A young man, driven to distraction by a glimpse of her bathing naked, crashes his motorcycle into a barbed wire fence. Holland realizes that Ellen is becoming a woman and that the surrounding country is hardly alive with suitable candidates to marry such a prize. He half-jokingly devises a competition for aspirant suitors. They must successfully identify each of his many eucalypts. The first one to do so will become Ellen's husband. Ellen seems neither to consent nor object.

As news of the competition spreads so suitors multiply. Most fall by the wayside on the first day, some so intimidated that they turn around without even trying. Throughout it all – the ritual of tea in the parlour before the test begins, the walk around the estate, the inevitable failure – Ellen remains aloof, detached from her fate, sure that the task is impossible.

Finally, an expert arrives. Roy Cave is a man whose eucalypt knowledge rivals Holland's own, but he is without charm, interest or, apparently, desire for Ellen. Slowly and inexorably, Cave walks the estate with Holland, casually naming each of the eucalypts. When Cave reaches the halfway point, Ellen is shaken by the idea that she may find herself wedded to this worthy but dull man and tries to communicate this to her father. He sees no honourable way out.

Out on one of her solitary walks, Ellen comes upon a sleeping man. When he wakes he tells her a story. The next day he finds her and tells her another. Her interest piqued, Ellen begins to look for the stranger every day. Meanwhile, Cave seems unstoppable. When her storyteller disappears and Ellen understands that Cave will complete the task she had thought impossible, she takes to her bed. When he names the last tree, she turns her face to the wall. It seems that Ellen is lost . . . until her storyteller appears once again to tell the story that will save her.

### ABOUT THE AUTHOR

Murray Bail was born in Adelaide in 1941 and has lived in both Bombay and London. As well as being a novelist, he has written non-fiction and many short stories which have been widely published. He is also the editor of the *Faber Book of Australian Short Stories*. His first novel, *Homesickness*, won both the National Book Council Award for Australian Literature and the *Age* Book of the Year Award. His second novel, *Holden's Performance*, won the Vance Prize for Fiction. *Eucalyptus* is his third novel.

### FOR DISCUSSION

▷ Why do you think Holland sets up the competition? It seems the act of a tyrannical father but Holland is far from that. Why do you think Ellen goes along with it? Do you think she wants to get married? What sort of man do you think she wants to marry?

▷ What do you think of Holland's interest in eucalypts? When Cave talks about his pursuit of eucalypt knowledge he says, 'Mind you, it's given me a life of sorts.' What do you make of this? Do you think Cave and Holland have much in common besides eucalypts?

▷ What do you make of Ellen? Do you think she is happy? How do you think the loss of her mother when she was a baby has shaped her life? There are no women in Ellen's life in New South Wales. How do you think this has affected her?

▷ Each chapter is headed with the name of a eucalypt. Why do you think Bail chose this structure? Do you think it works? Can you think of other ways he might have structured the novel?

▷ *Eucalyptus* is much more about storytelling than about eucalypts. How important do you think storytelling is in our lives? Storytelling is usually associated with fiction. Do you think that it is valid to argue that non-fiction tells a story rather than simply reporting the facts and, if so, why?

▷ Do you think there is a pattern to the stories that the stranger tells Ellen? Do they share a theme? If so, what is it and why has he chosen it?

▷ Do members of the group have a favourite among the many stories in the novel? If so, which one? What was it that you particularly enjoyed about the story? Do you think it has a particular significance in the novel and, if so, what is it?

▷ Near the end, Bail writes 'the formidable instinct in men to measure, which is often mistaken for pessimism, is counter-balanced by the unfolding optimism of women, which is nothing less than life itself'. What do you think he means by this? Do you agree with this assessment of men and women? Do you think it is borne out by the male and female characters in the novel? If so, can you point to examples?

## SUGGESTED FURTHER READING

▶ *Tales From One Thousand and One Nights* C.C. Addison
▶ *The Canterbury Tales* by Geoffrey Chaucer (c.1387)
▶ *Nights at the Circus* by Angela Carter (1984)
▶ *Periodic Table* by Primo Levi (1975)
▶ *In Babylon* by Marcel Möring (1999)
▶ *Life, a User's Manual* by Georges Perec (1978)

## OTHER BOOKS BY MURRAY BAIL
**NOVELS**
▶ *Homesickness* (1980)
▶ *Holden's Performance* (1987)
**SHORT STORIES**
▶ *The Drover's Wife and Other Tales* (1986)
**EDITED**
▶ *The Faber Book of Contemporary Short Stories* (1988)
▶ *Camouflage* (2001)

# The Crow Road (1992)
## Iain Banks

### ABOUT THE BOOK

Part thriller, part family saga, part coming-of-age story, *The Crow Road* is one of Iain Banks's warmest and most accessible books. Set in the early 1990s, this multi-layered novel is criss-crossed with flashbacks and leavened with humour. Narrated by Prentice, the middle son of the youngest generation of McHoans, the story is firmly located in Gallanach, a small, close-knit Scottish community. The main themes of the novel are introduced in the first chapter when family and friends are assembled for Grandma Margot's funeral.

Prentice is staying with his aunt and uncle because of a row with his father. Kenneth is an emphatic atheist and their quarrel has arisen from Prentice's difficulty in dealing with the death of a close friend without the consolation of faith.

In the funeral oration, Grandma Margot is said to be survived by her sons, including Prentice's uncle Rory; but is Rory still alive? No one has heard from him since he rode off on a friend's motorbike in 1981. Prentice is convinced that a man his friend Ashley met in a Berlin hotel who made mysterious references to Gallanach, may know something about Rory's disappearance.

At the funeral Prentice's obsessive infatuation with his cousin Verity is reawakened. His brother Lewis, a rising star on the alternative stand-up comedy circuit, arouses some less than charitable feelings in Prentice. When it becomes clear that Lewis and Verity are in love, Prentice is presented with a challenge to which he finally rises after a number of spectacular hiccups.

Through a series of flashbacks we learn about Kenneth's generation – childhood accidents, unlikely friendships, confessions and betrayals – which all form clues to the resolution of the novel. Kenneth is a storyteller, successful enough as a children's author to make a comfortable living. He is a man of strong convictions and principles who wants to prepare his children for the injustices of life. In contrast to Kenneth, firmly rooted in Gallanach, Uncle Rory travelled around India, using his journals as the basis for a successful travel book. Kenneth's other brother Hamish, with whom he is amiably at odds, manages the local glassworks and practises his eccentric religious beliefs. The family has already suffered one tragic death when their sister Fiona, married to Fergus Urvill, a member of the local gentry, died in a car crash. Overshadowing the family is the question of what has happened to Rory.

When Kenneth dies, struck by lightning whilst climbing the lightning conductor of Gallanach church after a heated, drunken debate with Hamish about religion, Prentice is faced with the terrible fact that their rift can never be healed. Among Kenneth's papers, he finds Rory's notes for a book, together with some old computer disks and matchbooks from various hotels around the world, including one from the Berlin hotel where Ashley met the mysterious stranger. Painstakingly fitting together the clues and with a good deal of help and support from Ashley, Prentice comes to a conclusion which is shockingly close to home and he confronts the person he believes to be Rory's murderer.

## ABOUT THE AUTHOR

Born in Dunfermline, Fife, in 1954, Iain Banks was an only child but surrounded by a multitude of aunts, uncles and cousins. He published his first novel, the controversial *Wasp Factory*, in 1984. It was successful enough for him to give up his day job and to write full time. Since then he has divided his writing between science fiction, under the name Iain M. Banks, and mainstream fiction, both of which have met with critical and popular acclaim. The *Crow Road* was made into a four-part television drama series. Iain Banks lives in Fife.

## FOR DISCUSSION

▷ Humour is an important element in *The Crow Road*. How would you describe Banks's particular brand of humour? Why do you think he uses humour?

▷ Prentice reflects on his parents' different attitudes towards bringing up their children. How do you think these two attitudes are reflected in Prentice's character? Do you think that Kenneth was a good father and if so can you say why? If not, why not? Why do you think that the rift between Prentice and his father is so great? Why are they unable to bridge it?

▷ How do you think Prentice changes during the book? Are there particular points in the book at which those changes take place? How would you describe Prentice's philosophy of life at the end of the novel? How do you think he has arrived at this?

▷ Religious and political differences are crucial in the book. How would you describe Kenneth's politics? Do you think they have influenced his determined atheism or vice versa? Why do you think Hamish drops his eccentric religious views after Kenneth's death and becomes a fully fledged Christian?

▷ The Urvills, the McHoans and the Watts all come from very different backgrounds. How are class differences portrayed in the book? How important is class as an issue in the book? How do attitudes to class change between the generations?

▷ When Janice gives Prentice the first set of notes for Rory's book, the file is labelled 'Crow Road'. Janice explains that taking the Crow Road meant dying. Why do you think Rory chose that title? Why do you think Iain Banks uses it? How important is death in the book?

▷ How does Banks work clues into the structure of the book? Did the plot fall into place for you at the end? If not, what did you think was unresolved?

▷ What do you make of the relationship between Ashley and Prentice? How important do you think Ashley is in the development of Prentice's character? Were you surprised when their relationship took a different turn?

## SUGGESTED FURTHER READING
▶ *The House of Sleep* by Jonathan Coe (1997)
▶ *Everything You Need* by A. L. Kennedy (1997)
▶ *The Buddha of Suburbia* by Hanif Kureishi (1991)
▶ *The Funnies* by J. Robert Lennon (1999)
▶ *The Ice Storm* by Rick Moody (1994)
▶ *The Catcher in the Rye* by J. D. Salinger (1951)

## OTHER BOOKS BY IAIN BANKS
▶ *The Wasp Factory* (1984)
▶ *Walking On Glass* (1985)
▶ *The Bridge* (1986)
▶ *Espedair Street* (1987)
▶ *Canal Dreams* (1989)
▶ *Complicity* (1993)
▶ *Whit* (1995)
▶ *Song of Stone* (1998)
▶ *The Business* (1999)
▶ Dead Air (2002)

## AS IAIN M. BANKS (SCIENCE FICTION)
▶ *Consider Phlebas* (1988)
▶ *The Player of Games* (1988)
▶ *The State of the Art* (1989)
▶ *Use of Weapons* (1990)
▶ *Against a Dark Background* (1993)
▶ *Feersum Endjinn* (1994)
▶ *Excession* (1996)

▶ *Inversions* (1998)
▶ *Look To Windward* (2000)

# The Voyage of the Narwhal (1998)
## Andrea Barrett

### ABOUT THE BOOK

Exploration and an overriding desire to extend the boundaries of knowledge were two hallmarks of the nineteenth century. Too often the thirst for knowledge was accompanied by an equal thirst for glory, coupled with an enthusiastic amateurism which frequently ended in disaster. In *The Voyage of the Narwhal*, Andrea Barrett captures both the spirit of adventure that fired explorers and public alike and the incalculable destruction wrought in the name of discovery.

The novel opens in 1855 when Zeke and Erasmus are organizing their voyage to search for the remains of the Franklin expedition which left ten years before. Their captain is anxious; they are late leaving and the ship is not prepared for an Arctic winter. Erasmus feels a particular responsibility for Zeke, who is engaged to his sister Lavinia.

Young and inexperienced, Zeke's authority is undermined when he suffers terribly with seasickness. Almost as soon as the voyage begins in earnest, it is beset by difficulties. Disease strikes the dogs and a minor injury to one of the crew results in lockjaw. When the battle for authority between Zeke and Captain Tyler intensifies, the crew becomes nervous.

As winter approaches, ice impedes the *Narwhal*'s passage. When Zeke visits an Eskimo encampment, he finds artefacts from the Franklin expedition. The *Narwhal* outstays its welcome and when they are all invited to a feast, the interpreter realizes that the Eskimos want them to leave. Ill prepared for winter, the ship turns for home but becomes iced in. Zeke manages to keep the crew's spirits up but the officers stand aloof. When his pet fox dies he retreats into himself, becoming dangerously isolated.

With no fresh food available, the health of the remaining sailors declines; several of the crew have already died. When Dr Boerhaave fails to return from a foraging trip for fresh meat, Erasmus is grief-stricken by the loss of his dear friend. Zeke's request for volunteers to help him investigate further evidence of Franklin's expedition meets with silence. He decides to go alone and when he does not return, the crew petition Erasmus to abandon the *Narwhal* before another winter sets in. In despair, he can see no other option.

Woven through the narrative of the voyage are extracts from the journal of Alexandra, a young woman employed as Lavinia's companion. They tell of Lavinia's anxiety and of her own efforts to develop the engraving skills that may gain her financial independence.

On his return, Erasmus finds that Dr Kane has been fêted for an expedition that almost mirrored the *Narwhal*'s. With no specimens, very few journals and no firm news of Zeke's fate, Erasmus feels that he has failed everyone, most of all Lavinia.

Zeke miraculously reappears with two Eskimos, Annie and her son Tom. His determination honed by his ordeal, he hatches a plan to mount a lecture tour in which Annie and Tom will take part. When this ends in tragedy, Alexandra, Erasmus and his brother Copernicus do what they can to try to make reparations for the terrible wrongs that have resulted from the expedition.

## ABOUT THE AUTHOR

Andrea Barrett lives in Rochester, New York. Her collection of short stories, *Ship Fever*, won the American National Book Award in 1996. *The Voyage of the Narwhal* was her second novel.

## FOR DISCUSSION

▷ Barrett has chosen an extract from *Tristes Tropiques* by the anthropologist Claude Lévi-Strauss to preface her novel. What bearing does this quotation have on the major themes of the novel? To what extent do you agree with the ideas expressed in the quotation? The quotation is dated 1955 – how much do you think things have changed since then? All the chapters are prefaced with a quotation – are there any which strike you as particularly apt and if so, which are they and why?

▷ What impression do you have of Erasmus at the beginning of the book? What are the major forces that have shaped his character at this point? How does he feel about exploration by the end of the book? What has led him to these conclusions?

▷ Lavinia says of Zeke: 'He loves me . . . In his own way – I know he does.' To what extent do you think Zeke is capable of love?

▷ Why does Zeke become so isolated? What sort of man is he at the beginning of the book? How has he changed by the end?

▷ How does Ned change? He is not much younger than Zeke, but who would make the better leader and why?

▷ What part does class play in the book?

▷ What light do the extracts from Alexandra's journals throw on the position of women in nineteenth-century society? How is this explored in part three of the book?

▷ Officers and men alike are contemptuous of 'discovery men'. Captain Sturrock says that they 'get lost. Lose things. Franklin is lost, and his ships and his men, and Dr Kane's ship is lost, and yours and all your precious relics and specimens.' Why do you think the sailors feel this way? Do you have any sympathy with their view? If so, why are we still fascinated by people like Franklin?

▷ When the *Narwhal* leaves Boothia, Zeke says of his pet fox, Sabine: 'Don't you think I'm doing well with her?' The final sentence of the chapter reads: 'As they began to move she stood and howled to her relatives back on shore.' What do you think Barrett is trying to convey about Zeke in this passage?

▷ What does the book have to say about the motives of the men who mounted the great expeditions of the nineteenth century? Do you think that these ideas apply today? How did the explorers affect the Eskimos? Are there parallels today?

## SUGGESTED FURTHER READING
### FICTION

▶ *Water Music* by T. Coraghessan Boyle (1982)
▶ *Heart of Darkness* by Joseph Conrad (1902)
▶ *Rites of Passage* by William Golding (1980)
▶ **Remembering Babylon by David Malouf (1993)**
▶ *Moby Dick* by Herman Melville (1851)
▶ **Promised Lands by Jane Rogers (1995)**

**NON-FICTION**
▶ *Arctic Dreams* by Barry Lopez (1986)
▶ *Barrow's Boys* by Fergus Fleming (1998)

## OTHER BOOKS BY ANDREA BARRETT

**NOVELS**
▶ *The Middle Kingdom* (1992)
▶ *Servants of the Map* (2002)
**SHORT STORIES**
▶ *Ship Fever* (1996)

# Island Madness (1998)
## Tim Binding

### ABOUT THE BOOK

When the Germans invaded the Channel Islands in 1940, it was to be a 'model occupation' but as time wore on, food became scarce and a thriving black market sprang up. As the line between co-operation and collaboration began to blur, resentment and suspicion flourished on both sides. Ostensibly a murder mystery, *Island Madness* explores this sensitive episode in British history and investigates the psychology of Occupation from both points of view.

As the novel opens Major Lentsch is returning to Guernsey. Germany has suffered its first major reversal at Stalingrad. Lentsch is concerned about morale among his fellow officers but is distracted by Major Ernst's unwelcome interest in joining him at his requisitioned house, the Villa. Lentsch is smitten with both Guernsey and Isobel van Dielen, the daughter of the wealthy Dutch engineer responsible for developing the island's defences.

With both food and work scarce, many islanders have little choice but to co-operate with the Germans, demonstrating their suppressed animosity with small acts of defiance. They are as distrustful of the slave labourers building the island's defences as they are of the Germans. Seeing a way out of their circumscribed lives, the young women are more welcoming than the men, who view the women's affairs with German officers with increasing bitterness.

A welcoming party has been arranged for Lentsch. He expects Isobel to attend and when she doesn't arrive, his mood turns. New to the Villa's frequent parties, Veronica attempts to console him. When he humiliates her, she turns to Captain Zepernick, beginning a relationship which she convinces herself is her passport to a better life. That same night she meets Peter, a young slave labourer on whom she takes pity. This relationship will also be a decisive factor in shaping her future.

When Isobel's body is found, the balance of power shifts among the German officers. Distraught at the loss of his lover, Lentsch begins to lose his grip. Ernst gains ground in his aspirations to take over the Villa and Zepernick chafes against the restraints of rank. Lentsch finds himself drawn to Ned Luscombe, the local police inspector in charge of the murder investigation who has also had a brief affair with Isobel, and a friendship of sorts forms between them.

Apart from Isobel's note imploring him to meet her, Ned has few clues. He begins to uncover instances of corruption, some petty, some on a grand scale, involving both islanders and Germans. Long suppressed resentments and suspicions surface on both sides.

Lentsch's feelings about the Occupation, the aims of the war and his leader have changed since Isobel's murder. Both his inaction and his odd behaviour are noted by Zepernick, who spills out his bitterness to Veronica. When Lentsch smashes a portrait of Hitler, he is to be arrested and stripped of his rank.

When he learns that Hitler is to visit the island, Lentsch passes the information to Ned and tells him of his own impending arrest. As they discuss the implications of the visit they unravel a plot that could change the course of history. They construct a dramatic and courageous alternative. The unmasking of the murderer follows hot on the heels of this revelation.

## ABOUT THE AUTHOR
Tim Binding was born in Germany in 1947 and is a scriptwriter as well as a novelist. His second novel, *A Perfect Execution*, was shortlisted for the *Guardian* Fiction Prize in 1996.

## FOR DISCUSSION
▷ Right at the beginning of the book, Binding describes Hitler's fixation on the islands as 'island madness'. Is the title of the novel open to more than one interpretation? Are there particular characters who fall into the grip of island madness and, if so, who are they and why?

▷ What is Major Lentsch's attitude towards Hitler when the book opens? What does he see as the main aims of the war? How has his attitude changed at the close of the novel and what has brought this about?

▷ When Zepernick returns from taking a phone call at Lentsch's welcome-back party, Binding describes him as 'in so many ways the epitome of the Occupation'. What traits and behaviour seem to epitomize the Occupation for you?

▷ How have the inhabitants of Guernsey been changed by the Occupation? Have particular relationships changed and, if so, how? Have there been any benefits and, if so, what are they?

▷ Why is Veronica so eager to acquire a German officer as a boyfriend? What are the contradictions in her relationship with Captain Zepernick and her relationship with Peter, the young slave labourer? Binding writes of Veronica and Zepernick '[he] began to recognize a part of him in her, just as while listening she became aware of a part of her within him'. What is it that Veronica and Zepernick recognize in each other? How does Veronica redeem herself?

▷ How would you describe Ned Luscombe's character? What particular difficulties does he face as head of the island's police force and how does he deal with them?

▷ How satisfying do you find the dénouement when Isobel's killer is revealed?

▷ The issue of collaboration during the five-year Occupation of the Channel Islands has remained very sensitive. Who do you consider to be a collaborator in the novel and who is merely co-operating to ensure their survival? Where would you draw the line between the two?

## SUGGESTED FURTHER READING
**FICTION**
▶ *Captain Corelli's Mandolin* by Louis de Bernières (1994)
▶ *Charlotte Gray* by Sebastian Faulks (1998)
▶ **Stones From the River by Ursula Hegi (1995)**

▶ *Mephisto* by Klaus Mann (1936)
▶ *The Sword of Honour Trilogy* by Evelyn Waugh, published separately as:
*Men at Arms* (1952)
*Officers and Gentlemen* (1955)
*Unconditional Surrender* (1961)

**NON-FICTION**
▶ *The Model Occupation* by Madeline Bunting (1965)
▶ *The Channel Islands at War* by G. Forty (1999)

## OTHER BOOKS BY TIM BINDING
**NOVELS**
▶ *The Kingdom of Air* (1993)
▶ *A Perfect Execution* (1996)
**NON-FICTION**
▶ *On Ilkley Moor* (2001)

# Visible Worlds (1998)
## Marilyn Bowering

### ABOUT THE BOOK
*Visible Worlds* is a complex, tightly plotted novel. Two narratives alternate, each full of clues to the connections which bind three Canadian families both to each other and to a young woman determinedly struggling across the Arctic snows. Although slim in volume, the novel is epic in scale. It covers both the Second World War and the Korean War, humanizing the political forces that shaped the twentieth century by filtering them through the lives of the Storrs, the Bones and the Fergussons.

The main narrative is Albrecht Storr's. Beginning in 1934, in Canada, he sets the scene for each family. His own family is German and at odds over the Nazi regime. His father is convinced that war is inevitable while his mother, still yearning for an idealized Germany, insists on sending Gerhard, Albrecht's twin brother, to study music in Cologne.

On one side of the Storr's house live the Bones. Bill Bone is a circus animal tamer, rarely at home, leaving his wife to fret over his many infidelities. On the other side lives the clairvoyant Madame Pince-Jones, formerly known as Mrs Fergusson, more attuned, since her husband's death, to the spirit world than to the needs of her two daughters, Prudence and Mary.

The Bone family are riven by grief when their daughter fatally scalds herself while in the care of her brother Nate. Bill Bone leaves home for the last time. Overwhelmed with guilt, Nate is convinced that his sister's spirit has entered his body. When he finds a baby abandoned in the porch of his house, he interprets it as a sign of forgiveness and takes the child with him to join his father's circus in Germany.

On the eve of the Second World War, Mrs Storr visits Albrecht's twin brother, Gerhard, in Cologne where she stumbles upon Bill Bone with Nate and the baby, Elizabeth. Mrs Storr's indiscreet conversation with an SS officer results in the abduction of Elizabeth whose blonde, blue-eyed looks are judged too Germanic for a circus family. Nate implores Gerhard to use any influence he might have to protect Elizabeth.

In Canada, the ordeal suffered by Prudence Fergusson's sweetheart as a prisoner of war in Burma has left him unable to father a child. Their hopes of salving their grief at the loss of their first child, born before they were married and abandoned in a neighbour's porch, are dashed until Nate Bone offers to help. The families become further entangled when Albrecht Storr marries Prudence's sister Mary. Mary Fergusson's involvement in the development of chemical weapons sows the seeds for a future tragedy in which, once again, Nate Bone will become involved.

Interwoven with Albrecht Storr's story is a seemingly unrelated and more contemporary narrative which tells of a heroic Arctic journey by a young girl named Fika. After the death of her companions on a polar expedition, Fika continues against all odds, striving to reach the nearest US territory. As she fights for her survival, she tells her story: her childhood experiences in an orphanage; her life in a Russian labour camp where she met her protector, Gerhard; and the appearance of the young Canadian, Nate Bone, who convinced her that she, too, was Canadian.

## ABOUT THE AUTHOR

Marilyn Bowering was born in Winnipeg, Manitoba, and grew up in Victoria, British Columbia. She is widely travelled and has lived in Greece, Scotland and Spain. She now lives in British Columbia where she teaches part-time at the University of Victoria. In addition to being a novelist, she is one of Canada's leading poets. Her first book of poetry, *The Liberation of Newfoundland*, was published in 1973. She is also a playwright and was commissioned to write the critically acclaimed *Anyone Can See I Love You . . .*, a play about Marilyn Monroe, for BBC Radio Scotland. Her first novel, *To All Appearances a Lady*, was published in 1989. *Visible Worlds* is her second novel.

## FOR DISCUSSION

▷ The literary critic Alberto Manguel said of *Visible Worlds*, the reader 'reaches the end with the sense of having undertaken a long, complex, enthralling journey in the company of a throng of tragic, ordinary, brave human beings whom he has grown to love'. How did you feel when you reached the end of the novel? Do you agree with Manguel and, if so, why? If not, what didn't work for you?

▷ Why do you think Wilhelm is so wedded to the idea of Personal Magnetism? How does it affect his life? Do you think other characters in the novel have unorthodox personal philosophies? If so, who are they and how do they try to explain the world to themselves?

▷ The novel is made up of two narratives: Albrecht's and Fika's. Did you find this effective? How does Bowering establish links between the two narratives?

▷ There are many references to the natural world in both Albrecht's and Fika's narratives. Why do you think Bowering makes these references? What do you think she is saying about the relationship between humans and nature?

▷ Danger is a strong presence in the novel – floods, bitter cold, animals, war. Why do you think Bowering lays so much emphasis on danger? How do her characters react to it? Does their suffering change them and, if so, how?

▷ There are a variety of different attitudes towards war in the novel. How would you describe the attitudes of Wilhelm, Friedl, Fritz, Nate, Pietor, Albrecht and Mary? Why do you think they have reached these conclusions?

▷ Albrecht says: 'I am a twin without his other half. I am less than myself.' How would you describe the relationship between Albrecht and Gerhard? How do they differ from each other? What do you think Albrecht means by 'I am less then myself'?

▷ In the final passage of the book, when Fika finds Albrecht, he thinks 'I have a feeling of something about to happen, pins and needles of the brain, and at the same time I know it doesn't matter, there is no forever'. What do you think he means by 'there is no forever'? Why does he think it at this point? How do you think it relates to what has happened in the book?

## SUGGESTED FURTHER READING
▶ *Catch-22* by Joseph Heller (1961)
▶ *A Prayer for Owen Meany* by John Irving (1989)
▶ **Fugitive Pieces by Anne Michaels (1997)**
▶ *The Book of Lights* by Chaim Potok (1981)
▶ *The Story of My Disappearance* by Paul Watkins (1997)

## OTHER BOOKS BY MARILYN BOWERING
▶ *To All Appearances a Lady* (1989)

# Wise Children (1991)
## Angela Carter
### ABOUT THE BOOK
*Wise Children* is steeped in show business, from the Hazard Shakespearean dynasty to the music hall turns of the Chances. Told by Dora Chance, the story revolves around issues of paternity and legitimacy. It is packed with Shakespearean references with a plot worthy of one of the Comedies and written in language which is earthy, vivid and memorable.

Nora and Dora's mother dies in childbirth and the twins were brought up by 'Grandma', a boarding house landlady with a passion for naturism. The distinguished Shakespearean actor Melchior Hazard, who has never acknowledged his paternity, is happy to let his twin brother Perry pass as their father. The ebullient Perry, a flaming redhead, appears at infrequent intervals, his arms full of presents. On one of Perry's outings, the twins meet their father who greets them as Perry's daughters. By now, the ambitious, social-climbing Melchior has acquired Lady Atalanta Lynde as his wife and legitimate twin daughters, Saskia and Imogen, both with distinctive red hair.

The twins are enchanted by their first matinée and before long make their début in pantomime. Their professional paths cross their father's when their company puts on a Shakespearean revue. They are invited to the Hazard family seat to celebrate the show's success but the party literally turns to ashes when a guest's cigar starts a conflagration. Happily the cigar smoker, a Hollywood producer, announces that he wants to make a film of *A Midsummer Night's Dream*. He whisks the company off to Hollywood where Dora has her first serious affair, Melchior falls for the producer's wife, the spurned producer pursues Dora, and Nora conceives a passion for a Sicilian whose mama is appalled. When a triple wedding is arranged, Dora has a narrow escape, the Sicilian mama scuppers Nora's chances and only Daisy and Melchior are united.

War breaks out shortly after the Hollywood escapade. A bomb kills Grandma on her way to the off-licence and Perry disappears. Dora draws a veil over the twins' wartime antics apart from a few asides on their adventures with members of the armed forces.

Perry next appears at Saskia and Imogen's ill-fated twenty-first birthday party. When Melchior announces his third marriage, to Saskia's best friend, and his intention to cut off his daughters' allowances, the party ends in dramatic disarray. That same evening the Chances learn of Lady Atalanta's paralysis in an accident.

The Chances' careers become confined to dancing in *Nudes Ahoy* and *Nudes of the World*. Eventually, Lady Atalanta comes to live with them and a new set of twins, Tristram and Gareth, appear upon the Hazard stage. Both Saskia and Imogen find careers in television while their father burnishes his Shakespearean reputation. Saskia takes her revenge on her father by seducing Tristram. He becomes a quiz show host where he meets Tiffany, the twins' adopted darling, who falls in love with him and becomes pregnant. After an appearance reminiscent of Ophelia on Tristram's show, Tiffany disappears.

All is resolved at Melchior's birthday party when both Tiffany and Perry reappear and all the players are gathered together in front of the television cameras. The ensuing finale is worthy of the last act of a Shakespearean comedy.

## ABOUT THE AUTHOR

Angela Carter was born in 1940. After studying English at Bristol University, she spent two years in Japan. She lived and worked extensively in both Australia and the United States. In 1976 she was appointed Fellow in Creative Writing at Sheffield University, a position she held until 1978. She was a novelist, poet and essayist whose strikingly original work met with both popular and critical acclaim. Her fiction often drew upon the themes and symbolism of both fairytale and myth, underpinned by feminism and sometimes coupled with a rich humour. Her second novel, *The Magic Toyshop* (published in 1967), won the John Llewellyn Rhys Prize. Neil Jordan filmed *The Company of Wolves*, taken from her collection of short stories, *The Bloody Chamber*, in 1984. Angela Carter died in 1992.

## FOR DISCUSSION

▷ How would you describe Angela Carter's writing style? Can you see ways in which her style fits her subject matter? Were there passages in the book which you found particularly striking and, if so, which were they?

▷ Grandma's motto, often quoted by Dora, is 'Hope for the best, expect the worst'. How is this philosophy illustrated in the book? Do you think it was helpful to Dora and Nora, and, if so, in what way? At one point, Nora says that Grandma's ghost is trying to tell them something – 'Expect the worst, hope for the best'. Why do you think the order of the phrases is reversed here?

▷ What does the book have to say about illegitimacy? Because they are illegitimate, Nora and Dora are excluded from the 'legitimate' theatre and confined to music hall, although the two seem to come together in Hollywood. What do you think this says about attitudes in different types of culture?

▷ The issue of paternity is an important theme in the book. What do you think the book is saying about fatherhood? Does it also have something to say about motherhood and, if so, what?

▷ Dora says, 'It's a characteristic of human beings, one I've often noticed, that if they don't have a family of their own, they will invent one.' Do you think this is true and, if so, can you think of reasons why? How is this illustrated in the book?

▷ We often expect twins to share similar traits. Why do you think Melchior and Perry are presented as such different characters? What are the main differences between them?

▷ Nora and Dora are seventy-five, strong and lively. What do you think the book has to say about ageing and in particular about the ageing of women?

## SUGGESTED FURTHER READING
### FICTION
▶ *An Awfully Big Adventure* by Beryl Bainbridge (1991)
▶ *Nicholas Nickleby* by Charles Dickens (1839)
▶ *The Sword Cabinet* by Robert Edric (1999)
▶ *Juggling* by Barbara Trapido (1995)

### NON-FICTION
▶ *White Cargo* by Felicity Kendal (1998)

## OTHER BOOKS BY ANGELA CARTER
### NOVELS
▶ *Shadow Dance* (1966)
▶ *The Magic Toyshop* (1967)
▶ *Heroes and Villains* (1969)
▶ *The Infernal Desire Machines of Dr Hoffman* (1974)
▶ *Nights at the Circus* (1984)
▶ *Love* (1987)
▶ *The Passion of New Eve* (1993)

### SHORT STORIES
▶ *Fireworks* (1974)
▶ *The Bloody Chamber* (1979)
▶ *Black Venus* (1985)

### ESSAYS
▶ *The Sadeian Woman: An Exercise in Cultural History* (1978)
▶ *Nothing Sacred* (1982)
▶ *Expletives Deleted* (1992)
▶ *American Ghosts and Old World Wonders* (1993)

### EDITED
▶ *Wayward Girls and Wicked Women* (1986)
▶ *The Virago Book of Fairy Tales* (1990)
▶ *The Second Virago Book of Fairy Tales* (1993)


# The House of Sleep (1997)
## Jonathan Coe

### ABOUT THE BOOK
The many intricacies of this tightly plotted novel hinge upon the misunderstandings, sometimes comic, sometimes devastating, which result from Sarah's inability to distinguish her extraordinarily vivid narcoleptic dreams from reality. It needs to be read with close attention; many apparently insignificant details are crucial to the resolution of the plot. The narrative alternates between the student days of the 1980s and Terry's experiences at the sleep clinic in 1996.

The novel opens when Sarah is a student living in Ashdown. As she and

Gregory make love on his last night before starting his post-graduate psychiatric studies, Gregory indulges in his habitual power games. Sarah's anger explodes and she tells him just how lousy he is in bed. He quickly seizes the opportunity to end the relationship before Sarah gets the chance.

Sarah's narcolepsy has made her a social outcast but when Robert moves into Ashdown, there is an instant rapport between them. For Sarah, Robert is the brother she never had but he falls desperately in love with her, sadly looking on as she becomes attracted to Veronica. Sarah and Veronica share idealistic plans for the future; Veronica dreams of founding a theatre group while Sarah wants to be a teacher. When Veronica gets a job in financial services, Sarah storms out, shocked at her betrayal. Very drunk, she asks Robert to sleep with her but he refuses, cursing himself for his own decency. When he asks her if she could ever love him, she replies that if he were the twin sister he has told her about, he would be her ideal lover. This exchange eventually leads Robert to change his life irrevocably.

Pursuing his obsession with film, Terry finds a job on a cinema magazine. He asks Sarah if she wants a room in his shared house, a decision he will deeply regret when one of Sarah's narcoleptic episodes ruins his promising career. When they move to London, Robert disappears from their lives.

The 1996 narrative tells of Terry's experiences in Dr Dudden's sleep clinic at Ashdown, interwoven with scenes from Sarah's life.

Terry is now a freelance film critic, hooked on coffee and cinema. The elaborate fourteen-hour dreams that occupied most of his student life have long gone and he has hardly slept since he left university. When he hears that Ashdown has become a sleep clinic, he registers for treatment. Terry has lost touch with Sarah since the magazine débâcle but when he mentions her to Dr Dudden, the doctor becomes strangely agitated.

Rather than setting out to cure Terry of his insomnia, Dudden wants to emulate him. From the many hints that Dr Madison drops and a tour of his research laboratory, Terry begins to question Dudden's sanity. When Dudden attends a conference, Terry seizes the chance to do a little investigation and is appalled by what he finds. He and Dr Madison form an alliance and Terry finally finds out what has happened to Robert.

As the novel draws to its conclusion, its many conundrums are solved as the links between each character become clear.

## ABOUT THE AUTHOR

Jonathan Coe was born in Birmingham in 1961. He grew up in the Midlands and took degrees from Cambridge and Warwick universities. His novel *What a Carve Up!* won the John Llewelyn Rhys Prize in 1995. He spent some time as the film critic for the New Statesman and has written biographies of both James Stewart and Humphrey Bogart.

## FOR DISCUSSION

▷ Jonathan Coe has worked as a film critic as well as a novelist. Can you see ways in which cinema has influenced his writing style? Are there particular passages in the book which seem to you to be cinematic?

▷ Although it has a number of serious themes running through it, *The House of Sleep* is a comic novel. How would you describe the humour? Were there any passages that you found particularly funny? How does the humour of these passages work?

▷ Dr Dudden is often portrayed in the book as someone to be laughed at but he has some disturbing traits. Why do you think Coe chose to make him a comic figure?

▷ What does the book have to say about modern society? Can you think of specific examples?

▷ What did you think of the way the novel ended?

▷ The main characters, Dr Dudden, Sarah, Terry and Robert, are present in both the 1983–4 and the 1996 narratives? How does each of the characters change?

▷ *The House of Sleep* is constructed around the different stages of sleep. How far do you think each section reflects its equivalent stage as described by Dr Dudden?

## SUGGESTED FURTHER READING

▶ *Emotionally Weird* by Kate Atkinson (2000)
▶ **The Crow Road by Iain Banks (1992)**
▶ *The Road to Wellville* by T. Coraghessan Boyle (1993)
▶ *The Last Picture Show* by Larry McMurty (1966)
▶ *The Treatment* by Daniel Menaker (1998)
▶ *253* by Geoff Ryman (1998)

## OTHER BOOKS BY JONATHAN COE

▶ *The Accidental Woman* (1987)
▶ *The Dwarves of Death* (1991)
▶ *A Touch of Love* (1997)
▶ *What A Carve Up!* (1994)
▶ *The Rotters' Club* (2001)

## Being Dead (1999)
### Jim Crace

#### ABOUT THE BOOK
At the beginning of *Being Dead,* Jim Crace describes this story of a couple whose prosaic lives have been cut off by a random act of violence as a 'quivering'; the retelling of their lives as a rite of passage into death which he tells us was an ancient way of dealing with grief. As the 'quivering' proceeds, Crace shows us through visceral yet poetic descriptions of decay how nature makes a quick adjustment to death.

The novel has three narrative strands. The first is the story of Joseph and Celice's first meeting thirty years ago. The second describes the events of the day of their murder, beginning a half hour after it has happened and running backwards through the day. In the third, Crace describes what happens to the corpses in the 'six days of grace' between the murder and their discovery. The strands are drawn together as their daughter Syl arrives to identify the bodies.

Joseph and Celice have returned to Baritone Bay where they met as students. This is where they first made love and Joseph is hoping to celebrate their return in the same way. Less enthusiastic, Celice has decided to accommodate him. They have reached a stage in their marriage where each has adjusted to the other, moving on from the initial passions of youth to separate beds where their sleeping habits will be less disruptive. Celice seems to have attained a kind of peace but Joseph is haunted by a fear of ageing.

This uneventful yet resignedly contented life is interrupted when a psycho-pathic thief bludgeons to death first Celice, then Joseph, as they lie naked after their first attempt at making love.

The 'quivering' commences as Crace tells us how Joseph and Celice first met at a study week. Joseph, instantly attracted to Celice, played it cool by remaining aloof from the group. Celice, at first irritated then aroused by Joseph, goes off with him one morning to make love in the dunes. They emerge as a couple but their happiness is quickly overshadowed by the discovery that the building in which they were sleeping has burnt down with one of their colleagues still in it. A kerosene lamp had been left burning under a wooden table. Each of the students may have contributed to this negligence but Celice takes on the responsibility and carries it with her for thirty years.

As nature takes its course with their battered bodies, Joseph and Celice begin to be missed. Joseph's secretary gets in touch with their daughter Syl. The relationship between Syl and her parents is strained. Her visits are frequently requested but rarely happen and she has disappointed their aspirations with her aimless drifting. Her reaction to the news of her parents' disappearance is ambivalent but she finds herself heading home. She contacts the police, goes to the hospitals, tours the morgue until eventually she is told that the bodies have been found at Baritone Bay.

Joseph and Celice's 'six days of grace' are over. As Syl reclaims their bodies, the beach on which they lay begins its quick adjustment so that, only nine days after the murder, no trace of their presence remains.

## ABOUT THE AUTHOR

Jim Crace was born in Enfield, North London, in 1946. After taking his degree in English Literature in Birmingham he went to the Sudan as part of a Voluntary Service Overseas programme, where he worked in Khartoum as an assistant for educational television. On his return he worked as a freelance journalist for *The Sunday Times* and *The Daily Telegraph* magazine. His first novel, *Continent*, was published in 1986 and went on to win both the Whitbread First Novel Award and the *Guardian* Prize for Fiction. *Quarantine*, published in 1997, won the Whitbread Novel of the Year Award. *Being Dead* was also shortlisted for the Whitbread Fiction Prize.

## FOR DISCUSSION

▷ The book deals with disturbing details of death and physical decay. What did you think of this as subject matter for fiction? What was your reaction to Crace's graphic descriptions of bodily corruption and decay? Why do you think he chose to describe this so explicitly?

▷ Joseph dies with his hand on Celice's leg, a detail that is referred to frequently in the novel. How important is this as a signal of the state of their relationship. How does your view of the relationship between the couple change from the opening chapter to the end of the book? How does Crace convey the nature of the relationship between Joseph and Celice, the details of their characters and their lives?

▷ How would you describe Crace's style and tone? The narrative has a strong authorial voice. What effect does this have? What did you think of his use of language? Can you give examples of passages that you found particularly effective?

▷ What would you say was the central message of the book? What does it say about death and attitudes towards death in modern society? How does Crace convey this?

▷ Crace writes of Joseph and Celice: 'Both know that life and death are inextricably entwined, the double helix of existence.' How does the book illustrate this idea?

▷ Nature and science are closely intertwined throughout the book – both Joseph and Celice are scientists who specialize in the natural world. What do you think Crace is saying about the links between science and nature?

▷ When *Being Dead* was published, it was noted by experts that many of the scientific details were inaccurate. How much does this matter in a work of fiction?

▷ The relationship between Syl and her parents is, at best, an uneasy one. When it becomes clear that something is wrong and Syl goes back to her parents' home, Crace asks, 'Why had Syl come?' Why do you think she went home? What is her reaction to her parents' death? Why do you think she feels this way?

▷ The novel ends with the sentence 'These are the everending days of being dead'. Why do you think Crace chose the word 'everending' which can so easily be read as 'neverending'? How does a misreading of this word change the meaning of the sentence?

## SUGGESTED FURTHER READING
**FICTION**
- ▶ *As I Lay Dying* by William Faulkner (1930)
- ▶ *The Death of Vishnu* **by Manil Suri (2000)**
- ▶ *Blackwater Lightship* by Colm Tóbín (1997)

**NON-FICTION**
- ▶ *The Undertaking: Life Studies from the Dismal Trade* by Thomas Lynch (1997)
- ▶ *And When Did You Last See Your Father?* **by Blake Morrison (1993)**
- ▶ *How We Die* by Sherwin Nuland (1996)

## OTHER BOOKS BY JIM CRACE
- ▶ *Continent* (1986)
- ▶ *The Gift of Stones* (1988)
- ▶ *Arcadia* (1992)
- ▶ *Signals of Distress* (1994)
- ▶ *Quarantine* (1997)
- ▶ *The Devil's Larder* (2001)

# A Home at the End of the World (1990)
## Michael Cunningham
### ABOUT THE BOOK
*A Home at the End of the World* is a thoughtful examination of what constitutes a family in modern society. Although the novel tells a story, it does not depend on plot to move it along. It is told from the point of view of four different characters, Jonathan, Bobby, Clare and, occasionally, Jonathan's mother Alice, each of

whom has their own perspective on the complex interplay of relationships between themselves and the other three.

The novel opens in the 1960s when both Jonathan and Bobby are children. Jonathan Glover's family is secure, his parents' marriage stable if a little strained. We hear of his mother's discontent and her lonely frustration at being at home all day. This stability is interrupted by the loss of her newborn baby, a small tragedy made larger by Alice's inability to bear other children.

The Morrows are also a stable family. Bobby and his idolized older brother, Carlton, are in love with the ideals of the Woodstock nation. At one of their parents' parties, Carlton walks through a glass door and dies in his mother's arms. The family, numb from this dreadful tragedy, takes on a stunned, almost somnolent quality. No one is sure whether Mrs Morrow's fatal overdose is deliberate or accidental.

When the two boys meet, Jonathan sets out to charm Bobby. They play music in Jonathan's room, experiment with drugs and, eventually, with sex. Alice sometimes visits them, sometimes dances with Bobby and even smokes a joint, unsure of her welcome from Jonathan. It is almost as if she is exploring a new personality. When she realizes that the boys' relationship has become sexual, she retreats. More accepting than shocked, it's as if she has always known that Jonathan is gay.

When Jonathan moves to New York City, Bobby stays with the Glovers, taking comfort from familiarity. In New York, Jonathan shares an apartment with his new friend, Clare. They go to the movies, decorate their home with funky garage sale junk and plan how they would bring up a child, indulging themselves in a cosy domesticity which lacks only sex. Jonathan's twice-weekly meetings with Erich fill that gap for him but his real life is with Clare, playing the Hendersons game in which Clare plays Mom and Jonathan plays Uncle Jonny.

When the Glovers move to Arizona, Alice tells Bobby he should make a real life for himself. He moves in with Jonathan and Clare, completing the family in the role of Junior Henderson. The dynamics of the household are overturned when Clare and Bobby become lovers. Jonathan, 'in love with both of them', disappears, leaving the couple grief-stricken.

When his father dies, Jonathan seeks out Bobby and Clare, who is pregnant. They move upstate and set up a home-style café, fulfilling all their old dreams. Clare's fierce, fearful love for her child sometimes overwhelms her but when Jonathan discovers that his old friend Erich has Aids, she insists that he move in with them, nursing him until he dies. Eventually, Clare's faith in the strength of her family is undermined and she finds herself facing a stark decision.

## ABOUT THE AUTHOR

Michael Cunningham was born in Cincinnati, Ohio, in 1952 and grew up in Pasadena, California. He took degrees from both Stanford University and the University of Iowa. His work has been widely published in magazines such as *Esquire*, *The New Yorker* and *Vogue*. In 1999, he was awarded the prestigious Pulitzer Prize for fiction for his novel *The Hours*, which was inspired by Virginia Woolf's *Mrs Dalloway*. Michael Cunningham lives in New York City.

## FOR DISCUSSION

▷ The novel is narrated in four different voices, Jonathan's, Bobby's, Alice's and Clare's. How does the writing style of each narrative reflect the character? How successful did you find this structure?

▷ Alice says, 'This is what you do. You make a future for yourself out of the raw material at hand.' What do you think of Alice's philosophy? How has it worked for her? Does she change it at any stage and, if so, how?

▷ The novel opens in the 1960s when Jonathan and Bobby are children. How much have their characters been shaped by the time in which they grew up? How is Alice's life shaped by the social climate of that period? How much do you think Alice's and Clare's experiences differ because of the generation into which they were born?

▷ Why do you think Clare, Bobby and Jonathan play the Hendersons game? How do the characters each of the players take on match their own characters? Do you think this changes throughout the course of the book? How far do you accept Clare, Bobby and Jonathan as a family?

▷ What do you think of Clare's final decision?

▷ On the last page Jonathan says, 'I was merely present, perhaps for the first time in my adult life.' What do you think he means by this and why does he feel it at that point?

▷ When Jonathan says he is in love with both Bobby and Clare, what do you think he means? Clare also says she is in love with both Jonathan and Bobby, do you think she means the same thing as Jonathan?

## SUGGESTED FURTHER READING
▶ *Love Invents Us* by Amy Bloom (1997)
▶ *The Short History of a Prince* by Jane Hamilton (1998)
▶ *The Hotel New Hampshire* by John Irving (1981)
▶ *Equal Affections* by David Leavitt (1989)
▶ *The Ice Storm* by Rick Moody (1994)
▶ **The Magician's Assistant by Ann Patchett (1998)**
▶ *A Regular Guy* by Mona Simpson (1996)

## OTHER BOOKS BY MICHAEL CUNNINGHAM
▶ *Flesh and Blood* (1995)
▶ *The Hours* (1999)

## Talking to the Dead (1996)
## Helen Dunmore

### ABOUT THE BOOK
For such a slim volume, *Talking to the Dead* is a richly complex book. On one level it has the pace of a thriller with clues scattered throughout the plot. On another and almost contradictory level, it is a long prose poem written in language which is as sensuous and languorous as the heat which seems to permeate every page. On yet another level it is packed with insight into the complications of family life and the secrets which may lie hidden for years but which can both shape and destroy our lives.

Nina is a photographer living in London, struggling to make a living but confident in her urban life. By contrast, her sister Isabel is caught up in what at first glance seems to be a rural idyll, living in her adored house in Sussex with her successful economist husband, cultivating her garden, expecting her first baby. But the birth is difficult and when Nina comes to help her sister with her new son,

Antony, she finds that Isabel has become almost agoraphobic, barely having left her house and garden for many months. Isabel's needs seem already to be catered for: Edward, her closest friend, provides support and comfort, despite his own emotional problems, and Susan, the young daughter of a neighbour, is rather bossily but very capably helping her with the baby. Nina's presence seems almost superfluous yet there are bonds between the two sisters that are viscerally deep, shared experience that no one else can comprehend but which makes Nina necessary to Isabel.

As Nina occupies herself with drawing and cooking so she begins to remember the childhood she shared with Isabel and to fill in the gaps left by always accepting Isabel's version of events. Isabel seems ill and overwrought after Antony's difficult birth and her subsequent hysterectomy but this is no ordinary bout of post-natal depression. Both Nina and Isabel are troubled by long-buried memories of the events that surround the death of their baby brother, Colin.

Almost as a backdrop to the disturbing cross-currents which run through the two sisters' relationship with each other is the sexually obsessive affair on which Nina embarks with her brother-in-law Richard. Yet what would seem to be shocking in its betrayal of one sister by another is tacitly permitted by Isabel. Just as Isabel is the opposite of Nina in her attitude towards food, so sensuously celebrated in the meal which Nina prepares, so too she sees sex as merely a means to an end, something that men need.

When Isabel proposes another celebratory meal, Nina allows her concern at her sister's state of mind to be overridden. She, Edward and Richard drive to Brighton to gather the materials. When they arrive home to find that Isabel has taken Antony and gone off to the beach alone, Nina is horrified and so begins a gut-wrenching lurch towards a climax which has haunted the novel since the first disturbing chapter.

## ABOUT THE AUTHOR

Helen Dunmore was born in Beverley, Yorkshire, in 1952. After studying English at York University, she spent two years teaching in Finland. She is a children's writer and an award-winning poet as well as a novelist. In 1996 she was the first winner of the Orange Prize, open only to women novelists, for *A Spell of Winter*. She lives in Bristol.

## FOR DISCUSSION

▷ How would you describe the relationship between Nina and Isabel at the beginning of the novel? How has your view changed by the end? Were there significant points at which your view changed?

▷ The story is told through Nina's voice. Do you feel that you gain as strong a view of Isabel's character as you do of Nina's? How would you describe Isabel? Does your view of her change? If so, why?

▷ Edward says to Nina: 'There's something missing in you.' Do you think this is true? If so, what is it? What reasons do you think there might be?

▷ Why do you think Nina sleeps with Richard? Do you find their affair shocking? If so, why? What does Isabel's attitude to the affair seem to be? How does your view of Richard change? Do you think the nature of their affair changes?

▷ In Chapter 9, Nina describes her preparation of the celebratory meal and the meal itself. What does this chapter tell us about each of the characters? Do you think that it is an important event in the development of the novel? If so, why?

▷ How do you think Colin died? Do you believe Isabel's version of events? Do you think the ending of the novel is ambiguous?

▷ Nina has several dreams which throw light on the past. Why do you think Dunmore has used this method to elucidate Nina and Isabel's childhood relationship?

▷ Do you think that Dunmore's writing style reflects the fact that she is a poet? If so can you find examples of language, imagery and metaphor in the novel to support this?

▷ Nina says: 'People do strange things when it's as hot as this.' Heat is present in the book almost as a character – do you think this has a purpose? If so, what do you think it is?

## SUGGESTED FURTHER READING
▶ **Behind the Scenes at the Museum by Kate Atkinson (1995)**
▶ *The Game* by A.S. Byatt (1967)
▶ *Telling Liddy* by Anne Fine (1998)
▶ *Limestone and Clay* by Lesley Glaister (1993)
▶ *Sleepwalking* by Julie Myerson (1994)

## OTHER BOOKS BY HELEN DUNMORE
### NOVELS
▶ *Zennor in Darkness* (1994)
▶ *Burning Bright* (1995)
▶ *A Spell of Winter* (1996)
▶ *Your Blue-eyed Boy* (1999)
▶ *With Your Crooked Heart* (1999)
▶ *The Siege* (2001)

### SHORT STORIES
▶ *Love of Fat Men* (1998)
▶ *Ice Cream* (2000)

### POETRY
▶ *Apple Fall* (1983)
▶ *The Sea Skater* (1986)
▶ *The Raw Garden* (1988)
▶ *Short Days, Long Nights: New and Selected Poems* (1991)
▶ *Recovering a Body* (1994)
▶ *Bestiary* (1997)
▶ *Bouncing Boy* (1999)
▷ *Out of the Blue* (2001)

### FOR CHILDREN
▶ *Going to Egypt* (1992)
▶ *In the Money* (1995)
▶ *Secrets* (poetry, 1995)
▶ *Amina's Blanket* (1996)
▶ *Fatal Error* (1996)
▶ *Go Fox* (1996)
▶ *Allie's Apples* (1997)
▶ *Great-Grandma's Dancing Dress* (1998)
▶ *Clyde's Leopard* (1998)
▶ *Allie's Rabbit* (1999)
▶ *Brother Brother, Sister Sister* (1999)

▶ *Aliens Don't Eat Bacon Sandwiches* (2000)
▶ *Allie Away* (2000)
▶ *Zillah and Me* (2000)
▶ *Snollygoster* (poetry, 2001)
▶ *The Ugly Duckling* (2001)
▶ *The Zillah Rebellion* (2001)

# Birdsong (1994)
## Sebastian Faulks
### ABOUT THE BOOK

Although not originally intended as a trilogy, three of Sebastian Faulks's novels – *Birdsong, The Girl at the Lion D'Or* and *Charlotte Gray* – are linked through location, history and several minor characters. *Birdsong* and *Charlotte Gray* are set in the arenas of war, but in both novels Faulks vividly depicts his characters' personal lives so that we never forget that they are ordinary people whose lives have been thrown into chaos by cataclysmic events. *Birdsong* is largely set at the Western Front of the First World War. It contains graphic scenes of bloodshed which, while gut-wrenching, are wholly necessary to the novel's themes.

*Birdsong* opens with Stephen Wrayford's arrival at Amiens in 1910. He has been invited to stay with Monsieur Azaire, the local textile factory owner. Stephen's obsession with his host's wife, Isabelle, leads to a passionate, sexually charged affair. Eventually Isabelle leaves her husband for Stephen but disappears when she finds she is pregnant.

The war chapters span the years from 1916 to 1918, covering the ferocious battles of the Marne, Verdun and the Somme. Losses were appalling. In the Somme campaign alone, around one million casualties were sustained out of an estimated three million participants. These chapters follow the fortunes of three main characters – Stephen, Jack Firebrace and Michael Weir.

Stephen, now a lieutenant in the British Army, is regarded as cold and eccentric by both officers and men. Alongside his battalion a company of miners and London Underground workers are attempting to penetrate German defences by constructing a system of tunnels. Like Stephen, Jack Firebrace manages to survive both the hazards of tunnelling and the carnage of battle. He sustains himself through dreadful physical conditions, the loss of his only child and, ultimately, the deaths of all his colleagues, stifling his emotions and seeking solace in memories of his wife and son.

Refusing all offers of leave, Stephen fights on, fired by a furious hatred of the enemy coupled with a peculiar curiosity to see how things turn out. Others are not so fortunate. As the war continues, Stephen's closest friend, Michael Weir, loses both his nerve and his capacity for hope and is eventually killed by a sniper's bullet.

In 1917 Stephen returns to Amiens and finds Isabelle's sister, Jeanne. He makes his peace with Isabelle, still unaware that he has a daughter. He continues to write to Jeanne, meeting her when he can, comforted by her quiet faith in him.

Stephen survives the war, rescued from collapsing earthworks by a German officer just as the guns fall silent, too late to save Jack who was in the tunnel with him. He and Jeanne marry and settle in Norfolk.

Alternating with the battlefield scenes is the story of Elizabeth Benson, thirty-eight, single, childless and engaged in an affair with a married man. Elizabeth stumbles on one of Stephen's war diaries. The diary is in code but Elizabeth sets out to uncover the details of her grandfather's life in an effort to discover her own history and find some meaning to her life. As Elizabeth begins her journey into the past, her own life changes irrevocably when she discovers she is pregnant.

## ABOUT THE AUTHOR

Sebastian Faulks was born in Newbury, England, in 1953. He graduated from Cambridge University in 1974 and took a job teaching in a London school. He wrote freelance book reviews for a variety of papers and in 1978 left teaching to become a reporter for *The Daily Telegraph*, later becoming a feature writer for *The Sunday Telegraph*. His first novel, *A Trick of the Light*, was published in 1984 and in 1986 he became literary editor at the newly established *Independent* newspaper. His second novel, *The Girl at the Lion D'Or*, was published in 1989, and in 1991 he left journalism to write fiction full time. *Birdsong* has remained a consistent bestseller since its publication in 1994.

## FOR DISCUSSION

▷ What do you think of Faulks's descriptions of the relationships between his male and female characters? How do they compare with his descriptions of the relationships between the male characters in the novel?

▷ Why do you think Isabelle leaves Stephen, having sacrificed home, family and reputation for him? What do you think the consequences are for both of them?

▷ Stephen Wraysford is described by various characters as 'cold' or 'strange'. How would you describe his character? Does he have traits which help him to deal with the horrors that he experiences and, if so, what are they? How is he changed by the war?

▷ Stephen is one of the few characters to survive the war, virtually the only character who has continuously fought at the Front. Why do you think he survives when others don't? Is it simply chance or does something else sustain him? Are there significant points at which his view of the war changes?

▷ How would you describe Firebrace's character? How is he changed by the war? Are there other events that change him, and if so what are they and how do they change him? Why does he seem relieved to die?

▷ How would you describe the relationships between officers and men? What are the different ways in which the officers try to motivate the men while dealing with their own horrors?

▷ How would you compare the experiences of the officers with those of the men at the Front? How do both officers and men try to cope with what would seem to be intolerable horror? How successful do you think Faulks is in conveying the state of mind of the forces at the Front?

▷ Firebrace reflects that 'None of these men would admit that what they saw and what they did were beyond the boundaries of human behaviour.' Why do you think this is so? The letters home on the eve of the first attack of the Somme are optimistic to the point of being almost anodyne, despite the horrors which surround the men. Why do you think this might be so?

▷ Why do you think Faulks introduces Elizabeth into the story? What purpose does she serve both in the development of the story and in any message that you feel Faulks is trying to convey?

▷ Stephen's life is ultimately saved by a German soldier. How significant is this? Why do you think Faulks chose a German Jew to save Stephen's life?

▷ How important do you think fiction is in helping us to understand history and the important issues that shape our lives? How successful do you think *Birdsong* is in this context?

## SUGGESTED FURTHER READING
### FICTION
▶ *The Regeneration Trilogy* by Pat Barker, published separately as:
  *Regeneration* (1992)
  *The Eye in the Door* (1994)
  *The Ghost Road* (1995)
▶ *A Very Long Engagement* by Sebastien Japrisot (1991)
▶ *All Quiet on the Western Front* by Erich Maria Remarque (1930)
▶ *War and Peace* by Leo Tolstoy (1805)

### AUTOBIOGRAPHY
▶ *Undertones of War* by Edmund Blunden (1928)
▶ *Testament of Youth* by Vera Brittain (1933)
▶ *Goodbye to All That* by Robert Graves (1929)

### FIRST WORLD WAR HISTORY
▶ *The Donkeys* by Alan Clark (1991)
▶ *The First World War* by Martin Gilbert (1994)
▶ *The Somme* by Lyn Macdonald (1983)

## OTHER BOOKS BY SEBASTIAN FAULKS
### NOVELS
▶ *A Trick of the Light* (1984)
▶ *The Girl at the Lion D'Or* (1989)
▶ *A Fool's Alphabet* (1992)
▶ *Charlotte Gray* (1998)
▶ *On Green Dolphin Street* (2000)

### NON-FICTION
▶ *The Fatal Englishman: Three Short Lives* (1990)

### EDITED (WITH JORG HENSGEN)
▶ *The Vintage Book of War Stories* (1997)

# Cold Mountain (1997)
## Charles Frazier

### ABOUT THE BOOK
*Cold Mountain* is the story of two journeys. Inman's journey is homeward. It takes him through a stricken land, shattered by the brutality of the American Civil War. His sweetheart Ada's journey is one of self-discovery as she learns that the love of knowledge and beauty cherished by her father has left her lamentably unprepared for survival. Frazier alternates their stories, drawing them ever closer in a novel that is as much about the human ability to adapt and endure as it is about love.

The novel opens with Inman's recuperation in hospital from a severe neck wound. Rather than be sent back to fight a war in which he has lost all faith, he decides to walk home to North Carolina. Despite the hazards of the journey, travelling through backwoods, avoiding both the Unionist Federal forces, who will shoot him as an enemy, and the Confederate Home Guard, who will shoot him as a deserter, Inman is convinced that his chances of survival are greater than returning to the bloody battlefields he has endured for four years.

His journey is filled with incident and reflection. It is long and arduous, passing through difficult country, beset by dangers from vigilantes and robbers. Veasey, a preacher found trying to drown a young woman pregnant with his child, becomes his unwelcome companion. The two are eventually betrayed to Teague's Home Guard which roams the land in search of deserters. Veasey is killed but Inman narrowly escapes. Continuing his journey, Inman finds that there is still kindness and generosity to be found in this devastated country. A hermit woman tends his wounds and gives him a good supper. Even the poorest refuse to take the money he offers for food they can hardly spare. In turn, Inman is still capable of self-sacrifice, risking his life to return a hog stolen by armed thugs to a young woman bereft but for the hog and her baby. Throughout his travels, he comforts himself with a book of nature writings, his memories of Cold Mountain and his decision to ask Ada to marry him.

Alternating with Inman's journey is the story of how Ada learns to survive. Her father brought her up to believe in the sustaining qualities of beauty and knowledge but not the sort of knowledge that Ada desperately needs to keep herself alive. After her father's death, she is left poor and alone with no idea of how to run the farm he has left her. When Ruby arrives, Ada is almost starving. Proclaiming that she is no servant but that she will stay and help run the farm, Ruby sets about teaching Ada some practical skills. Ruby's arrival marks not only the beginning of an enduring friendship but also the start of Ada's quest for a different kind of knowledge.

Just as Inman thinks of her on his journey home, so Ada becomes sure of their love. Not knowing where he is or if he is still alive, she thinks of him, pondering his last letter which simply says he will return.

## ABOUT THE AUTHOR

Charles Frazier was born in North Carolina in 1950. He took degrees at Chapel Hill and Appalachian State followed by a Ph.D. in twentieth-century American literature at the University of South Carolina. He has taught at the University of Colorado and North Carolina State University. *Cold Mountain* was inspired by family stories of his ancestors' experiences in the American Civil War and written using *The Odyssey* as its model. In interviews Frazier has said that Inman is loosely based on his great-great-uncle. *Cold Mountain* is Charles Frazier's first novel and won the American National Book Award in 1997.

## FOR DISCUSSION

▷ How would you describe Inman's character before he went to war? How has he been changed by the war? How does Frazier illustrate this?

▷ Why do you think that Inman thinks of Cold Mountain as a place where 'all his scattered forces might gather'?

▷ Throughout the war and his journey home, Inman has taken comfort from the book by Bartram that he carries with him. How has the book sustained him and what does it tell you about him?

▷ A traveller tells Inman that the road is 'a place apart, a country of its own ruled by no government but natural law, and its one characteristic was freedom'. How is this idea either illustrated or disproved in the book?

▷ What effects has the war had upon the country Inman walks through? What do people's attitudes seem to be to the war? How have they been affected by it?

▷ How would you describe the relationship between Ada and Ruby? Which of them is changed most by it and how?

▷ Ada writes to her cousin Lucy that she has found something 'akin to contentment'. How would you describe that contentment and how do you think she has achieved it?

▷ What do you think of Monroe and the way that he has brought up Ada?

▷ A young man gestures to the battlefield and says to Inman: 'Right there's what mostly comes of knowledge.' Are there similar comments or illustrations of this attitude to knowledge in the book and, if so, what do you think Frazier means by it?

▷ Slavery was a central issue of the American Civil War. Do you think that this is evident in *Cold Mountain*? What do you think the book says about slavery?

## SUGGESTED FURTHER READING

▶ *Birdsong* by Sebastian Faulks (1983)
▶ *On the Occasion of My Last Afternoon* by Kaye Gibbons (1998)
▶ *Oldest Living Confederate Widow Tells All* by Alan Gurganus (1990)
▶ *The Odyssey* by Homer
▶ *Gone with the Wind* by Margaret Mitchell (1936)
▶ *All True Travels and Adventures of Lidie Newton* by Jane Smiley (1998)

## Sheer Blue Bliss (1999)
Lesley Glaister

### ABOUT THE BOOK

Lesley Glaister alternates the voices of a deeply disturbed young man and an elderly woman trying to cope with the disruption and excitement of having her work exhibited at the National Portrait Gallery. Tony's obsessive nature becomes apparent in a narrative suffused with unease and menace. Connie's memories of her youth, in poignant contrast to the pain and sheer hard work of old age, are threaded through the narrative of her trip to London. The two strands are drawn together, and the pace of the novel quickens, as it moves towards its taut climax.

Tony sees the forthcoming retrospective of Connie's work as a sign from his hero, Patrick Mount, who outlined the Seven Steps to Bliss in his memoir. Connie's portrait of Mount, painted shortly before his disappearance in 1965, is being exhibited for the first time. Tony sees Mount's elixirs as a way of easing the pain of his cruel childhood and of controlling a sexuality that threatens to engulf him as it has done once before. Apart from his neighbour in whose girlish flat he finds some sort of comfort, Tony's life is filled by his obsession.

When he visits the exhibition, Tony meets a young woman who recently wrote an article about Connie's Norfolk home. Seizing his chance, he asks her out, manages to get Connie's address and makes his way to Norfolk, confident that he will attain the elixir of bliss.

Connie is thinking about the retrospective with a mixture of excitement and regret. Used to isolation, she is suddenly the centre of attention and unsure of how she feels about it. Memories of her years with Patrick Mount come flooding back to Connie. She tells herself the story of how she came to live with Mount and his wife Sacha as a fourteen-year-old evacuee during the Second World War. When her family were killed in a bombing raid, Connie stayed on, finding some comfort in her consuming desire to paint. Soon after her sixteenth birthday, she and Patrick became lovers, apparently with Sacha's blessing, and lived together until his disappearance in 1965. She continued to paint while he developed his elixirs and wrote the memoir which sparked off Tony's obsession many years later.

Connie spends a week in London, buying clothes, attending her private view and enjoying the perplexity that results from her mild eccentricity. Soon she longs for peace, quiet and isolation but when she returns to Norfolk, she finds she is not alone. A strange and beautiful young man is waiting for her. Unsure of Tony's intentions but soon aware of his instability, Connie takes up a feisty stance but eventually accepts his demands to paint his portrait. When she is too tired to continue, Tony's fragile control begins to unravel and when Lisa, the young journalist, arrives, his carefully constructed world shatters, with chilling results for all of them.

## ABOUT THE AUTHOR

Lesley Glaister was born in 1956 and grew up in Suffolk. She is a graduate of both the Open University and of Sheffield University where she has worked as a writing tutor in the School of Continuing Education. She has also tutored at the Arvon Foundation. She is an occasional book reviewer and has contributed to the *Spectator* and *The Times*. In 1991 her novel *Honour Thy Father* won a Somerset Maugham and a Betty Trask award. Lesley Glaister lives in Sheffield.

## FOR DISCUSSION

▷ An atmosphere of unease pervades *Sheer Blue Bliss* almost from the beginning. How does Lesley Glaister achieve this?

▷ How would you describe Tony? How does Glaister convey Tony's character? Why is he so disturbed? Why do women upset him so much? The only woman with whom he seems remotely comfortable is Donna. Why is this?

▷ Connie's memories of her youth are very vivid. How do you think she feels about getting older? Are her feelings about ageing different in London and, if so, why? What do other people's attitudes to Connie say about the way we see older people in contemporary society?

▷ What does the way Connie is treated in London say about the modern perception of celebrity? How does Connie feel about it?

▷ A year after the deaths of her family, Connie reflects: 'There are those who have suffered and those who haven't and that is the biggest difference between people.' How is this idea reflected in the rest of the novel? What do you think of it?

▷ How does the loss of her family shape Connie's life? How do Sacha and Patrick help her through her grief? To what extent does Sacha become a mother figure for Connie?

▷ What do you think about Patrick's 'phytosophical principle' and the Seven Steps to Bliss? Would Mount's memoir seem out of place in a bookshop today? Why do you think Tony is so attracted to Patrick's ideas?

▷ How big is the difference between Tony's view of Patrick and Connie's view of him? Red describes Patrick as a bully but Connie disagrees. What do you think?

▷ What do you think of Patrick's attitude towards sex? Would you describe Connie's sexual relationship with Patrick as a betrayal of Sacha? Do Patrick and Sacha truly have an 'open marriage'? How does Patrick feel about Connie having other lovers? What do you think of this?

## SUGGESTED FURTHER READING
▶ *The Blind Assassin* by Margaret Atwood (2000)
▶ *The Chymical Wedding* by Lindsay Clarke (1989)
▶ *Nothing Natural* by Jenny Diski (1983)
▶ *Burning Bright* by Helen Dunmore (1994)
▶ *Enduring Love* by Ian McEwan (1997)
▶ *The Artist's Widow* by Shena Mackay (1998)

## OTHER BOOKS BY LESLEY GLAISTER
▶ *Honour Thy Father* (1990)
▶ *Trick or Treat* (1991)
▶ *Digging to Australia* (1992)
▶ *Limestone and Clay* (1993)
▶ *Partial Eclipse* (1994)
▶ *The Private Parts of Women* (1996)
▶ *Easy Peasy* (1997)
▶ *Now You See Me* (2001)

# Disobedience (2000)
## Jane Hamilton

### ABOUT THE BOOK
When seventeen-year-old Henry discovers his mother's infidelity he is faced not only with his own distress and confusion but also with a series of moral dilemmas. Should he confront his mother, reveal her secret or keep quiet? He chooses to keep quiet but is haunted by the affair, unable to resist reading the email correspondence between the lovers. Through Henry, Jane Hamilton explores the tangled relationships of the Shaw family, giving this story of adultery and betrayal a rather unusual spin by telling it from an adolescent boy's point of view filtered through the experience of his adult self.

The novel opens with Henry's discovery of his mother's passion for Richard Polloco, a Ukrainian violin maker she met when playing the piano at a family wedding.

The Shaws moved to Chicago from Vermont three years before when Henry's father, Kevin, lost his job as a high school history teacher. Beth, Henry's mother, is a musician and his sister, thirteen-year-old Elvira, is a passionate Civil War re-enactor who rarely takes off her authentic drummer boy uniform. Although Kevin greatly admires Elvira, Beth is both appalled and humiliated by her daughter's unfeminine and eccentric behaviour. They frequently row about her. In contrast, Henry is a 'middle-aged teenager' whose only act of rebellion appears to be his ponytail.

Before he found out about her affair, Henry's relationship with his mother had been particularly close. She describes him as 'perfectly amiable' to her fellow book club members, who regularly meet to briefly discuss the book they are reading before launching into the real business of men and their failings.

Henry tries to go about his life as usual. He continues his close friendship with Karen, but does not confide his mother's affair to her although he does tell her about Lily with whom he falls in love when away at camp. After reading one of his mother's emails, he visits a psychic, fascinated by her suggestion to Beth that Henry and she were married in a past life. He reluctantly accompanies Beth when she takes Elvira to see her lover's log cabin in Wisconsin.

When Lily comes to stay, Henry tells her about his mother's affair and is confused by her failure to condemn Beth. A new bitterness slips into his feelings for his mother, crystallized when Beth uncharacteristically slaps his face over a trivial incident at a book club meeting. Although he knows that both Richard and Beth are trying to break off their relationship, Henry cannot recover from the slap.

Both parents have agreed that Elvira can't maintain her drummer boy persona much longer. They have devised a gentle and dignified way round the problem but events overtake them when Elvira is cruelly unmasked at a re-enactment on the celebrated battlefield of Shiloh. Both Beth and Kevin come to Elvira's aid in very different ways and their mutual concern kick-starts their marriage. As the members of the family pick up their lives, Henry is left to try to make sense of this most troubling of years and, a decade later, remains haunted by it.

## ABOUT THE AUTHOR

In 1989 Jane Hamilton's first book, *The Book of Ruth*, was awarded the PEN/ Hemingway Foundation Award for best first novel. Both her first novel and her second, *A Map of the World*, were selected for Oprah Winfrey's book club while her third, *The Short History of a Prince*, was shortlisted for the 1999 Orange Prize. She lives and works in her orchard farmhouse in Wisconsin.

## FOR DISCUSSION

▷ What is the significance of the title of the book? Which of the characters have been disobedient and what form has that disobedience taken? What do you think of Hamilton's choice of the word 'disobedience'?

▷ How has the young Henry's electronic eavesdropping shaped the adult Henry? For instance, how do you think it contributes to the kind of relationships he has with women, which we learn about from hints and asides in his narrative? Do you think his knowledge of the affair or the way that he gained that knowledge was more damaging? Do you think his behaviour was excusable?

▷ What kind of parents are Beth and Kevin Shaw? Their main point of conflict appears to be Elvira's passion for Civil War re-enactment. Why does Kevin think it is acceptable whereas Beth, despite her apparent unconventionality, does not? What does their disagreement and the different way that they handle the situation tell us about their characters?

▷ Henry is looking back over the year of the affair nearly ten years later. Why do you think Hamilton chose to have him do this rather than reporting the events as they happen? What difference does it make to your interpretation of events?

▷ Henry says: 'As a child I had no idea that the Shaws, the four of us, were removed from our century.' Elvira's removal is obvious but how are the others 'removed from our century'?

▷ Henry refers on several occasions to the 'ironic sensibility' of his generation. How does this manifest itself in his narrative? Do you think the use of irony adds to, or detracts from, the telling of the Shaws' story?

▷ Do you think that Henry would have behaved differently if he had been a girl and, if so, in what way?

▷ Henry refers to the Oedipal myth when he says: 'I was married to my mother, without having had to murder my father or pluck out my eyeballs.' Are there traces of Oedipus in Henry and, if so, how does this come out in his narrative?

▷ When his mother takes him and Elvira to meet Richard, Henry feels that he has had an epiphany, that he understands that his mother is having an affair because she is facing a 'blank' future when he leaves home. Do you think that this is what lies behind the affair or do you agree with Karen's assessment that this is the last sexual fling of a soon-to-be menopausal woman? What other reasons might there be for the affair?

▷ When the parents finally quarrel about Elvira shaving her head, Beth says that the boys who counted Elvira as one of them will 'feel hurt and ashamed and silly and embarrassed and betrayed' when they find she is a girl. Kevin replies that it will be 'a good training for what future women will do to them'. Does this prove to be the case? To what extent does this idea resonate through the rest of the novel? How significant is gender in the novel?

▷ What did you think of the book club scenes?

## SUGGESTED FURTHER READING
▶ *The Crow Road* **by Iain Banks (1992)**
▶ *A Crime in the Neighbourhood* by Suzanne Berne (1997)
▶ *Crooked Hearts* by Robert Boswell (1987)
▶ *Cold Mountain* **by Charles Frazier (1997)**
▶ *Exposure* by Katherine Harrison (1994)
▶ *The Ice Storm* by Rick Moody (1994)
▶ *A Thousand Acres* by Jane Smiley (1991)
▶ *Anna Karenina* by Leo Tolstoy (1874–6)

## OTHER BOOKS BY JANE HAMILTON
▶ *The Book of Ruth* (1989)
▶ *A Map of the World* (1994)
▶ *A Short History of a Prince* (1998)

# Stones From the River (1994)
## Ursula Hegi

### ABOUT THE BOOK
Spanning the years from 1915 to 1952, *Stones From the River* is a complex and searching portrait of a small German town seen through the unflinching gaze of Trudi Montag. As it struggles to deal with the blow to its pride inflicted by the humiliating defeat of the First World War, Burgdorf represents a microcosm of Germany, ripe for the rise of a political party fired by nationalistic fervour. In its examination of the effects of the Nazi regime on a small German community, the novel is a humane and profound attempt to understand how such a thing could happen and why silence descended when it ceased.

When Trudi is born in 1915, her mother is so emotionally disturbed that she refuses to touch her child. After three months Gertrud accepts her daughter but shortly after the stillbirth of her second child, she returns to the local asylum for the last time. She dies just before Trudi's fourth birthday. Trudi misses her terribly but forges a close and loving bond with her father. Wounded in 1914, Leo now runs the local library.

When the men return from the war dazed with defeat, they look to Leo to help them out of their confusion. In counterpoint to Leo, Herr Immers, whose broken back excused him from active service, has gradually convinced himself that he fought valiantly for his country, a fantasy which is sometimes indulged, often ignored but never contested by the other townspeople.

Trudi is a *zwerg*, a dwarf, and her 'otherness' leaves her prey to bullying. Her friendships are tentative and circumscribed by other people's reactions to her. Georg, whose mother dresses him as a girl, accepts her as a friend until he finally has his hair cut, dons lederhosen and joins the other boys. Afraid that her schoolmates will shun her, Eva Rosen's friendship stops at the school gates. Bruised and humiliated, Trudi finds comfort in her motherly neighbour, Frau Abramowitz.

By the time Trudi becomes an adult, Nazism has begun its inexorable rise. Jewish members of the Burgdorf community are forced to wear yellow stars, find their property damaged or confiscated and are finally arrested and taken to the camps. Fear and suspicion stalk the town. Some, including Leo and Trudi, help their Jewish neighbours and friends, but most do not. Many feel that, if they just keep quiet, things will blow over. When Trudi finds a Jewish woman hiding with her young son, she and her father take them in. Later they will hide Eva Rosen, now a dear friend.

After years of yearning for a lover, Trudi begins a passionate affair with a man who returns her love without reservation. Their affair is brought to an abrupt and cruel end when he disappears while searching for the Abramowitzs' daughter in Dresden on the day of the firebombing.

At the end of the war the men come home and Burgdorf begins to count its losses. Silence closes around the horrors of the Nazi regime but Trudi feels compelled to break it with her persistent questioning.

## ABOUT THE AUTHOR

Ursula Hegi spent the first eighteen years of her life in Germany, before going to live in the United States. She has been a regular reviewer for *The New York Times*, the *Los Angeles Times* and *The Washington Post*. She has also taught both creative writing and contemporary literature at Eastern Washington University. *Stones From the River* can be seen as a 'prequel' to her novel *Floating in My Mother's Palm*, set in 1950s Burgdorf. Two characters from the fringes of *Stones From the River*, Stefan Blau and Helene Montag, reappear in Hegi's fifth novel, *The Vision of Emma Blau*. In the course of her researches for *Stones From the River*, Hegi interviewed her German godmother who had lived through the period covered by the book.

## FOR DISCUSSION

▷ Why do you think Hegi makes her principal character a *zwerg* or dwarf? How do other characters respond to her 'otherness'? How does she cope with the cruelty of other children and how does it change her? Would this still happen today?

▷ When Trudi was fourteen years old she was dragged into a barn and assaulted by four young boys, one of whom was her first real friend. How does Hegi use this incident to develop Trudi's character, both immediately after the attack and throughout the rest of the book? Does she ever come to terms with it and, if so, how?

▷ Trudi collects stories about the people of Burgdorf, storing them up for future use. Why does she do this? How does the way she uses those stories change over the years? How does this illustrate the changes in Trudi's character?

▷ How do the Jewish members of the community fit in before the war? At what point does this begin to change? Were there signs of prejudice before the war and if so what were they?

▷ Frau Blau and Trudi discuss the possibility that Herr Immer's grandmother may have been Jewish. Trudi thinks: 'Until now, she'd never thought of the butcher as afraid. She'd only seen his loathing for the Jews, his malice, but now she wondered if all of that was just fear and, perhaps, contempt for himself.' To what extent do you think this idea can explain prejudice? What other reasons might people have for hating those who can be described as 'other'?

▷ How do Hegi's characters react as Nazism begins to take hold? Are particular characters more receptive than others? If so, who are they and why? Conversely, are there characters whose resistance surprises you?

▷ Trudi and her father show enormous courage in helping Jews during the war. How does this change Trudi? How does it change the way people respond to her?

▷ When Herr Pastor Beier and Sister Agathe are discussing her feelings of guilt, after the war, he says: 'Don't say that. That would make us all accomplices.' She replies: 'But we are. Don't you see?' What does she mean by this, and to what extent do you agree with her?

▷ Given Hegi's German background, why do you think she decided to write *Stones From the River*? How difficult do you think it is for post-war generations in Germany to deal with the emotional aftermath of the Second World War? How do the people of Burgdorf cope with it? What changes happen in the community? Why won't Trudi let things rest? What is the community's attitude towards the Jews and their experiences in the camps?

▷ Has the book helped you to understand how such an atrocity as the Holocaust could take place? If so, how has it done that?

## SUGGESTED FURTHER READING
### FICTION

▶ *The Archivist* by Martha Cooley (1998)
▶ *Middlemarch* by George Eliot (1872)
▶ *The Tin Drum* by Günter Grass (1959)
▶ *A Prayer for Owen Meany* by John Irving (1989)
▶ *Schindler's List* by Thomas Keneally (1982)
▶ *The Time of Light* by Gunnar Kopperud (1998)
▶ **Fugitive Pieces by Anne Michaels (1997)**
▶ **The Reader by Bernhard Schlink (1997)**
▶ *Sophie's Choice* by William Styron (1979)
▶ *A Model Childhood* by Christa Wolf (1976)

**NON-FICTION**
- ▶ *The Past is Myself* by Christabel Bielenberg (1970)
- ▶ *Anne Frank: The Diary of a Young Girl* by Anne Frank (1947)
- ▶ *The Drowned and the Saved* by Primo Levi (1986)

## OTHER BOOKS BY URSULA HEGI
- ▶ *Intrusions* (1981)
- ▶ *Floating in My Mother's Palm* (1991)
- ▶ *Salt Dancers* (1995)
- ▶ *The Vision of Emma Blau* (2000)

# Empress of the Splendid Season (1999)
## Oscar Hijuelos

### ABOUT THE BOOK

*Empress of the Splendid Season* is a tender portrayal of the life of a Cuban immigrant in New York whose pride never lets her forget that she has come down in the world. Although both Lydia and her husband are proud to be Cuban their aspirations for their children are based on the American Dream. Through the España family, Oscar Hijuelos gently explores the difficulties of building a life in a new country without losing touch with the old.

Lydia's story is told through a series of closely linked vignettes which crisscross the years from the 1950s to the 1980s. They provide snapshots of her employers' lives and a vibrant portrait of the immigrant community of Spanish Harlem as well as a narrative of Lydia's life.

Lydia left Cuba in disgrace at sixteen when her father, a wealthy business-man, threw her out after she spent the night with a visiting bandleader. Using a small inheritance, she found her way to New York where she worked as a seamstress, struggling to adjust to her poverty. She still holds herself just a little apart, carrying herself so proudly that the children on the street call her 'Queenie'.

Lydia gave up work when she married Raul. His job as a waiter brought in just enough to raise a family and pay maintenance to his first wife for their son, a thorn in Lydia's side. Lydia has many aspirations for their own two children. Raul is a good, hard-working husband, whose only fault is his failure to curtail his smoking and drinking which exacerbate his poor health. Although Lydia indulges her sensuality by fantasizing about other men, she and Raul have a satisfying marriage.

When Raul has a heart attack, Lydia has to support the family and finds work as a cleaner, a change in status she finds painful. Her employers are many and varied, from an Aleister Crowley devotee, to a psychotherapist who used to work with Freud, to Susannah Morales, a Cuban diva and one of Lydia's idols. She has an enduring relationship with the Ospreys, a wealthy family who embody everything to which she aspires. She enjoys romantic fantasies about Mr Osprey while quietly admiring his well-preserved wife. It is Mr Osprey who comes to the rescue when her son gets into trouble, finding him a scholarship which eventually leads to a career as a psychotherapist, sought after by the very people for whom his mother cleans.

As the children grow up and lead the sort of lives that their mother had always wanted for them, a gulf opens up between them and their parents. Lydia still finds solace in the company of other cleaning ladies, and she and Raul still go to parties with their Cuban friends. When Raul suffers a final heart attack, Lydia is bereft. She continues to clean for Mr Osprey, who has also been widowed, even after she breaks her hip, until his decision to sell up and travel abroad draws the novel to a gentle close.

## ABOUT THE AUTHOR
Oscar Hijuelos was born the son of working-class Cuban immigrants in New York in 1951. He took a BA and a Masters at New York's City College where he studied writing under the novelist Donald Barthelme. Before taking up writing full-time, Hijuelos did a series of odd jobs from raising insects in Wisconsin and selling shoes in Macy's to writing advertisements for display in New York City subway cars. His first novel, *Our House in the Last World*, won him the American Academy Arts and Letters 1985 Rome Prize, enabling him to spend a year in Italy where he began the Pulitzer Prize-winning *The Mambo Kings Play Songs of Love*, later made into a film. Hijuelos still lives in New York City.

## FOR DISCUSSION
▷ Although not written in the first person, the novel attempts to give us an insight into Lydia and her world. How successful is Hijuelos at portraying a woman's perspective?

▷ How would you describe Lydia? Are there contradictions in her character and, if so, what are they? How does the Lydia at the beginning of the book differ from Lydia at the end?

▷ How does their position as the children of working-class immigrants shape the characters of Lydia's children, in particular Rico? How have their adult relationships with their parents been affected?

▷ What does the book say about social divisions in America? Are these divisions along the lines of race, class, money or all three? How does Lydia maintain her self-respect despite the change in her status from upper-middle-class Cuban to working-class American?

▷ How would you describe the relationship between Lydia and the Ospreys? How do you think they feel about her? Why is Lydia so drawn to them?

▷ How does Lydia feel about Cuba? Do you think she feels Cuban, American, or neither? Are her feelings different from Raul's and, if so, how does this manifest itself?

▷ Much of the novel is written as a series of linked vignettes from Lydia's life. What effect does this have? What is Hijuelos trying to achieve by italicizing passages in the novel and regularly placing comments in brackets? How successful do you find this technique?

## SUGGESTED FURTHER READING
▶ *The Infinite Plan* by Isabel Allende (1994)
▶ *Dreamland* by Kevin Baker (1999)
▶ *Tortilla Curtain* by T. Coraghessan Boyle (1995)
▶ *For Kings and Planets* by Ethan Canin (1998)
▶ *This Side of Brightness* by Colum McCann (1998)
▶ *Accordion Crimes* by Annie Proulx (1996)
▶ *The Hundred Secret Senses* by Amy Tan (1995)

## OTHER BOOKS BY OSCAR HIJUELOS
▶ *Our House in the Last World* (1983)
▶ *The Mambo Kings Play Songs of Love* (1989)
▶ *The Fourteen Sisters of Emilio Montez O'Brien* (1993)
▶ *Mr Ives' Christmas* (1995)

## Animal Dreams (1991)
## Barbara Kingsolver

### ABOUT THE BOOK
In *Animal Dreams*, Barbara Kingsolver explores the dislocation of the rootless metropolitan life that Codi, the central character, has left behind and the interdependence of those who live in the small community of Grace. Interweaving Native American beliefs with the discovery of an impending environmental disaster, Kingsolver highlights the gulf in attitudes towards the natural world between those who have lived off it for centuries and those to whom profit is paramount.

Codi has been drifting through her life in Tucson. Since dropping out of medical school she has had a succession of dead-end jobs. Her beloved sister Hallie has left to offer her horticultural expertise to the beleaguered farmers of Nicaragua, and her ten-year relationship is going nowhere. When she is offered a one-year contract as a science teacher back in her home community of Grace, she packs up and goes, staying with Emelina, the only person there with whom she is still in contact.

In the main, the novel is written from Codi's point of view, with occasional short chapters in which her father tries to untangle memories of his daughters from the confusion into which Alzheimer's has thrown him. Codi's mother died when she was three, shortly after giving birth to Hallie. She has not seen her father since he told her about his illness two years ago. Theirs is a difficult relationship, constrained by the multitude of rules which her father felt necessary to impose while bringing up two girls on his own.

Absent from Grace for fourteen years, Codi is welcomed by all but feels an outsider, remembering almost nothing of her childhood. She sets about making a life for herself, winning over her students with an inspired lecture on contraception. When, as a result of an experiment, she and her students discover that the local river is contaminated with sulphuric acid, she seeks the help of the matriarchs of the Stitch and Bitch Club, a sewing circle with attitude. Their ideas for fundraising are successful enough to find a way to combat the Black Mountain mining company whose attempts to leach copper deposits from the defunct mine have resulted in the pollution.

When Codi becomes reacquainted with a Native American, Loyd Peregrina, with whom she had a brief relationship when she was fifteen, she finds herself attracted to him once again. Loyd is everything that Codi is not, comfortable with himself and his place in the world, firmly rooted in his culture and his community – qualities to which Codi is both attracted and resistant.

Still missing her sister, Codi relies upon letters to reassure her of Hallie's safety. Hallie's letters are a mixture of delight at what she and the farmers manage to achieve and anger at the destruction wreaked by the American-funded Contras in Nicaragua. When Hallie is kidnapped, Codi's world is shaken, her new-found roots torn up. Then she discovers a family secret that helps her to understand both her father and the ambivalence which she has always felt about her own place in Grace.

## ABOUT THE AUTHOR

Barbara Kingsolver was born in Annapolis, Maryland, in 1955 and grew up in rural Kentucky where her father was the local physician. She won a scholarship to DePauw University, Indiana, where she majored in biology, took a creative writing course and became active in the last anti-Vietnam War protests. After graduating in 1977, she lived and worked in a variety of places including France and Greece. In the early 1980s she took a masters degree in biology and ecology at the University of Arizona. She took up a position as a science writer at the university, and went on to write features for journals and newspapers such as *The New York Times* and *Smithsonian*. Kingsolver took up writing fiction when she suffered from insomnia while pregnant. Her first novel, *The Bean Trees*, was published in 1988. She remains keenly interested in ecology, a recurrent theme in her novels, and is an active environmentalist and human rights supporter.

## FOR DISCUSSION

▷ Codi and Hallie are very different from each other. How would you describe Hallie's attitude to life? How does it differ from Codi's approach? What are the most important factors in shaping that approach and why?

▷ Why does Codi feel such an outsider when she comes back to Grace? How do those feelings change and why?

▷ The natural world is an important theme in *Animal Dreams*. Codi asks her class: 'Do you, or do you not, think the world was put here for you to use?' What do you think Loyd's answer to this question would be, and why? How do you think the board of the Black Mountain mining company would answer? What would your answer be?

▷ Arizona was originally in Spanish hands and was only incorporated into the United States early in the twentieth century. It is also home to some of the largest Native American communities in the US. How important are cultural differences in *Animal Dreams*? How do the different cultures of Grace get along together?

▷ Would you describe *Animal Dreams* as a political novel and, if so, which aspects of the novel meet this description? Is the book successful in conveying a message and, if so, how does it achieve this and what is the message?

▷ Why do you think Kingsolver chose to call the novel *Animal Dreams*? How important are Codi's dreams?

▷ What kind of parent do you think Codi's father was, and why? Why is their relationship so difficult? How does Kingsolver convey their difficulties? Do you think they understand each other better by the end of the book and, if so, how has this come about?

▷ Both Homero and Codi have difficulties in remembering things. How does Kingsolver use Homero's loss of memory to develop the novel? How does it illuminate our understanding of his feelings for his daughters? Why does Codi seem to have so few memories of her early life in Grace? What is the effect of her recovering those memories?

▷ Apart from Homero and Loyd, the male characters in the novel seem to fade into the background. Do you think this is a deliberate choice and, if so, why? How do reactions to the contamination of the river by the Black Mountain mining company divide along gender lines? To what extent do you think this is accurate and why?

## SUGGESTED FURTHER READING
**FICTION**
▶ *The Monkey Wrench Gang* by Edward Abbey (1975)
▶ *Reservation Blues* by Sherman Alexie (1995)
▶ *A Friend of the Earth* by T.C. Boyle (1999)
▶ *The Beet Queen* by Louise Erdrich (1986)
▶ *Goodnight Nebraska* by Tom McNeal (1998)
▶ *The Grass Dancer* by Susan Power (1994)

**NON-FICTION**
▶ *The Jaguar Smile* by Salman Rushdie (1987)

## OTHER BOOKS BY BARBARA KINGSOLVER
**NOVELS**
▶ *The Bean Trees* (1988)
▶ *Pigs in Heaven* (1993)
▶ *The Poisonwood Bible* (1999)
▶ *Prodigal Summer* (2000)

**SHORT STORIES**
▶ *Homeland and Other Stories* (1989)

**ESSAYS**
▶ *High Tide in Tucson: Essays from Now and Forever* (1995)
▶ *Small Wonder* (2002)

# The Vintner's Luck (1999)
## Elizabeth Knox

**ABOUT THE BOOK**

Although the relationship between an angel and a vintner is central to *The Vintner's Luck*, the novel is firmly rooted in the earthy reality of a nineteenth-century French village. The angel Xas is a physical, muscular presence, insatiably curious about the world. He and Sobran share theological debates along with their wine just as Sobran and the Comte's niece debate new ideas emerging from scientific advances.

The novel begins in 1808 with Sobran's disappointment at his rejection by Céleste. Taking two bottles of wine, he climbs a hill above the family vineyard to drown his romantic sorrows. He sees what he thinks at first to be a statue on the hillside. When he realizes that it is a living creature he faints, falling into the Xas's arms. Recovering himself, he tells Xas his problems, shares his wine and agrees to meet him the following year.

Sobran and Xas meet almost every year until Sobran's death. The structure of the novel follows the pattern of those years – each year has its own section.

Sobran marries Céleste who quickly presents him with his first child. He has his troubles. His relationship with his brother is difficult and will be until Léon's violent death. A murder of a young girl remains unsolved and, seven years later, another girl is killed. When a third is murdered, shortly before Léon's death, Sobran thinks he has solved the crime.

In 1811 Sobran follows his closest friend to war, surviving the terrible Russian winter only to see Baptiste perish. After his father's death, Sobran merges Baptiste's vineyards with his own. The Comte begins to turn to him for advice, telling his niece, Aurora, to do the same.

When Sobran's daughter dies in 1819 he seeks comfort with Xas. Desire creeps into their relationship. Xas reluctantly agrees to visit Sobran's daughter in heaven and is wounded by another angel. Unhinged by grief, Céleste becomes unpredictable and drifts away from Sobran.

On the twentieth anniversary of their first meeting, Sobran lays out a feast for Xas and shares the year's news. The Comte has died and Aurora has asked Sobran to take charge of her vineyard. Sure that he will be reunited in heaven with everyone he loves, Sobran's world seems complete. When Xas reveals that he is a fallen angel, Sobran runs away, appalled. The madness that consumes him is replaced by an obsessive piety. He will not see Xas for three years.

His business relationship with Aurora deepens into a friendship based on a mutual interest in philosophy. Rumours circulate, adding fuel to speculation about Sobran's nocturnal wanderings on 27 June each year. When Aurora finds she has breast cancer, Sobran promises that he will share his secret if she submits to the surgeon's knife. She survives but excuses herself on the night of Sobran's meeting with Xas, watching them in secret.

Xas arrives one day, unannounced and horribly wounded after a second encounter with the Archangel. Aurora comes to Sobran's aid but Xas is only saved by the arrival of Lucifer who takes drastic action.

In the following years, Xas travels the world, sometimes writing to Sobran, sometimes staying with him. Sobran's friendship with Aurora becomes his mainstay. The next generation prospers and the wine continues to improve. When Sobran dies, both Céleste and Xas are at his side.

## ABOUT THE AUTHOR

Elizabeth Knox is a native of New Zealand where she lives with her husband and family in Wellington. In interviews, she has said that the idea behind *The Vintner's Luck* had come to her in a dream when she was delirious with pneumonia.

## FOR DISCUSSION

▷ 'Could a stone escape the laws of gravity? Impossible. Impossible for evil to form an alliance with good' (Comte de Lautréamont). Why do you think Knox chose this epigram to start her book?

▷ How difficult did you find it to suspend your disbelief when embarking on a novel in which the principal character was an angel? Did you find Xas convincing? How does Knox develop his character? How does he differ from traditional depictions of angels?

▷ Why does Sobran think that Xas visits him in the early years of their relationship? What difference does this make to his life? How is he affected by Xas's revelation of his fall from grace? Why does he decide to see Xas again?

▷ Early in the book the Comte describes Sobran as 'a sharp-tongued, high-handed bully'. To what extent do you agree with the Comte and why? How is Sobran changed over the years and what changes him? How would you describe him, at his death?

▷ Why does Xas visit Sobran? What does he mean when he says: 'I had to have you – someone I could lose forever.' How is Xas's friendship with Apharah different from his relationship with Sobran? How is Xas changed after Lucifer's visit and how does this affect his relationship with Sobran?

▷ Aurora is a determined atheist. Does her relationship with Xas change her views at all and if so, how? What are Xas's views on faith?

▷ Does Xas change other characters in the book besides Sobran and Aurora? If so, who are they and how are they affected?

▷ The relationship between Sobran and Aurora seems more important than his relationship with his wife. What is its basis? How does Knox develop the relationship? How important is it in the development of the novel?

▷ *The Vintner's Luck* is set at a time when many long-held beliefs were being challenged. How important is theology in the book? How does science begin to change the world in which Sobran lives?

▷ How does Knox root her story so firmly in its period?

## SUGGESTED FURTHER READING

▶ *The Leper's Companion* by Julia Blackburn (1999)
▶ *The Rationalist* by Warwick Collins (1993)
▶ *Quarantine* by Jim Crace (1997)
▶ *A Case of Curiosities* by Allen Kurzweil (1992)
▶ ***Ingenious Pain* by Andrew Miller (1997)**
▶ *Paradise Lost Books 1 and 2* by John Milton (1667)
▶ *Lemprière's Dictionary* by Lawrence Norfolk (1991)
▶ *Perfume* by Patrick Süskind (1985)

## OTHER BOOKS BY ELIZABETH KNOX

▶ *Black Oxen* (2001)
▶ *Billie's Kiss* (2002)

# Charming Billy (1997)
## Alice McDermott

### ABOUT THE BOOK

Central to *Charming Billy* is a deception that has been closely guarded for over thirty years. Unable to face breaking the news to his cousin Billy of his sweetheart's betrayal, Dennis tells him that she is dead. When, after Billy's funeral, Dennis tells his own daughter the truth, she pieces together the cousins' story. Her narrative criss-crosses the period immediately after the Second World War to the 1980s, as she recounts his story to her husband, exploring Billy's effect on the lives of all who knew him.

The novel opens with the funeral lunch in a Bronx bar. All forty-seven guests remember Billy with affection. Dennis sits close to his widow Maeve, supporting her as he has throughout the long years of Billy's alcoholism. His daughter's curiosity is aroused as Billy's relatives remember the girl from Ireland with whom he was passionately in love and debate whether his condition was the result of heartbreak or disease. After the funeral Dennis tells his daughter the truth about Billy's first love.

When the cousins return from the war, Dennis's stepfather asks them to renovate his holiday home on Long Island. It's a glorious summer. One day they join two young women playing with a group of children on the beach, as charmed by the children as they are by their nursemaids. Billy is drawn to Eva, who is helping her sister Mary for the summer. When Eva returns to Ireland, Billy is so unhappy that Dennis asks his stepfather to give Billy an advance on his wages so that he can send Eva her fare. Billy receives only one more letter after sending $500 to Eva. When Mary tells Dennis that Eva has married someone in Ireland and is keeping the money to set up a business, he breaks off his relationship with her. Unable to face Billy with the truth, he tells him that Eva has died of pneumonia.

Billy's drinking becomes serious. He is never absent from work, always good company, but frequently drunk. When Maeve visits the shoe shop where he works, it is through her alcoholic father that they get to know each other. The couple marry but Billy fails to control his drinking and in 1975 he goes to Ireland to take a pledge to give it up. Almost inevitably, he decides to visit Eva's grave. Dennis's lie is uncovered and the pledge rapidly broken. Although Billy tells Dennis that he knows the truth, their relationship seems unchanged.

Billy's alcoholism is a fact of Dennis's life – as much a part of it as his wife, his four children and his job. He's called out at all hours and uncomplainingly goes to Billy's aid. Billy reminds his friends of Dennis's father – ebullient, loquacious and generous. The loss of his sweetheart is part of his romantic persona.

When Dennis gets the final call to go to the hospital to identify Billy's body, it comes as no surprise. At first, he is sure that the bloated, discoloured corpse must be someone else and it is with a terrible sadness that he has to accept that it is Billy.

## ABOUT THE AUTHOR
Alice McDermott was born in 1954 and brought up in Elmont, New York. *Charming Billy*, McDermott's fourth novel, won the American National Book Award for fiction. In addition to writing she teaches part-time at Johns Hopkins University.

## FOR DISCUSSION
▷ Dennis's daughter narrates the book. Why do you think McDermott chose a character from the next generation to recount Billy's story? What effect does this achieve? What impression do you get of the narrator?

▷ 'If you knew Billy at all, then you loved him,' says a guest at Billy's funeral, a sentiment which echoes throughout the book. What was it that people loved about Billy? Do you think Billy was capable of loving other people?

▷ Why does Dennis choose to tell Billy that Eva is dead rather than tell him the truth? How does it change the course of Billy's life? What effect does it have on Dennis and his family?

▷ How important is faith in the book and how does it manifest itself? Why is it so important to Billy? Is faith necessarily linked with religion in the book? What problems does Dennis experience with faith and why?

▷ How would you describe Dennis? How does his character compare to Billy's? What are the most important factors in shaping Dennis's character?

▷ Billy's sister Rosemary describes Billy's alcoholism as 'a disease' but Dan Lynch emphatically challenges this, saying: 'Don't say it was a disease that blindsided him and wiped out everything he was.' Which of these views seems to apply to Billy? Why do both Rosemary and Dan defend their positions so passionately?

▷ *Charming Billy* is set firmly in an Irish neighbourhood in New York. How important is their Irish identity to the characters? How does this manifest itself?

Are there characters to whom it is particularly important and, equally, are there characters that distance themselves from it? Why do you think this is so?

▷ How would you describe McDermott's writing style? What tone does it take and how is this achieved?

## SUGGESTED FURTHER READING

▶ *For Kings and Planets* by Ethan Canin (1998)
▶ *Telling Liddy* by Anne Fine (1998)
▶ ***Empress of the Splendid Season* by Oscar Hijuelos (1999)**
▶ *Cal* by Bernard MacLaverty (1983)
▶ *The Folded Leaf* by William Maxwell (1945)

## OTHER BOOKS BY ALICE MCDERMOTT

▶ *A Bigamist's Daughter* (1982)
▶ *That Night* (1987)
▶ *At Weddings and Funerals* (1992)

## Brightness Falls (1992)
### Jay McInerney

### ABOUT THE BOOK

Set in New York in the months before the stockmarket crash of 1987, *Brightness Falls* captures an atmosphere of frenzied recklessness through the story of Russell and Corrine, an attractive and likeable young couple. With a cast of characters ranging from Victor Propp, who negotiates regular increases in advance payments for his twenty-year-old unfinished novel, to the homeless Corrine sees at the soup kitchen, Jay McInerney takes a swipe at the rash profligacy of the 1980s and the high price that was paid for it.

It's 1987, six years into the Reagan era, and Corrine's thirty-first birthday party. Corrine is a stockbroker and Russell the rising star at Corbin, Dern, a small publishing house. Their social calendar is packed with dinner invitations, gallery openings and parties. They live just a little beyond their means and Russell has begun to dabble on the stockmarket. When Victor Propp, the literary jewel in Corbin, Dern's crown, suggests that a bright young man could take over the company, Russell is seduced by the idea, despite Corrine's cautious advice. Aggrieved by the souring of his relationship with his boss and intoxicated by his investment successes, he is sure he can do it and contacts Trina, an old acquaintance working in mergers and acquisitions. Caught up in the adrenaline-fuelled 'deal time', working long hours, attention fixed on one aim, Russell has little time for Corrine or his friends. When he finds his best friend in the toilet of a club, a tourniquet around his arm, Russell ducks the issue.

Her shaky confidence further eroded by Russell's neglect, Corrine convinces herself that he wants an affair. She would like children but Russell seems reluctant. At work she feels out of step, her caution at odds with the frenzy that intensifies at every rise in the Dow Jones index. Needing to do something worthwhile, she works at a soup kitchen one night a week.

As Russell's deal gains momentum he and his partners, Washington and Whitlock, lose their jobs. They set up offices, taking with them Victor and many other authors, excited at the prospect of a young company. Money seems always to hand but Washington's unfinished business with Donald Parker, who has been picketing Corbin, Dern in protest at their rejection of a book by a black author, is a problem.

Things are a little rough around the edges. Parker continues to stir up bad publicity. Victor talks of a new contract with another publisher and the deal remains unsigned. The strain between Russell and Corrine begins to tell, particularly when she decides to leave her job after a miscarriage.

During the exhilarating 'deal time' Trina and Russell have been thrust into a sexually charged proximity. Russell has no real intention of sleeping with her but when Trina turns up in his hotel room in Frankfurt, things get out of hand. He returns home to find that Corrine has left him.

Just after Corrine leaves her stockbroking job, the market crashes, bringing Russell's still unsigned deal down with it. Russell and Corrine are left to begin the painful business of rebuilding their shattered lives.

## ABOUT THE AUTHOR

Jay McInerney was born in Connecticut in 1955 and has lived in London, Tokyo and New York. His writing has appeared in a number of magazines such as *Esquire* and *Atlantic*. His first novel, *Bright Lights, Big City*, published in 1984, was made into a film for which he wrote the screenplay.

## FOR DISCUSSION

▷ In Jeff's musings as he watches Russell and Corrine walk up the hill to the hospital at the beginning of the novel, he sees them as a golden couple. Is this an accurate portrayal of their relationship? How would you describe their marriage as the novel opens? How is it changed at the end? What chance do you think it would have of survival and on what basis?

▷ Corrine is portrayed as a 'modern woman' with a foot on the career ladder. Would you describe her as being in charge of her life? How does her view of life differ from Trina's?

▷ When Russell takes Victor Propp for lunch, Victor says to him: 'Men are the great romantics, the dreamers and fools. Women are realists.' Do you think this idea is borne out in the novel and if so, how? To what extent would you apply it to the real world?

▷ What sort of friend is Russell to Jeff and vice versa? Near the end of the book Jeff says to Russell: 'I sometimes think of everything I've done since college as an inverse image of your life.' Why do you think that the two friends took such different paths? Is Jeff's suggestion, that Russell's marriage to Corrine saved him, an adequate explanation?

▷ How important is money in the novel? What part does it play in the disintegration of Russell and Corrine's marriage? Is it the driving force behind the need for Trina and Melman to make deals? If not, what is?

▷ How would you describe the social world in which Russell and Corrine move? How does McInerney use peripheral characters to build up a picture of New York in the 1980s?

▷ Much is made of the fact that Washington, one of the colleagues who join Russell in his new venture, is black. How is the issue of race treated in the novel?

▷ Corrine is a volunteer at the soup kitchen. Does McInerney offer any explanation for the gulf between Corrine's life and the life of people on the streets and, if so, what is it?

## SUGGESTED FURTHER READING

▶ *The Fall* by Albert Camus (1956)
▶ *The Great Gatsby* by F. Scott Fitzgerald (1925)
▶ *Goodbye to Berlin* by Christopher Isherwood (1939)
▶ *Martin Dressler* by Steven Millhauser (1996)
▶ **In a Land of Plenty by Tim Pears (1997)**
▶ *The Custom of the Country* by Edith Wharton (1913)
▶ *Bonfire of the Vanities* by Tom Wolfe (1987)

## OTHER BOOKS BY JAY MCINERNEY

NOVELS

▶ *Bright Lights, Big City* (1984)
▶ *Ransom* (1985)
▶ *Story of My Life* (1988)
▶ *The Last of the Savages* (1996)
▶ *Model Behaviour* (1998)

SHORT STORIES

▶ *How It Ended* (2000)

# The Orchard on Fire (1995)
## Shena Mackay

### ABOUT THE BOOK

Childhood is popularly portrayed as a time of carefree innocence yet children are often haunted by worries that are dismissed as trivial by adults and sometimes beset by very real terrors that they feel unable to confide. *The Orchard on Fire* is set in a small Kent village in the 1950s, but deals with aspects of childhood which are relevant anywhere and at any time. By telling the story of the friendship between April Harlency and Ruby Richards through April's fresh and often funny eight-year-old voice, Shena Mackay vividly depicts both the dark fears and the happy excitements of childhood.

April's eight-year-old narrative is sandwiched between the opening chapter, in which the grown-up April decides to visit Stonebridge, where she and Ruby met, and the closing chapter, where she reflects on the changes she finds when she gets there.

April first meets Ruby when her parents shelter from the rain in the Rising Sun, Ruby's parents' pub. The girls soon strike up the kind of friendship which offers a safe haven from the rest of the world. When they stumble upon a disused railway carriage in the orchard, they set up camp. Here they read, plan their adventures, take refuge from the teasing of other children and, for Ruby, escape the beatings and verbal abuse which seem to be an open secret in the village.

Mr Greenidge and his dachshund Liesel are the only regular visitors to the Harlencys' new venture, the Copper Kettle tea rooms. Her parents encourage April to take up Mr Greenidge's invitations to visit his wife for tea. Lured by the idea of taking Liesel out for walks, April accepts but doesn't know what to do when Mr Greenidge kisses her. As he ingratiates himself with her parents, April is helpless in the face of their determination that she be polite and Mr Greenidge's disappointment if she avoids him. When Betty Harlency finds she is pregnant, April is appalled to hear that she will be spending the weeks before Christmas with her grandmother, missing the pantomime and deserting Ruby. But when her baby brother is born she is as delighted as everyone else.

As summer approaches, Joe Silver holds a garden party for the village. Ruby defies her parents who have forbidden her to go. When her drunken father tries forcibly to take her home, Ruby is humiliated in front of the whole village. She manages to escape and disappears. When she is still missing the next day, April realizes that she is at their camp but keeps quiet, convinced that she will get Ruby into trouble. It is Mr Greenidge who drops the hint. Ruby sets a fire in the orchard and April catches her last glimpse of Ruby as she is carried home. The Richards leave the Rising Sun in the middle of the night, and although Ruby and April write for a while, April's last letter comes back marked 'gone away'.

April's anger with Mr Greenidge arms her against his reproaches when she won't see him. When Mrs Greenidge dies, it is April who sets the whisper going that he may have poisoned her. As the Copper Kettle continues to fail, the Harlencys decide to move back to London.

## ABOUT THE AUTHOR

Shena Mackay was born in Edinburgh. As well as serving on the London Arts Board, she has been a judge for a number of literary prizes including the Whitbread Prize and the Macmillan Silver Pen Award. In 1993 her work was the subject of a BBC Bookmark film. She won the Fawcett Society Prize for her novel *Redhill Rococo*, published in 1986. *The Orchard on Fire* was shortlisted for the 1996 Booker Prize, the Saltire Prize and the McVitie's Prize. Shena Mackay lives in London.

## FOR DISCUSSION

▷ *The Orchard on Fire* is told through the voice of April, an eight-year-old girl. How successful do you feel Mackay is in portraying the world through a child's eyes? Are there particular things that you feel she gets right or wrong and what are they?

▷ What does the book have to say about adults' attitudes towards children? Why does April feel she can't tell her parents about Mr Greenidge? Do you think they would have believed her? What do you think their reaction would have been? How damaging to you think Mr Greenidge has been to April?

▷ Are Percy and Betty good parents to April? How do you think their upbringing of April would compare with the parents of an eight-year-old today? How different do you think today's children are from the children in the novel?

▷ How would you describe Ruby? How does she deal with her parents' bullying behaviour? Do you think that people like the Richards would be treated any differently today and, if so, how?

▷ How would you describe the grown-up April of the first and final chapters of the novel? How has the loss of Ruby affected April?

▷ How authentic do you think April's memories of her childhood are likely to be? How do attitudes to childhood change as people get older? How does that attitude change if people have children of their own?

▷ How does Mackay anchor *The Orchard on Fire* so firmly in the 1950s?

▷ April says of the 'kitchenalia' shop: 'They are trying to buy their way into the past they think we had, they want to be snug and safe down Rabbit Lane.' How much safer, if at all, do you think life was in the 1950s? How safe was life at Stonebridge?

## SUGGESTED FURTHER READING

**FICTION**

▶ **Behind the Scenes at the Museum by Kate Atkinson (1996)**
▶ *Cat's Eye* by Margaret Atwood (1989)
▶ *Hideous Kinky* by Esther Freud (1993)
▶ *The Ten O'Clock Horses* by Laurie Graham (1996)
▶ **Anita and Me by Meera Syal (1996)**

**NON-FICTION**

▶ *Cider With Rosie* by Laurie Lee (1959)

## OTHER BOOKS BY SHENA MACKAY

**NOVELS**

▶ *Music Upstairs* (1965)
▶ *Old Crow* (1967)
▶ *An Advent Calendar* (1971)
▶ *A Bowl of Cherries* (1984)
▶ *Redhill Rococo* (1986)
▶ *Dunedin* (1992)
▶ *The Artist's Widow* (1998)
▶ *Heligoland* (2002)

**NOVELLAS**

▶ *Dust Falls on Eugene Schlumburger/Toddler on the Run* (published in one volume, 1964)

**SHORT STORIES**

▶ *Babies in Rhinestones* (1983)
▶ *Dreams of Dead Women's Handbags* (1987)
▶ *The Laughing Academy* (1993)
▶ *Collected Stories* (1994)
▶ *The World's Smallest Unicorn and Other Stories* (1999)

**EDITED**

▶ *Such Devoted Sisters* (short story anthology) (1994)
▶ *Friendship* (essays) (1997)

## Remembering Babylon (1993)
David Malouf

### ABOUT THE BOOK

In the mid-nineteenth century, when news of free land in Australia reached Britain many were inspired to set out in search of a prosperous future. *Remembering Babylon* is both an examination of the arrival of an outsider in a small, close-knit community and a commentary on colonialism.

The novel opens as Gemmy dances out of the bush towards the paddock in which Lachlan and his two cousins are playing. When Gemmy leaps on to the paddock fence crying: 'Do not shoot . . . I am a B-b-british object!' he stamps an indelible image on the minds of both Lachlan and his cousin Janet.

Gemmy's sixteen years in the bush have left him bereft of his own language, unsure of who he is or where he belongs. His antics in trying to convey something of his history are like a game of charades. The adults are amused but uncomprehending; it is the children, led by Lachlan, who understand. Gemmy forms a special bond with Lachlan, giving the boy a sense of power that catches him by surprise but gives him great pleasure. Lachlan knows what it is to be an outsider, having arrived from Scotland to live with his Aunt Ellen and Uncle Jock after the death of his father. The family provides Gemmy with shelter in return for a few chores.

Mr Frazer, the community's minister, tries to make a record of Gemmy's life and his knowledge of the bush while suspicions rumble away among the rest of the community. Fears are focused on a possible conspiracy between Gemmy and the aborigines who are perceived as a constant threat. Trust in Jock begins to wane because he is sheltering Gemmy. Things come to a head when a disgruntled worker sees Gemmy with two aborigines. Seizing his moment of glory, the worker embroiders the episode. Unpleasant little incidents follow. Three of Ellen's geese are killed and the shed on which Gemmy is working is smeared with human excrement. Finally, under cover of darkness, an attempt is made to drown Gemmy.

Shocked out of his ambivalence and concerned for his family, Jock finds a home for Gemmy with the eccentric Mrs Hutchence, whose class protects her from the rest of the community. Painfully aware of the fragility of his position, Gemmy begins to remember his past; his life as a rat catcher's boy in London, his rebellion against his master, his abduction and life aboard ship and, finally, his arrival in Australia and acceptance by the aborigines. Eventually, he disappears back into the bush.

The novel ends with an incident far in the future. Lachlan, now a government minister, has taken up the case of a naturalized German who is being persecuted in the wake of the battle of Paschendale. He has received a letter which passionately defends the German, signed 'Sister Monica'. When the letter is leaked to the press, 'Sister Monica' is revealed as Lachlan's cousin. Once again, Janet and Lachlan are united in their defence of the underdog, each of them holding in their mind's eye the image of Gemmy Fairley astride the paddock fence.

## ABOUT THE AUTHOR

David Malouf was born in Brisbane in 1934. His father's family emigrated to Australia from the Lebanon in the 1880s. His mother's family came from London on the eve of the First World War. After graduating from the University of Queensland, he taught in the English department for two years. In 1959 he moved to the United Kingdom, working as a teacher, first in London and later, in Birkenhead, returning to Australia in 1968 to teach at the University of Sydney. In 1977 he took up writing full time and moved to Tuscany, returning to Australia in 1985. He is internationally acclaimed both as a novelist and a poet and has also written several opera libretti. His novel *The Great World*, winner of the Miles Franklin Award in 1990, also won both the Commonwealth Writers Prize and the Prix Femina Etranger in 1991. *Remembering Babylon* was shortlisted for the Booker Prize in 1993 and won the 1996 International IMPAC Dublin Literary Award.

## FOR DISCUSSION

▷ David Malouf is a poet as well as a novelist. How do you think this has influenced his writing in *Remembering Babylon*? Can you find particular examples to support your view?

▷ How would you describe Lachlan's reaction to Gemmy when he arrives? How important is his relationship with Gemmy in shaping his life both as a child and an adult? Why do you think Gemmy made such an impression on Lachlan? How important was Gemmy to Janet?

▷ How would you describe the community's reactions to Gemmy when he arrives? Is everyone's reaction the same and, if not, how do they differ? How do people's feelings towards Gemmy change over time? Why do you think they change?

▷ How would you describe the majority of the settlers' feelings towards the landscape around them? What do they feel about the aborigines? Why do you think they feel this way? Are there characters that don't share this view? Can you explain why this might be?

▷ Why does Jock continue to protect Gemmy at the risk of antagonizing his neighbours? How does giving Gemmy a home change him? How does the relationship between Ellen and Jock change? What do you think provokes those changes?

▷ There are references to nature throughout the novel – in the descriptions of the landscape, Frazer's botanizing and Mrs Hutchence's bee-keeping. How important do you think nature is as a theme in the novel? How does the aborigines' attitude to the bush differ from the settlers'?

▷ Why does Gemmy feel at ease with Frazer? What do you think Frazer is saying about colonialism in the extracts from his field notebook quoted in chapter 14? Are these ideas illustrated elsewhere in the novel and, if so, where? What do you think of them?

▷ Why does Gemmy make the settlers so uneasy?

## SUGGESTED FURTHER READING

▶ *The Songlines* by Bruce Chatwin (1987)
▶ *A Passage to India* by E. M. Forster (1924)
▶ *Rites of Passage* by William Golding (1980)
▶ *Snow Falling on Cedars* by David Guterson (1995)
▶ **Promised Lands by Jane Rogers (1995)**

## OTHER BOOKS BY DAVID MALOUF

**NOVELS**

▶ *Johnno* (1978)
▶ *An Imaginary Life* (1978)
▶ *Fly Away Peter* (1981)
▶ *Child's Play* (1982)
▶ *Harland's Half Acre* (1985)
▶ *Antipodes* (1985)
▶ *The Great World* (1990)
▶ *The Conversations at Curlow Creek* (1996)
▶ *Dream Stuff* (2000)

**POETRY**

▶ *Bicycle and Other Poems* (1970)
▶ *Neighbours in a Thicket* (1974)
▶ *The Year of the Foxes and Other Poems* (1976)
▶ *Wild Lemons* (1980)
▶ *First Things Last* (1981)
▶ *Selected Poems 1959–1989* (1994)

# Fugitive Pieces (1996)

## Anne Michaels

### ABOUT THE BOOK

Although *Fugitive Pieces* has a beginning, a middle and an end, plot is not its most significant element. It is more a novel of ideas, a many-layered exploration of the way in which even the deepest wounds may be healed. The first two parts of the novel are narrated by Jakob Beer, the young Jewish boy whom Athos Roussos saves from the Nazis. The third part is narrated by Ben, the child of concentration camp survivors. We know, from the beginning, that Jakob has recently been killed in an accident.

When a mud-encrusted little boy appears before Athos as he excavates the ancient Polish city of Biskupin, Athos hides him from the German guards and takes him back to his house on the Greek island of Zakynthos. Jakob has fled the village where his parents were murdered. He does not know what has happened to his sister. Memories of her are threaded through Jakob's narrative – she is always just out of reach, on the fringes of his consciousness.

Zakynthos is under occupation and Jakob remains in hiding. The scholarly Athos immerses him in knowledge, poetry and words. They exchange languages, share Athos's passion for geology and his consuming interest in Scott's expedition to the South Pole. While Athos wants to soothe Jakob's pain, he does not want him to forget his past. When the war is over, Athos takes up an invitation to teach at the University of Toronto.

In Toronto, Jakob has a new language to learn. He attends the university where he meets Maurice Salman, who becomes a dear friend. Athos becomes obsessed with the Nazi falsification of history. When he dies, Jakob finds a set of notes which he prepares into a book called *Bearing False Witness*.

By the time Jakob meets Alex, the book has been published. Alex is thoroughly European, a vibrant young woman with a passion for music who finds it hard to penetrate the darkness into which Jakob periodically sinks. When their marriage is over, he returns to Greece to live in Athos's family home on the island of Idhra.

Occasionally visited by Maurice and his family, Jakob spends his time translating memoirs of the Holocaust and writing poetry. On a visit to Toronto, he meets Michaela and falls deeply in love. They marry and return to Idhra. A life of quiet happiness is destroyed when Jakob is killed in a car accident. Michaela dies two days later.

At this point, the narrative passes to Ben, a professor at Toronto University and a friend of Maurice. Ben has grown up in the shadow of the Holocaust, the child of camp survivors to whom every knock at the door is terrifying. His parents seem unable to connect with him in the way that they do with his wife, which Ben increasingly resents. This resentment hardens after the death of his parents, when he discovers a family secret that his wife already knows. He leaves her and travels to Greece in search of Jakob's journals. In Jakob's poetry, Ben recognizes something of his own experience and his journey to Greece teaches him much about himself.

## ABOUT THE AUTHOR

Anne Michaels was born in Toronto in 1958. She was educated at Toronto University where she spent several years teaching creative writing. Her first volume of poems, *Weight of Oranges*, was published to great acclaim in 1986 when it won the Commonwealth Poetry Prize for the Americas. *Fugitive Pieces*, her first novel, won both the Orange Prize and the Guardian Fiction Award. Michaels has since published another two volumes of poetry.

## FOR DISCUSSION

▷ Even before the book opens we learn that Jakob Beer has been killed in an accident. How did the foreknowledge of Jakob's death affect your reading of the book? Why do you think that Michaels chose this moment for Jakob to die?

▷ 'When the prisoners were forced to dig up the mass graves, the dead entered them through their pores and were carried through their bloodstreams to their brains and hearts. And through their blood into another generation.' What echoes does this graphic image have later in the book? How does the influence of the dead run through the lives of the living and of the next generation? Does this still apply today?

▷ Michaels weaves Jacob's memories through Kostas' and Daphne's stories of the German occupation of Athens and the violence orchestrated by the Communist partisans which erupted after their departure. Why do you think that Michaels chose to put across their memories in this way?

▷ Jakob writes: 'I already knew the power of language to destroy, to omit, to obliterate. But poetry, the power of language to restore: this is what Athos and Kostas were trying to teach me.' How has the destructive power of language been revealed to Jakob? How is the restorative nature of poetry illustrated in the book? What part does language play in Jakob's life?

▷ Michaels is primarily a poet and *Fugitive Pieces* is her first novel. How are her skills as a poet reflected in the language of the novel? Were there particular words, phrases or passages that you found striking and, if so, what were they? What was it that you found so arresting in your examples?

▷ Music runs through the book as vital to several of the characters – Bella, Alex and Naomi are all passionate music lovers and Jakob also finds solace in it. Why is music so important to each of these characters?

▷ Jakob's narrative is threaded with memories of his sister Bella, although we learn little of his parents. Why does Bella's absence seem to haunt Jakob more than his parents' murder?

▷ Jakob states: 'History is amoral: events occurred. But memory is moral; what we consciously remember is what our conscience remembers.' How is this idea illustrated in the novel? What conclusions does Jakob draw about history?

▷ When Jakob reasons his way through the Nazis' justification of their treatment of the Jews, what do you make of his argument? Have you read other arguments and, if so, how do they compare?

▷ Ben describes a flash of recognition when reading one of Jakob's poems. How does Ben's indirect experience of the Holocaust differ from Jakob's?

How are they similar? Why do you think Michaels chose to call the first sections of both Ben's and Jakob's narratives 'The Drowned City'?

▷ Towards the end of the book Ben describes the different ways in which his parents deal with loss: 'Loss is an edge; it swelled everything for my mother and drained everything from my father.' Why do they react so differently? Are there aspects of their characters that govern the way they cope with the legacy of their terrible experiences?

▷ Why are both of Ben's parents able to reach out to Naomi but not to Ben? Why does this anger Ben so much?

▷ The last line of Ben's narrative, and of the novel, reads: 'I see that I must give what I most need.' What is it that Ben most needs and to whom will he give it?

▷ What did the title of the novel mean to you? What are the 'fugitive pieces' in the book?

## SUGGESTED FURTHER READING
**FICTION**
- ▶ *Captain Corelli's Mandolin* by Louis de Bernières (1994)
- ▶ *The Archivist* by Martha Cooley (1998)
- ▶ ***Stones From the River* by Ursula Hegi (1994)**
- ▶ *Schindler's List* by Thomas Keneally (1985)
- ▶ *Yosl Rakover Talks to God* by Zvi Kolitz (1996)
- ▶ *The Time of Light* by Gunnar Kopperud (1998)
- ▶ *The English Patient* by Michael Ondaatje (1992)
- ▶ ***The Reader* by Bernhard Schlink (1997)**
- ▶ *Music For the Third Ear* by Susan Schwartz Senstad (1999)

**AUTOBIOGRAPHY**
- ▶ *Anne Frank: The Diary of a Young Girl* by Anne Frank (1947)
- ▶ *If This is a Man/The Truce* by Primo Levi (1960)

**HISTORY**
- ▶ *Konin* by Theo Richmond (1996)

## OTHER BOOKS BY ANNE MICHAELS
**POETRY**
- ▶ *Weight of Oranges* (1986)
- ▶ *Miner's Pond* (1991)
- ▶ *Skin Divers* (1999)

# Ingenious Pain (1997)
## Andrew Miller

### ABOUT THE BOOK
Set in the eighteenth century, *Ingenious Pain* straddles the old world of quack shows and superstition and the new world of religious doubt and scientific enquiry. James Dyer's inability to feel physical or emotional pain may appear enviable but it precludes an understanding of suffering, isolating him from the rest of humanity. Both an exciting adventure story and a vivid depiction of a world on the brink of modernity, *Ingenious Pain* is also an exploration of the essential nature of compassion.

Dyer is an odd child. Born in 1739, nine months after a stranger took his mother by surprise, he is mute until he is eleven, feels no pain and his wounds heal almost immediately. When his family succumbs to smallpox, he deserts his only surviving relative and seeks out a quack doctor Gummer, who passed through the village the previous year.

His condition is a great asset in selling Gummer's bogus remedies but their antics are under surveillance. Dyer is abducted and taken to the house of a wealthy dilettante where he meets a pair of Siamese twins awaiting separation on their eighteenth birthday. He becomes interested in medicine and studies anatomy. When he meets Gummer a year after the twins have died during their horribly botched operation, Dyer leaves with him.

During a celebratory pub-crawl, Dyer and Gummer are press-ganged. On board ship Dyer attaches himself to the surgeon, Robert Munro. Taking advantage of Munro's drunkenness, he seizes every opportunity to practise his new skills. He later finds Munro in Bath and becomes his assistant. Happy to indulge himself in drink, Munro ignores his wife's passion for Dyer until scandal forces him to challenge Dyer to a duel. They both survive but when Munro later kills himself, even Dyer's brilliant reputation cannot withstand the disgrace.

Dyer enters the race to St Petersburg to inoculate the Empress of Russia against smallpox and it is on this journey that he meets Reverend Lestrade. Bad weather forces Lestrade's company to seek shelter in a monastery, and on the way they find Dyer and a wounded servant. Gummer has finally turned on Dyer and made off with his money. When Lestrade later sees a woman running for her life he and Dyer take her back to the monastery. With her filed teeth and tattoos, she is a strange and intriguing figure. They name her Mary.

The party leaves for St Petersburg, taking Mary with them. Dyer's behaviour is suddenly tinged with compassion and Lestrade finds Mary and Dyer engaged in a ritual which he can hardly believe, let alone understand.

With compassion arrives a terrible awareness of pain, both physical and mental. A lifetime of wounds make themselves known and madness overtakes Dyer. He finds himself in Bedlam where he suffers terribly at the hands of surgeons but finds a love which eases his way to redemption. When he sees Mary from his window, he persuades his physicians to let him go.

Mary leads him to the home of Reverend Lestrade and Dyer spends his last few years in the house of the man who becomes his closest friend.

## ABOUT THE AUTHOR
Born in Bristol in 1960, Andrew Miller grew up in the west of England. He has lived in Holland, Spain, Japan, France and Ireland. *Ingenious Pain*, his first novel, met with a good deal of critical acclaim and went on to win both the James Tait Black Memorial Prize in 1997 and the Dublin IMPAC Literary Award in 1999.

## FOR DISCUSSION
▷ Why do you think Andrew Miller chose the title *Ingenious Pain* – what is ingenious about pain?
▷ Reverend Lestrade muses to himself: 'What does the world need most – a good, ordinary man, or one who is outstanding, albeit with a heart of ice, of stone?' To what extent do you feel that the novel answers this question and what answers does it provide? How would you answer the question?
▷ How does the absence of pain affect Dyer's ability as a surgeon? What leads him to make the decision to become a surgeon?

▷ Several people describe Dyer as 'dangerous'. What is it that is dangerous about him? How does this manifest itself in the book?

▷ When Dyer lives in Mr Canning's house, he is attracted to the library. The librarian seeks out books for him – 'Not poetry, of course, or stories – the boy is blind to them.' Why is Dyer blind to poetry and stories? Are there other instances of literature which leave him untouched and how does Miller use literature to illustrate the change that is brought about in him towards the end of the book?

▷ When Dyer awakes to pain, Miller writes of Mary: 'He knows that she is his only hope, the beginning and the end of the nightmare.' What is the relationship between Mary and Dyer? Would you describe her as a healer? Why do you think she smiles when Dyer dies?

▷ Miller depicts a world on the threshold of the Enlightenment. What elements do you recognize of the modern world in the book? How are the new ways beginning to change the old?

▷ What do you think of Miller's use of language in the novel? Are there images or descriptions which you find particularly striking and, if so, what are they and why?

## SUGGESTED FURTHER READING
**FICTION**

▶ *Mr Vertigo* by Paul Auster (1994)
▶ *Nights at the Circus* by Angela Carter (1984)
▶ *The Rationalist* by Warwick Collins (1993)
▶ **The Vintner's Luck by Elizabeth Knox (1998)**
▶ *A Case of Curiosities* by Allen Kurzweil (1992)
▶ *Lemprière's Dictionary* by Lawrence Norfolk (1991)
▶ *Perfume* by Patrick Süskind (1985)
▶ *The Lightning Cage* by Alan Wall (1999)

**NON-FICTION**

▶ *The Enlightenment* by Norman Hampson (1996)
▶ *English Society in the Eighteenth Century* by Roy Porter (1982)

## OTHER BOOKS BY ANDREW MILLER

▶ *Casanova* (1998)
▶ *Oxygen* (2001)

# The World Below
Sue Miller

## ABOUT THE BOOK

Catherine Hubbard is a thoroughly modern woman – twice divorced, independent, in charge of her life and considering the prospect of new possibilities now that her three children are grown up. Her grandmother Georgia's diaries reveal a life far more complex than it had appeared to Catherine when she sought a safe haven with her grandparents during a childhood overshadowed by her mother's schizophrenia and eventual suicide. Interweaving Catherine's narrative and Georgia's story, Sue Miller explores the lives of these two women, peeling back the layers to reveal unexpected parallels between them.

The novel opens with the funeral of Georgia's mother when Georgia was just sixteen years old. Determined to make life easier for her beloved father, Georgia steps in and takes over the running of the house alongside her studies.

Georgia's story, reconstructed by Catherine from the diaries and letters that she finds in the attic of her grandparents' house, is woven through Catherine's own narrative of her time in Vermont. For Catherine, life in the small town of West Barstow is quiet. She takes up an unexpected assignment as a sports writer, making up for her lack of knowledge by enlisting the help of Samuel Eliasson, the retired professor who had been renting her grandmother's home. She makes a few friends and reflects on her life, her marriages, her lovers and her children. Catherine has proved to be a strong, independent and resourceful woman but now feels restless and cast adrift, unsure about what to do with her future. Her grandparents' house represents security and stability, a place in which to take stock. It is the home she chose as a teenager after her mother's suicide, drawn by the enduring bond between her grandparents. But, as Georgia's diaries reveal, their marriage had required patience, understanding and a tireless negotiation between both partners.

Left exhausted by her mother's death and the running of the family home, Georgia had succumbed to tuberculosis and, on the advice of her doctor, spent four months in a sanatorium. Life in the 'san' was surprisingly liberated and in its sexually charged atmosphere, Georgia found herself drawn into a brief affair with Seward Wallace, a passionate young man snatching eagerly at whatever life was left to him. Shortly after she left the 'san', Georgia accepted her doctor's marriage proposal, despite the twenty-year age difference, after carefully explaining that she was 'damaged goods'. Amazed and delighted by his apparent understanding and forgiveness, Georgia contentedly embarked on her married life. When her husband found her in tears at the news of Seward's death, they both discovered that misunderstanding and deception lay at the heart of their marriage and each was left to find a way back to the other.

Alongside her journey into her grandmother's past, Catherine has been considering her own future, tentatively exploring the possibility of a relationship with Samuel Eliasson, but the premature birth of her granddaughter resolves her indecision. She ends her Vermont sojourn, turning her back on West Barstow with no regrets but with a better understanding of both who she is and where she has come from.

**ABOUT THE AUTHOR**

Sue Miller was born in Chicago in 1943. She married shortly after graduating from Harvard and held a variety of jobs until her son was born in 1968. Her first short story was published in 1981 and, after teaching a number of creative writing programmes around Boston, she held a writing fellowship at Radcliffe from 1984 to 1985. Her first novel, *The Good Mother*, was published in 1986 and was later made into a film starring Liam Neeson and Diane Keaton. Her sixth novel, *While I Was Gone*, was chosen for Oprah Winfrey's Book Club in June 2000. Now divorced from her second husband, she has recently moved to Cambridge, Massachusetts, after living in Boston for many years.

**FOR DISCUSSION**

▷ The narrative switches back and forth from the first to the third person as Catherine reconstructs Georgia's life from her diaries and letters, occasionally quoting from them directly. How successful did you find this structure? Why do you think Miller chose this way of telling Georgia's story rather than simply using the diaries themselves?

▷ 'But they'd all gotten skilled by this time at never acknowledging what they knew, at pretending they didn't see what they saw.' Fanny's family becomes adept at convincing themselves that there is nothing seriously wrong with her. Why do you think they do this? How does Miller explore the links between illness and shame in the book? Is this still a problem for us today?

▷ When remembering the silence that surrounded her mother's schizophrenia Catherine put forward her own philosophy on hard truths with the statement: 'I explained everything to my children, long before their questions could have been framed.' Is this philosophy reflected throughout Catherine's life? How does it fit with her reflections on reading Georgia's diary when she says that she 'would never have wanted my children – or their children when they came – to know the way I made the decisions that resulted in their lives'?

▷ Ostensibly, Catherine and Georgia have lived very different lives yet the diaries reveal many parallels. What are they? Are there character traits that the two women share? How do the two women's lives differ? How would you compare Georgia's marriage with Catherine's, first to Peter and then to Joe?

▷ Georgia describes the sanatorium as 'a place that existed out of time'. What does she mean by this? Why do you think the atmosphere in the 'san' was so much more liberated than outside it? What are the lasting effects of her time there? To what extent does it set her apart from other women of her generation?

▷ When Georgia hears of Seward's worsening condition in Colorado, she feels no terrible grief. Can her feelings for Seward be described as love? What might have attracted her to him? Would the relationship have formed in other circumstances?

▷ John says to Catherine that being Georgia's doctor had given him 'Too much power in her life'. Do you think this is the case? How has he exercised that power? Are there ways in which he has balanced it? What has the overall effect been on their lives?

▷ Catherine considers the possibility of a relationship with Samuel. Why does she choose to turn away? Why do you think Miller chose to portray Samuel as so much older than Catherine?

▷ Catherine has mixed feelings about whether diaries should be read by anyone other than the diarist. What do you think of the debate between Catherine and Samuel on this subject? Whom do you most agree with?

▷ Why is Catherine drawn back to Vermont? What purpose has her sojourn there served for her? How has it changed her attitude to the future? What are the factors that have brought her to the decision that she doesn't want to 'begin again' as she tells Fiona?

▷ Why do you think Miller chose the title *The World Below*? To what do you think it refers?

▷ Miller has been described as a writer with feminist sympathies. Although, perhaps, not a feminist novel in the traditional sense, would you say that there are feminist aspects to *The World Below*?

## SUGGESTED FURTHER READING

▶ *Behind the Scenes at the Museum* by Kate Atkinson (1995)
▶ *Sights Unseen* by Kaye Gibbons (1995)
▶ *A Short History of a Prince* by Jane Hamilton (1998)

▶ *Animal Dreams* by Barbara Kingsolver (1990)
▶ *Charming Billy* by Alice McDermott (1999)
▶ *The Stone Diaries* by Carol Shields (1993)
▶ *Fortune's Rocks* by Anita Shreve (2000)

## OTHER BOOKS BY SUE MILLER
### NOVELS
▶ *The Good Mother* (1986)
▶ *Family Pictures* (1990)
▶ *For Love* (1993)
▶ *The Distinguished Guest* (1995)
▶ *While I Was Gone* (1999)
### SHORT STORIES
▶ *Inventing the Abbotts* (1997)

# The Boy in the Moon (1997)
## Kate O'Riordan

### ABOUT THE BOOK
*The Boy in the Moon* is a disturbing but rewarding novel which tackles the deepest fears lurking beneath ordinary domestic lives. When Sam falls to his death while under his father's supervision, his parents' lives are struck by the very tragedy that his father constantly fears but perversely courts. Julia O'Riordan's description of the anguish of both parents is starkly vivid but Brian's and Julia's eventual acceptance of Sam's death and the beginnings of reconciliation leave us with a sense of the resilience of the human spirit.

At the beginning of the novel the family prepares for its Christmas visit to Ireland. Julia is reluctant, averse to the idea of a comfortless house and to Jeremiah, Brian's brusque, domineering father. As Brian lies in his two-hour bath and Julia rushes around packing for the holiday, both of them reflect on their life together.

When the family breaks the journey at a service station, Sam briefly goes missing. When he reappears, Julia releases a volley of anger at Brian, cataloguing the risks that he takes with Sam. Brian cannot explain why he seems to put Sam in danger even though the loss of his son is the thing he fears most.

The family spends one night with Brian's brother. On a family outing the following day, Sam slips from Brian's grip and falls to his death from the top of a bridge. Furious and distraught, Julia can no longer bear to live with Brian. After five months with her parents, she decides that she must go to Ireland to try to find a way of coping with her anger and grief.

Brian retreats into himself. He spends his days watching television and his nights sleeping in Sam's room, which he has papered with photographs of his dead son. As he struggles to come to terms with Sam's death, memories of his twin brother Noel flood his mind. Noel fell to his death after a fight with Brian and, as he descends into a suicidal depression, Brian convinces himself that he is responsible for the deaths of both boys.

In Ireland, Jeremiah accepts Julia's presence rather than welcoming her. She slips into a routine, helping out on the farm, responding to Jeremiah's grunted commands, finding satisfaction in mastering new skills. Cathal, a neighbouring farmer, makes daily calls to help Jeremiah, and Julia makes friends with his wife.

When she discovers Brian's mother's diary, a meticulously written record of household accounts, weather and the occasional reference to family life, Julia begins to understand the harshness of Brian's childhood. The depths of Jeremiah's bitterness and the destructive nature of his tyranny become clear. The discovery of the shocking truth behind Noel's death, a truth that Jeremiah has twisted into yet another weapon with which to torture his sons, unleashes a visceral anger.

Brian's arrival in Ireland after his recovery from his suicide attempt and the revelation that he is not to blame for Noel's death, mark the beginning of a new understanding between the couple and a tentative hope of a future together.

## ABOUT THE AUTHOR

Kate O'Riordan was born and brought up in the west of Ireland. A playwright and screenwriter as well as a novelist, she has had several plays performed on the London stage. She has also won the *Sunday Tribune*/Hennessy Prize for 'Best Emerging Writer. *The Boy in the Moon* is her second novel.

## FOR DISCUSSION

▷ The first chapter of the book is headed 'Is it Love?' What do you think the answer to this question is, at this point in the book? How does your view change, if at all, and at what point?

▷ What sort of mother do you think Julia is? What sort of father is Brian? What does the incident in the service station, when Sam gets lost, and its aftermath say about the way they work together as parents?

▷ Why do you think Brian takes risks with Sam? Has Brian's position as Noel's protector and Noel's subsequent fatal accident influenced his behaviour with Sam? Why has he 'always been afraid' and why is this the first time in his life that he can acknowledge it?

▷ Why do you think Julia returns to Ireland after Sam's death, despite the aversion she has to it in the opening chapters? Does she find any comfort there and, if so, what form does it take?

▷ Despite Jeremiah's cruel and bullying behaviour, people around him – Brian, Cathal and even Julia – seem to adapt themselves to his requirements. How do you explain this? Why does Edward not do this?

▷ To what extent does Julia begin to understand Brian after living under the same roof as Jeremiah? How has her own behaviour towards Brian shaped their relationship? At various points Julia compares herself to Jeremiah. Do you think this is fair and, if so, which elements of Julia's behaviour towards Brian might remind him of his father? In what ways has Julia's upbringing affected her ability to show love?

▷ When Brian visits Jennifer and Richard, they find themselves laughing hysterically. Does this reaction surprise you? How can you explain it within the context of grief?

▷ The encounter between Julia and the dog that has been bullying Jeremiah's collie is very powerfully described. What do you think O'Riordan is trying to convey in this incident and in the recurrent persecution of the collie that leads up to it?

## SUGGESTED FURTHER READING

▶ *The Sweet Hereafter* by Russell Banks (1991)
▶ *Talking to the Dead* by Helen Dunmore (1996)

▶ *Mothers' Boys* by Margaret Forster (1994)
▶ *The Child in Time* by Ian McEwan (1987)
▶ *The Dark* by John McGahern (1965)
▶ *The Pilot's Wife* by Anita Shreve (1996)
▶ *Thin Air* by Kate Thompson (1999)

## OTHER NOVELS BY KATE O'RIORDAN
▶ *Involved* (1995)
▶ *The Angel in the House* (2000)
▶ Kate O'Riordan has also contributed to the short story anthology *Ladies' Night at Finbar's Hotel* (1999), edited by Dermot Bolger

## The Magician's Assistant (1998)
### Ann Patchett
#### ABOUT THE BOOK
In *The Magician's Assistant,* Parsifal proves to be a master of illusion both on and off stage. Ann Patchett's novel gently unravels the life that he has woven around himself while demonstrating the many forms that love can take, from Parsifal's deep love for his gay partner to Sabine's love for a man unable to return it in the way that she wished, to the love of the Fetters family for the man who so firmly cast them off.

The novel opens with an emphatic statement: 'PARSIFAL IS DEAD. That is the end of the story.' But for Sabine it is the beginning of a new and very different life. Waking with a blinding headache, Parsifal died suddenly that afternoon. Like his lover Phan who died fourteen months before, Parsifal had Aids but Sabine had not expected his death so soon. He and Sabine had married after Phan's death – not just for tax reasons, Parsifal had said, but because he loved her. She had loved him since he called her up on stage to assist him at the Magic Hat twenty-two years ago, when she was a nineteen-year-old waitress. He made no secret of his homosexuality but Sabine had been powerless to resist him.

Shocked and bereft, she takes to her bed and dreams of Phan, who tells her that Parsifal is happy but too embarrassed to come to her. Her dreams are startlingly vivid and wonderfully comforting. When she hears that Parsifal's family is eager to talk to her, Sabine is astonished. She had understood that they had been killed in a car crash when he was very young. Her suspicions are aroused when Dot Fetters calls from Nebraska to arrange a visit to Los Angeles. Parsifal was a wealthy man. He had inherited Phan's sizeable estate and made his own money from trading in oriental rugs. Dot and her daughter want to see how Parsifal, or Guy as they knew him, lived. Sabine grudgingly gives them a tour of Los Angeles, encountering condolences at every turn. When Dot invites her for a late night drink at her hotel, Sabine feels she can't refuse and an unexpected bond forms between them.

After Dot and Bertie Fetters fly home, Sabine retreats into her grief, immune to her parents' attempts to console her. Drawn to Parsifal's family, she is persuaded by Dot to join them for Bertie's wedding. Leaving the Californian warmth for a chilly Nebraskan winter she hopes to find something of the man she thought she knew. When she meets Kitty, Parsifal's eldest sister and his first assistant, Sabine is struck by her resemblance to her brother. Kitty lets slip the real reason for

Parsifal's absence – a shocking act of violence that liberated the family from a tyranny they had endured for years. A warm friendship develops between the two women and when Kitty's husband's jealousy explodes Sabine pleads with her to bring her sons to Los Angeles.

The novel ends with Bertie's wedding. Pressed to perform some magic, Sabine chooses a complicated card trick that came to her in her last dream. The trick amazes everyone. Sabine's passage from assistant to magician is complete.

## ABOUT THE AUTHOR

Originally from Los Angeles, Ann Patchett took her first degree at Sarah Lawrence College in 1984 and her masters from Iowa University in 1987. Before taking up writing full time, she worked as a waitress and as a college professor. Her first novel, *The Patron Saint of Liars*, was published to critical acclaim in 1992. *The Magician's Assistant* was shortlisted for the 1998 Orange Prize for Fiction. Her fourth novel, *Bel Canto*, won the prize in 2002.

## FOR DISCUSSION

▷ Why does Patchett start the novel 'PARSIFAL IS DEAD. That is the end of the story'? A few pages on she writes: 'It was, in a way, the end of Sabine.' What is it that ends for Sabine with Parsifal's death? What is it that begins for her?

▷ How would you describe the relationship between Parsifal and Sabine? Is their marriage simply one of convenience? What effect has their rather unorthodox arrangement had on Sabine's life?

▷ Sabine seems to take a slightly condescending view of Dot and Bertie when she first meets them, but which of them proves to be more capable of dealing with loss and grief? What is it that changes her attitude towards the Fetters?

▷ Sabine must deal not only with the loss of the man she loved but also with the revelation that he was not what he seemed. Does Parsifal become Guy for Sabine and, if so, at what point and why? How different is Parsifal from Guy? Does Guy ever become Parsifal for any of the Fetters?

▷ Why does Patchett choose to make Parsifal a magician? How important is the theme of illusion in the novel?

▷ Sabine goes to Nebraska to find out what she can about Parsifal. What else does she find there?

▷ What part does violence play in the Fetters' lives? Kitty is a strong and capable woman. Why do you think she endures Howard's behaviour for so long? What makes her finally leave?

▷ Early in the novel Patchett writes: 'But Sabine never remembered her dreams, or maybe she didn't have them', yet Sabine's dreams of Phan and Parsifal are extraordinarily vivid. What are we to make of them? In particular, what is the significance of her final dream at the Magic Castle?

## SUGGESTED FURTHER READING

▶ *Mr Vertigo* by Paul Auster (1994)
▶ *Love Invents Us* by Amy Bloom (1997)
▶ ***A Home at the End of the World* by Michael Cunningham (1990)**
▶ *The Giant's House* by Elizabeth McCracken (1997)
▶ ***Charming Billy* by Alice McDermott (1999)**
▶ *The Pilot's Wife* by Anita Shreve (1998)
▶ *Ladder of Years* by Anne Tyler (1995)

## OTHER BOOKS BY ANN PATCHETT
▶ *The Patron Saint of Liars* (1992*)*
▶ *Taft* (1995)
▶ *Bel Canto* (2001)


# In a Land of Plenty (1997)
## Tim Pears

### ABOUT THE BOOK

Seen through the eyes of the inhabitants of Northtown, somewhere in middle England, and focusing on the fortunes of one family, *In a Land of Plenty* explores the ways in which Britain adapted to the slow, quiet social and economic revolution that took place between the 1950s and the 1990s.

It is 1952. Charles Freeman takes his fiancée to the house overlooking Northtown that is to be their home. The house has cost him almost everything he has but he is already expanding his family's small engineering firm. Caught up in Charles's enthusiasm, Mary feels overwhelmed by his energy.

They have four children – Simon, James, Robert and Alice. Mary suffers periodic depressions. Her household, garden and children are looked after by staff who become absorbed into the family. She writes poetry, attends readings and holds writing groups; Charles is uncomprehending and dismissive.

The children develop their own lives and ambitions. James's plans for a football career are scuppered by a three-month spell in hospital. On his final day, Mary tells him that she is leaving Charles but he returns to find that she has died in an accident. He retreats behind his mother's camera and looks at the world through its lens.

When James returns from a summer on his Aunt Margaret's farm, the house is in chaos. Laura, the cook's daughter, pregnant with Robert's child, has had an abortion for which she has been badly beaten by her father. James storms out of the house after attacking Robert and does not return for many years. He turns to his cousin Zoe, briefly joining her in her cinema, before finding a job as a photographer with the local paper.

Alice goes to boarding school then university. Harry Singh single-mindedly pursues her until they eventually marry and join Charles and his extended family in the house on the hill. Harry has built up a property development business that seems unstoppable. When Alice becomes pregnant, she relinquishes her feminist resolutions for full-time motherhood.

Simon has risen through the ranks of the family firm, based on his popularity and status as eldest son. Robert remains a shadowy figure dealing in cars and drugs, with a reputation for toughness. His clandestine affair with Laura continues until they have a daughter, Adamina.

Charles's fortunes finally begin to turn. His conversion to Thatcherism has soured his relationship with his employees. He has ventured into areas about which he knows nothing – buying the local paper, resulting in James's resignation, then a cable TV company. The Freeman empire hits rock bottom and when creative accounting can no longer conceal reality, Harry comes to the rescue.

When Laura needs a brochure to publicize her new catering business she asks James to be her photographer. They begin an affair that eventually leads to marriage and reconciliation between James and Charles. They marry on a glorious day in June. All seems set for a happy new phase in the fortunes of the Freeman family, until they are overtaken by a shocking tragedy.

## ABOUT THE AUTHOR

Tim Pears was born in 1956. He grew up in Crewe and Devon, and left school at sixteen. He has worked in a variety of jobs and has published both poetry and travel writing as well as fiction. He is a graduate of the National Film and Television School. His first novel, *In the Place of Fallen Leaves*, was published to great acclaim in 1993 and won both the Hawthornden Prize for Literature and the Ruth Hadden Memorial Award. *In a Land of Plenty* was dramatized by the BBC in 2001.

## FOR DISCUSSION

▷ The novel documents many social changes that have occurred since the early 1950s. Which would you say were the most important changes and how do they affect individual characters in the book? Have comparable changes happened since the close of the novel in 1993?

▷ James identifies two conditions of loneliness and freedom that seem to be both inseparable and inescapable in his life. How have these two conditions come to be so important for him and how do they influence the way he lives his life? To what extent does he want to escape them?

▷ Charles Freeman builds up an industrial empire and becomes the 'man in charge'. By the end of the book, Harry could be said to have taken over that position. What are the different approaches the two men take to their businesses and to their private lives? How are those approaches shaped by the times they live in? How do they affect other characters?

▷ From the outset we know that James is in a coma. How does this colour your reading of the book? Pears uses a technique of prefiguring events throughout the book. Why do you think he chose to do this? What effect does it achieve?

▷ Why do you think Pears chose to bring the book to such a tragic climax?

▷ To what extent do you recognize the world that Pears depicts in the novel? Are there particular aspects that strike a chord for you and, if so, what are they? How successful is Pears in recreating the atmosphere of the period? How does he attempt to do this?

▷ Pears has been to film school and his encyclopaedic knowledge of film is evident in Zoe. Are there other ways in which cinema influences the book and, if so, what are they?

## SUGGESTED FURTHER READING

- ▶ *Winesburg, Ohio* by Sherwood Anderson (1919)
- ▶ *Short Cuts* by Raymond Carver (1993)
- ▶ *What a Carve Up!* by Jonathan Coe (1994)
- ▶ *Flesh and Blood* by Michael Cunningham (1995)
- ▶ *Middlemarch* by George Eliot (1872)
- ▶ *The Facts of Life* by Patrick Gale (1995)
- ▶ *The Hotel New Hampshire* by John Irving (1981)
- ▶ ***Brightness Falls* by Jay McInerney (1992)**
- ▶ *White Teeth* by Zadie Smith (2000)

## OTHER BOOKS BY TIM PEARS
▶ *In the Place of Fallen Leaves* (1993)
▶ *A Revolution of the Sun* (2000)
▶ *Wake Up* (2002)

# The Shipping News (1993)
Annie Proulx

### ABOUT THE BOOK
*The Shipping News* is the story of a man whose life seems doomed to misfortune. Shambling and clumsy from boyhood, mocked by his father and his brother, a failure at most things he puts his hand to, Quoyle seems destined for unhappiness. But when his aunt arrives after a series of crises, Quoyle takes a step along a path that ends in a worthwhile and happy life. Annie Proulx's novel is a classic redemption story that encompasses family, friendship, love, tragedy and murder, leavened with her own brand of humour.

Quoyle has a 'great damp loaf of a body', is ugly, graceless, a college dropout and a failure at almost everything he has ever done. He has managed to hold a job at the local paper in Mockingburg, New York, largely thanks to his friend, Partridge. He fell desperately in love with Petal Bear, who loved him back for one month but has spent most of the last six years in other men's beds. He has two daughters, Bunny and Sunshine, whom he dearly loves.

When Quoyle finally loses his job, it coincides with his parents' joint suicides and the departure of Petal, later found dead in a car wreck. His two daughters are discovered in the nick of time, with the man who 'bought' them from Petal. In shock, Quoyle begs his aunt to stay with him and help him look after his children. Instead, she takes him back with her to Newfoundland, determined to reclaim the family home that has stood empty for years.

Quoyle finds a job on the local newspaper reporting car crashes and the shipping news. Surrounded by a startlingly eccentric staff, he carves out a niche for himself and finds, much to his surprise, that he can write. The family settles into the community. Dennis and Beety look after the girls while Quoyle works. Aunt Agnis sets up her yacht upholstery business and Quoyle slowly gets to know a young widow and her son.

Aunt Agnis has to move to St Johns to expand her business and as winter sets in it's clear that the isolated house on Quoyle Point is not fit for rough weather. When Quoyle's colleague Nutbeem announces his departure, Quoyle looks over his trailer as a possible place to live but a spectacular leaving party puts paid to that idea. When at last the family find a house to rent, Quoyle's tenuous relationship with Wavey seems also to become more solid as each lays the ghost of their philandering partners. Quoyle is put in charge of the paper by the owner, Jack Buggit, who would rather be out fishing than looking after a newspaper, and his life seems set.

Then he gets a call telling him that Jack has been found drowned at sea. Quoyle decides to devote the front page to the man who has become his friend but a miraculous event at Jack's wake changes everything, setting the seal on Quoyle's happiness.

## ABOUT THE AUTHOR

Annie Proulx was born in 1935 to a French-Canadian father and an American mother. She wrote magazine articles for many years on a multitude of subjects from cider making (co-authoring a book on the subject with Lew Nichols) to canoe making, but her first collection of short stories, *Heart Songs*, was not published until she was in her early fifties. In 1993, Proulx became the first woman to win the prestigious PEN/Faulkner Award for her first novel, *Postcards*. *The Shipping News* won the Pulitzer Prize for Fiction, the American National Book Award and the *Irish Times* International Fiction Prize. Something of a modern classic, the novel has remained a consistent bestseller since its publication in 1993. In 2001 it was made into a film starring Kevin Spacey as Quoyle. After many years in Vermont, Annie Proulx moved to Wyoming and quietly dropped the 'E.' from E. Annie Proulx, the name under which *The Shipping News* was originally published

## FOR DISCUSSION

▷ How does Proulx use language to evoke the landscape and weather of Newfoundland? What makes her use of language so distinctive? Are there particular examples that appealed to you or that you felt were particularly effective?

▷ How important are the landscape and the weather to the people who live in Newfoundland? What effect does it have on their lives? What sort of community has grown out of it?

▷ Proulx prefaces many of her chapters with quotations from *The Ashley Book of Knots*. What did this add to the narrative for you? Were there particular quotations that struck you and, if so, what were they?

▷ Most of the characters in *The Shipping News* have suffered unhappiness, even tragedy, in their lives and yet the book is suffused with humour. How would you describe Proulx's humour? What amused you in the book?

▷ Proulx writes of Quoyle: 'It came to him he knew nearly nothing of the aunt's life. And hadn't missed the knowledge.' The narrative explicitly concentrates on Quoyle's life but what is the aunt's story? Why has she been drawn back to Newfoundland? What makes her dispense with her brother's ashes in the way that she does?

▷ When Quoyle picks up his daughters from Dennis and Beety's house he thinks that at this time of the day 'his part in life seemed richer, he became more of a father, at the same time could expose true feelings which were often of yearning'. What is it about Dennis and Beety that makes him feel this? What is it that he is yearning for and does he find it?

▷ When Dennis tells Quoyle about Wavey and Beety setting up the Saving Grace group, Quoyle finds himself thinking of Petal, 'my lovely girl'. Why does Petal continue to have such a hold over Quoyle despite the six years of hell that he spent with her? How does his relationship with Petal influence the way he approaches Wavey?

▷ Quoyle muses that in Newfoundland 'it was as though he had found a polarised lens that deepened and intensified all seen through it'. What are the changes that have brought about this new clarity and intensity in his life?

▷ Jack Buggit says to Quoyle: 'There's two ways of living here now. There's the old way . . . Then there's the new way . . .' What other old ways and new ways have been illustrated in the book? Where does Quoyle fit in to this?

▷ Why does Quoyle turn his back on Nolan, his elderly relative, even though he finds out about him soon after he arrives in Killick-Claw? Have Quoyle's attitudes to his family and where he comes from changed by the time the novel ends and, if so, how?

## SUGGESTED FURTHER READING
▶ *The Short History of a Prince* by Jane Hamilton (1998)
▶ *The Colony of Unrequited Dreams* by Wayne Johnston (1999)
▶ **Animal Dreams by Barbara Kingsolver (1990)**
▶ *Fall On Your Knees* by Ann-Marie MacDonald (1996)
▶ *Goodnight, Nebraska* by Tom McNeal (1998)
▶ *The Bird Artist* by Howard Norman (1994)

## OTHER BOOKS BY ANNIE PROULX
### NOVELS
▶ *Postcards (1992)*
▶ *Accordion Crimes* (1996)
### SHORT STORIES
▶ *Heart Songs and Other Stories* (1988)
▶ *Broke Back Mountain* (1998)
▶ *Close Range* (1999) includes the novella, *Broke Back Mountain.*

# Promised Lands (1995)
## Jane Rogers

### ABOUT THE BOOK
*Promised Lands* is a complex and ambitious novel that focuses on characters fired by their own particular mission. The main narrative concerns William Dawes, a young marine lieutenant charged with setting up an astronomical observatory in the new colony of Australia, whose Christian conscience sometimes clouds his judgement of human nature. Stephen Beech is a teacher in our own times; his idealistic efforts to revolutionize education have ended in failure and he has dedicated himself to telling William's story. Olla, Stephen's Polish wife, is entirely focused on the survival of her severely handicapped child.

William's first sighting of Australia is as the First Fleet sails towards Botany Bay in 1788. The task of setting up the colony proves to be arduous. The weather is appalling, food is scarce and the convicts are both unruly and sickly from their long voyage. At first, relations between the settlers and the aborigines are cordial but they become strained as the settlers deplete fish stocks and steal the aborigines' belongings.

Although William's primary task is to set up the observatory, he must also oversee the construction of the settlement. Frequently shocked by the convicts' dissolute behaviour, he struggles to avoid judging them while measuring their actions against his own exacting moral code. His involvement with a convict woman both troubles and excites him.

Throughout William's three years in the settlement relations with the aborigines deteriorate. Apart from his fellow officer Watkin Tench, his colleagues seem indifferent and in William's view, Governor Phillip's patronizing treatment of the aborigines only aggravates the situation.

When a smallpox epidemic wipes out many aborigines, William challenges

Phillip to acknowledge responsibility but the Governor refuses. The Reverend Robert Johnson and his wife adopt a young aborigine orphan who teaches William her language. He talks to her about her beliefs, hoping to convert her to Christianity.

William's conscience is tested to the limits when he is asked to help Watkin Tench take six natives prisoner after a convict is attacked and mortally injured. Although eventually persuaded that this might prevent the crisis spiralling into a serious conflict, he remains convinced that it is morally wrong. Shortly after this incident, he decides to go home to England, resign his commission and come back to New South Wales as a free man. He never returns.

William's story is frequently interrupted by Stephen's commentary. Stephen has been relegated to a desk job after his attempts to build a utopian comprehensive school have backfired horribly. He is haunted by the knowledge of his own failure, the guilt of his affair with a colleague's wife and his inability to accept his son's disability.

Olla, Stephen's wife, provides the third narrative strand. She has fled her drunken father in Poland after the death of her handicapped brother. Her marriage to Stephen seems ill matched: he is fired with idealistic liberal fervour while she is resigned to the vagaries of human nature and determined to limit her role to being a housewife. After several miscarriages and the death of an infant son, Olla is determined that Daniel will survive, convinced that he will reveal his messianic powers to the world.

## ABOUT THE AUTHOR

Jane Rogers was born in London in 1952 and grew up in Birmingham, Oxford and New York state. She read English at Cambridge and went on to take a postgraduate teaching certificate at Leicester University. She has taught in comprehensive schools and further education, and has been a writing fellow at Northern College, at Cambridge and at Sheffield Hallam University. She has also held a variety of jobs in children's homes, in a mental hospital and at a London housing association. In addition to her novels, she has written several TV dramas including the BBC adaptation of her book *Mr Wroe's Virgins*. *Promised Lands*, her fifth novel, won the Writers Guild Fiction Book Award when it was published in 1995.

## FOR DISCUSSION

▷ What is the significance of the title *Promised Lands*? What were the 'promised lands' of the book? To whom was the promise extended and was it fulfilled?

▷ William reflects on the idea of a land without people and concludes that 'the land was man's backdrop, his setting. Land without man would be as futile as a stage with no actors; it would have no meaning.' What are the consequences of this conclusion for the aborigines? Do you agree with it? What do you think of Stephen's reactions to the idea?

▷ The King's commission to Phillip clearly states that no harm must come to the original inhabitants of the land, yet they suffer terribly because of the colonizers. Their food is depleted, their belongings stolen and smallpox wipes many of them out. Can their suffering and the invasion of their land be justified? What do you think of the exchange between William and Phillip about Phillip's part in the smallpox epidemic in chapter 16? Would the fate of the aborigines have been any different if Governor Phillip had been more like William?

▷ William finally accompanies Watkin Tench on the expedition to take six aborigines prisoner after McEntire has been mortally wounded. To what extent do you think he was right to refuse in the first place? Is he guilty of the 'sin of pride' or simply idealistic?

▷ William learns several hard lessons about himself. What are they and how do they change him? How would you describe the William Dawes who first arrived in Australia? What sort of man is he when he leaves?

▷ The structure of the book is very complex. Stephen tells us William's story, frequently interrupting it to reflect on his own life. Olla gives us her version of her marriage to Stephen. To what extent did you feel the narratives meshed together? Were there parts of the structure that did not work for you and, if so, what were they?

▷ Are there parallels between William's story and Stephen's and Olla's narratives and, if so, what are they? How similar are William and Stephen? In what ways do their characters overlap? In what ways do they differ? How have these characteristics shaped their lives?

▷ Stephen and Olla both have very different views of humanity. How would you describe Olla's view of the world? What does Stephen think? How have these two very different attitudes affected their marriage?

## SUGGESTED FURTHER READING
FICTION

▶ *The Voyage of the Narwhal* by Andrea Barrett (1998)
▶ *Water Music* by T. Coraghessan Boyle (1981)
▶ *Oscar and Lucinda* by Peter Carey (1988)
▶ *The Songlines* by Bruce Chatwin (1987)
▶ *Strandloper* by Alan Garner (1996)
▶ *English Passengers* by Matthew Kneale (2000)
▶ *Remembering Babylon* by David Malouf (1993)
▶ *The Last Time I Saw Jane* by Kate Pullinger (1996)

NON-FICTION

▶ *The Fatal Shore* by Robert Hughes (1986)

## OTHER BOOKS BY JANE ROGERS
FICTION

▶ *Separate Tracks* (1983)
▶ *Her Living Image* (1984)
▶ *The Ice is Singing* (1987)
▶ *Mr Wroe's Virgins* (1991)
▶ *Island* (1999)

EDITED

▶ *The Good Fiction Guide* (2001) with Mike Harris, Douglas Houston and Hermione Lee

# The Reader (1997)
Bernhard Schlink (translated by Carol Brown Janeway)

## ABOUT THE BOOK

Set in post-war Germany, *The Reader* begins as an erotic love story between a fifteen-year-old boy and a thirty-six-year-old woman. But what begins as a love story becomes a philosophical enquiry into the effects of the Holocaust on a generation whose parents are perceived as either its perpetrators or complicit in its perpetration. Central to this difficult but rewarding novel is the question: what is to be done with the knowledge and guilt of the Holocaust?

When Michael Berg is taken ill on his way home from school, a stranger helps him out. After a winter spent sick with hepatitis, Michael's mother sends him off to thank the stranger. Finding his way into Hanna's house, he takes her by surprise when she arrives home from her job as a tram conductor. When she changes out of her uniform, Michael watches through the crack of the door, running away when she catches his eye. He returns and the affair begins. When Hanna picks up one of Michael's books, she asks him to read it to her and soon the reading becomes an essential part of their routine. One day Hanna disappears.

When Michael next sees her, she is on trial for crimes committed when she was an SS guard. Now a law student, Michael is attending the trial as part of a course on war crimes. The sight of Hanna in the dock triggers a terrible guilt in him. She is on trial for her part in the deaths of a group of women in transit from one camp to another. During a bombing raid, Hanna and her colleagues locked the women inside a church. All but two were burnt to death. The author of the report describing this terrible event is considered the most culpable of the defendants. Hanna refuses to deny that she wrote it despite the fact that, as Michael has finally realized, she is illiterate.

One of the two survivors tells how Hanna would select the most delicate young women to read to her in the evenings. Knowing that if he can convince the judge of Hanna's illiteracy she will be given a lighter sentence, Michael is confused. Given that Hanna's pride has not allowed her to confess it herself, would she want it exposed? He seeks advice from everyone he knows, including his father. No one is able to help and eventually he lets it go. Hanna is sentenced to life, leaving Michael haunted by the questions that her trial has posed. He marries and has a daughter but cannot tell his wife about Hanna. They divorce and he is unable to sustain another relationship with a woman, seeking solace in his work.

He begins to record his favourite books for Hanna and eventually receives notes from her. When the governor informs him that Hanna has won a plea of clemency, he sets up the beginnings of a life for her, visiting her just before she is to be released. It will be the last time that he sees her.

## ABOUT THE AUTHOR
Bernhard Schlink was born in Germany in 1944. He is a professor of law at the University of Berlin and the author of several prize-winning crime novels. He divides his time between Bonn and Berlin.

## FOR DISCUSSION
▷ Who do you think 'the reader' of the title is, or can it be applied to more than one character? At what point was it apparent to you that Hanna was illiterate? What is the importance of literacy in the book?
▷ How would you describe the tone and style of Schlink's writing in part one of the book? How does it differ from the second and third part? What effect does this difference achieve, if any?
▷ The relationship between Hanna and Michael begins with an act of kindness on her part but we later learn of her involvement in the concentration camps. Do you find that Hanna engages your sympathy at any point after you found out that she was a camp guard? How convincing are Michael's arguments

why Hanna became a guard and for her selection of girls to read to her? How can we explain why ordinary people commit atrocities without resorting to calling them monsters?

▷ Why does Michael find it so difficult to make a relationship with other women work? How does the affair with Hanna affect him as an adolescent?

▷ Michael says: 'And if I was not guilty because one cannot be guilty of betraying a criminal, then I was guilty of loving one.' Michael did not know of Hanna's crime during their affair so why does he feel guilty? How do other characters of his generation seem to feel about the Holocaust? What about his father's generation?

▷ Michael refers to the many images that have been produced of the camps, particularly in films. Is there a danger that continued exposure of Holocaust images lessens their impact until they become frozen into clichés as Michael suggests? How do you feel about the images of war recorded in the newspapers and on television?

▷ Is Hanna just a scapegoat for her co-defendants or in a more general way? When she turns to the judge and asks him what he would have done in her position, what does his answer imply? Could the judge be considered as guilty as Hanna if he knew about the camps but did nothing?

▷ Why do you think Hanna does what she does at the end of the novel? How do you think learning to read might have changed her view of what she had done in the camps?

▷ The novel poses the question: 'What should our second generation have done, what should it do with the knowledge of the horrors of the extermination of the Jews?' Does it answer this question? What do you think the answer might be or is it an unanswerable question?

▷ Does the novel give any grounds for hope of forgiveness and, if so, what are they?

## SUGGESTED FURTHER READING
**NOVELS**

▶ *The Archivist* by Martha Cooley (1998)
▶ *Crime and Punishment* by Fyodor Dostoevsky (1866)
▶ *The Tin Drum* by Günter Grass (1959)
▶ **Stones From the River by Ursula Hegi (1997)**
▶ *Schindler's List* by Thomas Keneally (1982)
▶ *The Time of Light* by Gunnar Kopperud (1998)
▶ **Fugitive Pieces by Anne Michaels (1997)**
▶ *Sophie's Choice* by William Styron (1979)
▶ *A Model Childhood* by Christa Wolf (1976)
▶ *Music For the Third Ear* by Susan Schwartz Senstad (1999)

**NON-FICTION**

▶ *Eichmann in Jerusalem* by Hannah Arendt (1963)
▶ *If This is a Man/The Truce* by Primo Levi (1966)
▶ *The Holocaust and Collective Memory* by Peter Novick (1999)
▶ *Night* by Elie Weisel (1960)

## OTHER BOOKS BY BERNHARD SCHLINK

▶ *Flights of Love* (2002)
▶ *The Reader* and *Flights of Love* are the only titles available in English. Other titles include:

*Selbs Betrug*
*Selbs Justiz*
*Die Gordische Schleife*

# Larry's Party (1997)
Carol Shields

## ABOUT THE BOOK

This is the story of an ordinary guy who leads a reasonably uneventful life, told with a lingering and playful delight in everyday detail. Spanning twenty years in the life of Larry Weller, from the evening when he mistakenly picks up an altogether smarter version of his own Harris tweed jacket, to the dinner party at which his two ex-wives first meet, Carol Shields builds a subtle and many-layered narrative of a life that many of us might recognize.

We encounter Larry as he suddenly becomes aware that he has picked up the wrong jacket at the café where he drinks his usual late afternoon cappuccino. As he glories in the jacket's smartness, its superior cut and the silkiness of its lining, he realizes that he can't keep it and throws it away, striding off into the chilly Winnipeg evening.

In 1977, Larry is a florist, a career he stumbled into entirely by accident. He lives with his parents and has just fallen in love with Dorrie. When Dorrie becomes pregnant, the couple marry, spending their honeymoon in England courtesy of Larry's parents. On a visit to Hampton Court, Larry loses himself in the maze, conceiving a passion that will eventually lead him to a new profession as a maze maker.

Dorrie continues to work after the birth of their son, climbing the ladder at Manitoba Motors towards an executive position. The couple begin a slow drift apart; neither seems quite to know what the other wants. Larry moves out when Dorrie hires a bulldozer to destroy his first maze, laid out in the garden of their house.

Discontented with his job as manager at Flowercity, Larry summons the courage to move to Illinois to work under an expert maze maker. Here he meets and marries Beth, a feisty academic specializing in the lives of women saints. Their life is a settled one until Beth's application for a Guggenheim Fellowship fails, but Larry's unexpectedly succeeds. The couple spend a year exploring the mazes of the world and Beth, at first reluctant and humiliated by her failure, begins to understand Larry's passion.

Shortly after their return Beth is offered a job at an English university. When she accepts, Larry's life enters a new and lonelier phase as they try to sustain their relationship across two continents. Almost inevitably, they fail, and Larry moves back to Canada to take up a prestigious commission.

He settles into life in Toronto, meeting Charlotte with whom he builds a quietly happy relationship. When he finds that both Beth and Dorrie are to be in Toronto at the same time, Charlotte suggests she helps him to organize a dinner party. Finally, the two wives are to meet and Larry will find that his life is about to take another unexpected turn.

## ABOUT THE AUTHOR

Carol Shields was born in Oak Park, Illinois, in 1935. She was educated at Hanover College, Exeter University and the University of Ottawa where she took her MA. In 1957 she married and moved from the United States to Canada where she lived until her death in 2003. In between bringing up five children, she taught at the universities of Ottawa, British Columbia and Manitoba, and was Chancellor of the University of Winnipeg. Her first novel, *Small Ceremonies*, was published in 1976. She won many prizes for her fiction, including the 1995 Pulitzer Prize for *The Stone Diaries*, which was also shortlisted for the Booker Prize in the same year. In 1997, *Larry's Party* was awarded the Orange Prize for Fiction. She also ventured into biography with the publication of her book on Jane Austen in 2001.

## FOR DISCUSSION

▷ Why do you think Shields chose the unusual occupation of maze maker for Larry? What is it that so attracts Larry to mazes?

▷ Each of the chapters has a theme – 'Larry's Folks', 'Larry's Friends' – culminating in 'Larry's Party'. Why do you think Shields chose to structure the novel in this way and how does it shape the narrative?

▷ There is much reiteration of the detail of Larry's life as he moves through the years, each retelling subtly different from the last. Why do you think Shields chose to do this and what effect does it achieve?

▷ Shields writes of the Wellers: 'Nothing real will ever get said out loud in this house, though Midge will bleat and blast, and Larry will prod and suggest.' Why is this the case and what effect has it had on Larry? Are the Wellers any different from the average family in their lack of communication?

▷ 'The day will arrive in his life when work . . . will be all that stands between himself and the bankruptcy of his soul.' How important is work to Larry and how is this illustrated in the book? How important is work to the other principal characters and how does it affect their lives?

▷ How does Larry's second marriage to Beth differ from his first to Dorrie and why? How does each marriage change Larry?

▷ When Larry remembers taking his son around his first maze in Winnipeg, Shields writes: 'It may be that Larry has romanticised this particular memory.' Do you think he has and, if so, why? How does Larry's memory change the way he looks back over the years?

▷ Larry remembers Eric Eisner telling him that: 'Forty is the end of the party . . . What's left for us oldies is a freefall into hoary age and the thinning of imagination.' Does this prove to be the case for Larry? Does the fact that mid-life crisis is a cliché of our times make it any less painful? How does it affect Larry?

▷ What role do the women in the novel play in shaping Larry's life? How do his relationships with women change as time moves on and what prompts those changes?

▷ How much of Larry's life is shaped by accident? Can he be said to be a man in control of his life?

▷ How well do you feel you know Larry by the end of the book? Do you think Shields succeeds in conveying his character and the changes it has undergone during the twenty-year span of the book? How different is the Larry who picked up the wrong jacket in chapter 1 from the Larry who holds a dinner party for his two ex-wives?

▷ At the party the guests debate what it is to be a man in the late twentieth century. Do you agree with Ian's assessment – have men been 'walking on eggshells since about 1980' and, if so, why? What about the women's assessment of their position? How have these ideas been illustrated in the novel?

▷ Were you surprised by the way the novel ended? Were you convinced by the ending?

## SUGGESTED FURTHER READING
▶ *Preston Falls* by David Gates (1998)
▶ ***Empress of the Splendid Season* by Oscar Hijuelos (1999)**
▶ *A Widow For One Year* by John Irving (1998)
▶ *Ladder of Years* by Anne Tyler (1996)

## OTHER BOOKS BY CAROL SHIELDS
### NOVELS
▶ *Small Ceremonies* (1976)
▶ *The Box Garden* (1977)
▶ *Happenstance* (1980)
▶ *Mary Swann* (1987)
▶ *The Republic of Love* (1992)
▶ *The Stone Diaries* (1993)
▶ *A Celibate Season* (with Blanche Howard) (2000)
▶ *Unless* (2002)
### SHORT STORIES
▶ *Various Miracles* (1994)
▶ *Dressing Up For the Carnival* (2000)
### BIOGRAPHY
▶ *Jane Austen* (2001)

# The Last Time They Met (2001)
## Anita Shreve
### ABOUT THE BOOK
*The Last Time They Met* addresses themes of betrayal, forgiveness and passion while exploring the possibilities of a life unlived. The novel's reverse chronological structure is both unusual and challenging, but once the final sentences have been read, Shreve's reasons for using it become clear. The novel is split into three sections: the first takes place at a Toronto literary festival; the second tells the story of Linda and Thomas's affair in Kenya; and the third tells of their meeting in the 1960s.

Linda is a minor poet in her fifties, widowed with two grown-up children. As the novel opens she is arriving at her Toronto hotel – slightly reluctant to leave the luxury of her room, she slips quietly into the authors' party. When Thomas Janes, a reclusive but well-known poet, approaches her, all eyes are on them. She and Thomas have not met since the end of their affair twenty-six years ago. At Thomas's reading, Linda is moved by his poems about the drowning of his child. Her own reading passes in a blur. The couple spend the next day together, their joy in finding each other marred only by the jibes of a jealous author and Linda's discovery of her son's alcohol problem. They part, promising to meet again.

The Kenyan section is told from Thomas's point of view. When he meets Linda, he and his wife have been in Nairobi for a year. Their marriage has been strained by Regina's desperation to conceive after miscarrying their first child. Thomas is shocked into a semblance of politicization when his fellow poet Ndegwa is arrested for dissidence. On the day of the arrest he bumps into Linda, now married and teaching for the Peace Corps. They have not seen each other since the car crash that left them both badly injured. After visiting Ndegwa's wife, Thomas goes to Linda's village. Their lovemaking reignites a passion that began when they were seventeen. They write to each other and even snatch a night together. Their obsession intensifies until the affair becomes public. Believing Regina to be pregnant, Thomas reluctantly breaks with Linda.

In the final section, the narrative passes back to Linda. Abandoned by her father after her mother's death, Linda lives with her aunt. At thirteen, she is discovered in bed with her aunt's boyfriend and sent to Magdalene, a hostel for 'wayward' girls. She returns, aged seventeen, lonely and unforgiven. On her first day at high school, she sits next to Thomas. Their relationship begins with their discovery of a mutual love of poetry. Linda can only sleep with Thomas after she has made her confession to a priest about her aunt's boyfriend. Driving home after they have finally made love, Thomas swerves to avoid a child. The ensuing accident not only changes the course of his life but also turns the entire story upon its head.

*NB* Readers of *The Weight of Water* may recognize Thomas Janes as the husband of Jean, a photographer whose assignment to document the site of a nineteenth-century murder just off the New England coast ended in the drowning of their young daughter.

### ABOUT THE AUTHOR

Anita Shreve is American. She began writing fiction while working as a high school teacher. Although one of her early short stories was awarded the O. Henry Prize in 1975, she felt that she could not earn a living writing fiction and turned to journalism. She worked in Kenya for three years writing articles for a number of US magazines including *Newsweek*. When her first novel, *Eden Close*, was published in 1989 she took up writing fiction full time. In 1998 *The Weight of Water,* which can be read as a companion volume to *The Last Time They Met,* was shortlisted for the Orange Prize. *The Pilot's Wife*, published in 1998, became an Oprah Winfrey book club choice, ensuring Shreve a place on the US bestsellers list. She teaches writing at Amherst College and divides her time between Massachusetts and New Hampshire.

### FOR DISCUSSION

▷ Anita Shreve has chosen an unusual structure for *The Last Time They Met*. What effect does reversing the conventional chronological order of the narrative achieve? How does Shreve trace the threads of Linda's and Thomas's stories backwards through the years? What do you think might be the pitfalls of such a structure? How successful did you find it?

▷ At the literary festival, when Linda is quizzed about why she writes about love, she says: 'I believe it to be the central drama of our lives.' To what extent does this prove to be the case for her? When she suggests that marriage cannot be accurately described in fiction the Australian novelist agrees, saying: 'A marriage doesn't lend itself to art. Certainly not to satisfying structure or to dialogue worth reading.' To what extent do you agree with this? Are there literary examples that you feel disprove this idea?

▷ Although the three narratives that make up the novel are not written in the first person, they are clearly written from either Linda's or Thomas's point of view. What differentiates the two in style? How does Shreve convey their characters through the narratives? To what extent did you have to reassess your ideas about the characters when you finished the book?

▷ The name Magdalene runs through the novel like a motif. What is its significance for Linda and Thomas?

▷ Thomas says of living in Kenya: 'Living here is like watching an endless documentary.' This sentiment is echoed when he says: 'it is as though I watch an exotic, imagistic movie. It does not include me. I am in the audience. I suppose that allows me to critique the movie, but I don't feel capable of even that.' What do you think he means by these statements? How does his response to Africa differ from Linda's? Can you think of reasons why this might be the case?

▷ Linda is a Catholic but Thomas is not. How important is Linda's Catholicism in the novel – in particular, the concept of confession?

▷ The book ends in a particularly startling fashion. What did you think of the ending? How did it change your interpretation of the rest of the novel? To what extent did you feel that the ending was a success?

## SUGGESTED FURTHER READING
▶ *Out of Africa* by Karen Blixen (1937)
▶ *Cause Celeb* by Helen Fielding (1995)
▶ *Sin* by Josephine Hart (1992)
▶ *Rules of the Wild* by Francesca Marciano (1998)
▶ *Evening* by Susan Minot (1999)
▶ *Anna Karenina* by Leo Tolstoy (1874–6)

## OTHER BOOKS BY ANITA SHREVE
▶ *Eden Close* (1989)
▶ *Strange Fits of Passion* (1991)
▶ *Where or When?* (1993)
▶ *Resistance* (1995)
▶ *The Weight of Water* (1997)
▶ *The Pilot's Wife* (1998)
▶ *Fortune's Rocks* (2000)
▶ *Sea Glass* (2002)

# *The Death of Vishnu* (2000)
## Manil Suri

### ABOUT THE BOOK
In *The Death of Vishnu*, Manil Suri turns a single Bombay apartment block into a vibrant portrait of India in microcosm, with all its aspirations, intricate social structures and religious divisions. While Vishnu lies dying on the stairway where he has lived for almost eleven years, slipping in and out of consciousness, the dramas of the tenants' lives are played out around him. Social rivalries, strained marriages, the search for spiritual truth, romantic love and grief are all explored, as Vishnu's soul begins its ascent of the building's stairs. Suri underpins this tale

of all too human desires and preoccupations with a rich blend of Hindu mythology and an observation of human folly which is both humorous and astute.

The day begins. Mrs Asrani tops up the cup of tea she had left next to Vishnu's prostrate form the day before. Uppermost in her mind is the fulfilment of her daily duty of giving Vishnu his early morning tea as she has always done. None of the tenants seems able to shoulder the responsibility of what to do about the dying man.

The novel explores the lives of four sets of tenants. Mrs Asrani and her neighbour, Mrs Pathak, are deeply embroiled in a battle over their shared kitchen while their bemused husbands look on, carefully avoiding the flak. Mr Pathak inveigles Mr Asrani into sharing the payment for an ambulance for Vishnu but when it arrives, in the middle of the socially ambitious Mrs Pathak's card party, neither the Pathaks nor the Asranis will guarantee Vishnu's hospital fees.

Upstairs live the Jalals, the only Muslim family in the building. Their son, Salim, and nineteen-year-old Kavita Asrani plan to elope, an adventure that proves to be less romantic than Kavita had envisioned. As part of his quest for spiritual enlightenment, Mr Jalal decides to spend a night on the stairs with Vishnu where he has the dream or vision, as he chooses to interpret it, which leads to his downfall at the outraged hands of the Hindu stair-dwellers later in the day.

On the third floor lives Vinod Taneja, an elderly widower who spends his days sitting on his balcony recalling the brief joys of his marriage, oblivious to the dramas played out on the floors below.

Intertwined with the tenants' stories, Vishnu's narrative is filled with vivid memories, evoked by the sounds and smells around him. Lovemaking with the luscious Padmini, his mother brewing tea and the myths and stories that she told him all through his childhood, drift through his mind until his soul lifts itself from his body and begins its ascent. As Vishnu climbs the building's stair, he wonders: has he become his namesake, Lord Vishnu, as Mr Jalal seem to think, or is he just another dying man?

## ABOUT THE AUTHOR

Manil Suri was born in Mumbai (Bombay) in 1959. After taking his doctorate at the Carnegie-Mellon University, he took his first job as an assistant professor of mathematics at the University of Baltimore, Maryland, where he is now a full professor. He finished his first short story in 1985. *The Death of Vishnu,* his first novel, begun in 1995, was inspired by the true story of a man who lived and died on the steps of the Mumbai apartment block where he grew up. It is the first in a planned trilogy, the other two volumes of which will be based on the Hindu gods Shiva, the destroyer, and Brahma, the creator.

## FOR DISCUSSION

▷ The book is prefaced by a quotation from *The Bhagavad-Gita* in which the god Vishnu is described as 'sustaining the entire world with a fragment of my being'. Why do you think Suri chose this quotation? Are there ways in which it can be applied to Vishnu, the odd-job man, as well as Vishnu the god, and, if so, what are they?

▷ How does Suri use the senses to evoke memory and atmosphere? Are there particular examples that struck you and, if so, what are they? To what extent does the style of writing differ between Vishnu's narrative and the rest of the book?

▷ How important is religion to the book's main characters such as the Asranis, the Pathaks, the Jalals and Vishnu himself? How does this demonstrate itself in the tenants' attitude and behaviour towards Vishnu, both when he is well and while he is dying?

▷ The Jalals are the only Muslim family in the building. To what extent does this set them apart from the others? Were you surprised when the *lathi*-bearing mob was sparked off by Mr Jalal's description of his vision? Why do you think they were so brutal?

▷ The tenants' treatment of Vishnu while he lies dying is shocking, yet Suri infuses the situation with humour. Why do you think he decided to do this? What effect does it have and how does Suri achieve it?

▷ What impression do you gain from the novel of life in Bombay? What kind of social divides are apparent from the way people live their lives in the apartment block? What are the aspirations of the various characters?

▷ Bombay is the centre of the burgeoning Bollywood film industry and cinema is never far away in the novel. Some characters seem to visualize their actions as if they are acting a part in a movie. How does this affect their lives? Are there particular situations where the cinema comes into play? If so, what are they and why do you think Suri chose to do this? Could the book be described as 'cinematic', and, if so, why?

▷ Were there any characters in the book who engaged your sympathy? If so, who were they and what was it about them that attracted you? Which characters did you most dislike and why?

▷ At the screening of *The Death of Vishnu,* Vishnu watches himself as he climbs the stairs of the apartment block and 'wishes the movie would be more clear about what he is climbing towards. Whether he is the god Vishnu, or just an ordinary man'. Which do you think he is meant to be, and why?

▷ 'Who are you?' Vishnu asks the flute-playing boy on the final page of the book. The boy replies, 'You know who I am.' Who do you think he is and why?

▷ There has been something of a vogue in the West for fiction by Indian writers over the past decade. How does *The Death of Vishnu* compare with other novels such Arundhati Roy's *The God of Small Things* or Vikram Seth's *A Suitable Boy*? Are there similarities in style or subject with books by these and other Indian authors such as Salman Rushdie or do you think they are simply lumped together because of their race?

## SUGGESTED FURTHER READING
### FICTION

▶ *Love and Longing in Bombay* by Vikram Chandra (1997)
▶ *A Fine Balance* by Rohinton Mistry (1996)
▶ *Gods, Demons and Others* by R.K. Narayan (1965)
▶ *Life, A User's Manual* by Georges Perec (1970)
▶ *The God of Small Things* by Arundhati Roy (1997)
▶ *Midnight's Children* by Salman Rushdie (1981)
▶ *A Suitable Boy* by Vikram Seth (1993)

### NON-FICTION

▶ *The Bhagavad-Gita*
▶ *India: A Million Mutinies Now* by V.S. Naipaul (1990)
▶ *Hinduism* by K.M. Sen (1961)

## Anita and Me (1996)
Meera Syal

### ABOUT THE BOOK
Set in a Midlands village in the 1960s, similar to the one in which Meera Syal grew up, *Anita and Me* is as much about the difficulties of dodging parental concern in the quest for independence as it is about being different in a small community. It is narrated by nine-year-old Meena, whose propensity for telling stories frequently gets her into trouble and whose eagerness to be accepted leads to yet more problems when she pals up with the formidable Anita.

Meena is reluctant to admit that she stole a shilling from her mother's purse to buy sweets. Meena's father frog-marches her to the local shop, and when she finally confesses, her father leaves her sitting on the shop's doorstep. Anita, the village hussy, finds her and asks if she wants to tag along. Meena is thrilled. She wants nothing more than to be brash, tough and sassy like Anita, but her parents want her to be a good girl like her cousins. The Kumars have worked hard to be accepted; life is tricky as the only Indian family in a small village. Little is openly said but there are small affronts and occasional outright insults that cannot be ignored. The family's social life is confined to musical evenings with their Asian friends from Wolverhampton.

Anita's gang meet to compare notes about the latest issue of *Jackie*, have peeing competitions and boss the more diminutive members around. Although her relationship with the manipulative Anita is far from easy, Meena is proud of her friendship until an ugly incident at the local fete exposes the racism in the village. Local skinhead Sam Lowbridge shouts racist insults and Anita, far from springing to Meena's defence, is obviously impressed.

On the night of one of Meena's wildest adventures in the grounds of the mysterious Big House, Mrs Kumar gives birth to a baby boy. Her mother comes from India for a prolonged visit and Meena is charmed by her exuberant Nanima. The sedate musical evenings become quite boisterous as everyone celebrates her arrival, begging her for news from home.

When the local school falls victim to government education policy, the bulldozers arrive to tear it down and the whole village turns out to watch. Meena is amazed to see an Indian, smartly dressed and obviously in charge. Later she sees a report in the local paper about an Asian man found badly beaten. When she next sees Anita at Sherrie's farm, Anita proudly tells her that Sam Lowbridge has been 'Paki-bashing'. Meena jumps on Sherrie's horse and rides off. She falls, badly breaks her leg and spends the next four months in hospital.

The dramatic events of the night before Meena's eleven-plus exam, when Anita's sister Tracey comes knocking on her door in terrible distress, not only set the seal on the end of her relationship with Anita but also strengthen Meena's self-esteem when the ironic truth behind the mystery of the Big House is revealed.

### ABOUT THE AUTHOR
Meera Syal was brought up in the Midlands mining village of Essington, close to Wolverhampton. She studied English and drama at Manchester University, working as an actress at the Royal Court Theatre after graduation. She was commissioned by the BBC to write a three-part series, *My Sister Wife*, and went

on to write the screenplay for the critically acclaimed film, *Bhaji on the Beach*. She has regularly written for radio, including *Masala FM* and two series of *Goodness Gracious Me*. Her comedy, *It's Not Unusual*, in which she played a Tom Jones-obsessed cabbie, won a BAFTA for best short film. *Anita and Me*, Syal's first novel, won the Betty Trask Award and was shortlisted for the *Guardian* Fiction Prize.

## FOR DISCUSSION

▷ 'I'm not really a liar, I just learned very early on that those of us deprived of history sometimes need to turn to mythology to feel complete, to belong.' What does Syal mean by this and what bearing does it have on the rest of the novel? Are there other reasons why Meena tells so many stories? If so, what do you think they are?

▷ The novel is set in the 1960s and narrated by nine-year-old Meena. How successful do you think Syal is at capturing a nine-year-old's voice and at conveying the period?

▷ The book is infused with a good deal of humour – how amusing did you find it and what made you laugh?

▷ How different are Meena's feelings about Britain and the British from those of her parents and their friends? Do Meena's feelings about being Indian change in the book, and if so what triggers this change and how does it alter her view of life? How well does the family fit into the village and how does their effort to adapt affect them?

▷ There are instances of overt racism in the book but, on the whole, instances of prejudice are covert or unconscious. How does Syal convey this to her readers? To what extent do you think attitudes about race have changed since the 1960s? Would the Kumars have an easier time in Tollington today?

▷ What impression did you form of Anita? Why do you think she sought Meena out? How does her 'friendship' with Anita change Meena?

▷ What effect does Nanima's arrival have on Meena, her family and the rest of the village?

▷ How does Tollington change over the course of the novel and what triggers those changes?

## SUGGESTED FURTHER READING

▶ **The Romance Reader by Pearl Abraham (1995)**
▶ *Cat's Eye* by Margaret Atwood (1988)
▶ *Venus Flaring* by Suzannah Dunn (1996)
▶ *Fruit of the Lemon* by Andrea Levy (1999)
▶ **The Orchard on Fire by Shena Mackay (1995)**
▶ *The God of Small Things* by Arundhati Roy (1997)
▶ *Staying On* by Paul Scott (1977)
▶ *White Teeth* by Zadie Smith (2000)
▶ *The Sopranos* by Alan Warner (1998)

## OTHER BOOKS BY MEERA SYAL

▶ *Life Isn't All Ha Ha Hee Hee* (1999)

# The Hundred Secret Senses (1995)

## Amy Tan

### ABOUT THE BOOK

*The Hundred Secret Senses* explores the gap between two very different cultures. Kwan has grown up in a Chinese village and refuses to abandon her 'hundred secret senses' in the face of American scepticism. Determinedly rational, Olivia finds her sister's forays into the spirit world irritating and embarrassing. Kwan's stories of her previous life, caught up in the tumult of the nineteenth-century Taiping rebellion, punctuate Olivia's narrative as she charts their uneasy relationship and the break-up of her marriage.

Kwan's 'yin eyes', she believes, enable her to communicate with people from the spirit world. At her dying father's wish, she has been brought from China to live with his American family, including her half-sister Olivia. Olivia is Kwan's favourite. She bombards her with tales of the Yin people, telling Olivia stories of her previous life as Nunumu and her friendship with Miss Banner, a feisty young American. Her stories are of love, betrayal, war and loyalty. She swears Olivia to secrecy but, scared and irritated by this invasion of her privacy, Olivia tells her mother. Kwan is sent to a mental hospital where she endures electric shock therapy, but her love for Olivia is undiminished.

Kwan finds a job in a drugstore and talks to all her customers, consulting the Yin about them and handing out advice. She marries George and looks after his two sons but always has time for Olivia.

When Olivia meets Simon he seems obsessed with his former girlfriend. Finally he confesses that Elza died in a skiing accident for which he feels responsible. Overwhelmingly attracted to Simon and desperate to overcome his remorse, Olivia enlists Kwan's help. Kwan summons Elza from the Yin world and assures Simon that he must forget her. But Olivia is guilt-ridden by what she perceives to be a deception. The couple marry and set up a business together. For many years they are happy but discontent creeps in. In an attempt to save their marriage, they put together a proposal for an article about China, but Olivia's discovery of Simon's novel about Elza provokes a terrible row and he walks out. Kwan's campaign to reunite them only adds to Olivia's irritation. When a magazine accepts the China proposal Kwan presents Olivia with a *fait accompli* and all three of them set out on a journey to China that will change their lives.

Olivia and Simon suffer culture shock but Kwan is delighted to be home. They hire a driver for the knuckle-whitening journey to her village, passing an overturned bus on the way. When they arrive, Kwan realizes that her foster-mother has been killed in the accident.

The site of so many of Kwan's stories, the village seems strange yet familiar to Olivia. There is only one bed which the three of them share. Kwan gets up early, leaving Simon and Olivia asleep. Olivia is embarrassed when they wake, unsure of what she wants. After a tentative reconciliation they go for a walk together. When a row develops Simon disappears into a maze of caves. While they wait for him, Kwan tells Olivia the story of Nunumu and Miss Banner's last days and as Olivia listens she teeters on the brink of an intuitive leap into a new way of looking at the world.

### ABOUT THE AUTHOR

Amy Tan was born in 1952 in Oakland, California. She graduated from high school in Montreux, Switzerland, and took a masters degree in linguistics at

San Jose State University. Her first novel, *The Joy Luck Club*, was published in 1989, when it won the American National Book Award. It was later made into a film.

## FOR DISCUSSION

▷ How does Olivia feel about Kwan when the book opens? What are her feelings towards her when it ends? Why do you think this change has come about?

▷ How would you describe Kwan? What are her feelings for Olivia? Why is Kwan so forgiving when Olivia is so obviously irritated by her? Why does she so often ask Olivia what she thinks and tell her to keep things to herself?

▷ Nunumu says of Miss Banner: 'I wondered whether foreigners had feelings that were entirely different from those of Chinese people.' How important is this idea in the novel? How is it illustrated in the relationship between Kwan and Olivia?

▷ What do you think of the missionaries' attitude towards the Chinese? How would you describe the Chinese reactions to them?

▷ The idea of the 'loyal friend' is very important to Kwan, both in her present life and her past as Nunumu. What does Kwan/Nunumu mean by a 'loyal friend'? What does Miss Banner mean by it?

▷ Why does Olivia leave Simon? What effect does Elza's death have on their relationship? What does Olivia expect of her marriage and how realistic do you think her expectations are?

▷ What are the 'hundred secret senses'? Does Olivia understand what they are by the end of the book?

▷ What do Olivia and Simon learn from their visit to China? How different is it from their expectations? How do the Chinese view American culture? Are there any similarities between the way that Americans and Chinese view each other in the nineteenth-century narrative and the twentieth century? If so, what are they?

▷ How satisfactory did you find the ending of the book? What do you think happened to Kwan?

## SUGGESTED FURTHER READING

▶ *The House of Spirits* by Isabel Allende (1985)
▶ *Fruit of the Lemon* by Andrea Levy (1999)
▶ *Eating Chinese Food Naked* by Mei Ng (1998)
▶ *Pears on a Willow Tree* by Leslie Pietrzyk (1998)
▶ *The Last Time I Saw Jane* by Kate Pullinger (1996)

## OTHER BOOKS BY AMY TAN
### NOVELS

▶ *The Joy Luck Club* (1989)
▶ *The Kitchen God's Wife* (1991)
▶ *The Bonesetter's Daughter* (2001)

### EDITED

▶ *The Best American Short Stories 1999*

# Morality Play (1995)
## Barry Unsworth

### ABOUT THE BOOK

*Morality Play* is set in the late fourteenth century, a time marked by terrible calamity; plague and famine stalk the land while the century-long wars with France still rage. The long-established feudal system has begun to crumble. Millenarian sects prophesying the Last Days spring up in protest against the corruption of the clergy. This is the backdrop against which Martin and his players set the story of the murder of Thomas Wells, using the structure of the allegorical dramas known as morality plays. Told in the style of the period, the novel is narrated by a young priest.

When Nicholas Barber comes across a group of players mourning the death of their friend, he is already in trouble. He is outside his diocese without his bishop's permission, he has just committed adultery and he is about to compound these sins by joining a group of performers. The players decide to take their friend's body to the nearest town and ask Nicholas to join them.

They are charged such an exorbitant rate for the burial that they decide to put on a play to replenish their meagre finances. When Martin, their leader, hears that a young woman is to be hanged for the murder of twelve-year-old Thomas he suggests that this story should form their play. He overcomes the group's reluctance to breach dramatic convention with persuasion and the promise of money.

The players piece together the evidence which suggests that the motive was money. Jane, the convicted woman, and a monk were both seen in the vicinity of the body. The monk found a purse belonging to the victim's parents in Jane's home. Armed with this information, the players put together their play. Although they have agreed a framework based on the conventions of the morality play, they improvise freely until Martin throws suspicion on the monk in a startling departure from the accepted story. Despite their fears of the consequences, Martin persuades them to play one more night.

The next day Nicholas discovers that Jane's father belongs to a sect which deplores the corruption of the Benedictine clergy to which the monk belongs. Martin and Nicholas visit Jane in prison. She can neither speak nor hear. They communicate using the stylized gestures of their art. Martin is both smitten by Jane and convinced of her innocence. They have also discovered that Thomas is the fifth boy lost to the village.

At the second performance, Martin talks of the five other young boys. Springer, in the character of Thomas, takes off his mask and asks the audience where and by whom he was killed. After a disturbance the monk is found dead, hanged in a penitent's shirt. Martin asks: 'Why was the monk hanged?' As the players begin to draw their terrible conclusions the lord's steward arrives and takes them to the castle.

In great fear, they tell the lord that they will play the Play of Adam but each knows why they are there. When Nicholas seizes an opportunity to escape he runs for help. As the players are rescued, the awful truth behind the murder of Thomas Wells and its political implications is revealed.

### ABOUT THE AUTHOR

Barry Unsworth was born in a mining village near Durham in 1930. He was educated at Stockton-on-Tees Grammar School and Manchester University. He lived for some time in the eastern Mediterranean, taught English in Athens and Istanbul and has more recently lived in Italy. His first novel, *The Partnership*, was published in 1966. *Pascali's Island*, later made into a film, was shortlisted for the Booker Prize in 1980. In 1992 Unsworth was joint winner of the Booker Prize for *Sacred Hunger*, which tied with Michael Ondaatje's *The English Patient*. *Morality Play* was also shortlisted for the Booker.

## FOR DISCUSSION

▷ When Martin announces that the players are to play the murder they are all shocked. What is it about the idea that particularly upsets them? How is it different from the plays they usually perform? How do Nicholas's reactions differ from those of the others, and why? What is he afraid of when he says: 'if we make our own meanings, God will oblige us to answer our own questions'? Are his fears fulfilled?

▷ What are Martin's motives in staging such a provocative play? How do they change? What makes him give such a brave and dangerous performance in de Guise's castle?

▷ What risks is the company courting by staging *The Murder of Thomas Wells*? As the players improvise their parts on stage, it is as if they are impelled to reveal the truth. Why do you think they do this?

▷ How does Unsworth evoke the atmosphere of fear and foreboding which pervades the book?

▷ To what extent do you think justice was done at the end of the book? What are the implications of the conversation that Nicholas has with the Justice? Why does Nicholas decide to remain as a player rather than rejoin the clergy?

▷ What does Nicholas mean when he says, 'the player is always trapped in his own play but he must never allow the spectators to suspect this, they must always think that he is free'? How can this idea be applied in the rest of the novel?

▷ How do you interpret the meaning of the novel's title? Are there several meanings and, if so, what are they?

▷ We now accept the idea of using drama, fiction or art as a means of holding up a mirror to society in order to discover the truth. Are there particular examples that you believe to have been effective and, if so, what are they and what was the effect?

## SUGGESTED FURTHER READING

**FICTION**
- ▶ *Hawksmoor* by Peter Ackroyd (1985)
- ▶ *A Perfect Execution* by Tim Binding (1996)
- ▶ *The Leper's Companion* by Julia Blackburn (1999)
- ▶ *The Alienist* by Caleb Carr (1994)
- ▶ *A Maggot* by John Fowles (1985)

**NON-FICTION**
- ▶ *English Mystery Plays* edited by Peter Happe (1975)
- ▶ *A Distant Mirror* by Barbara Tuchman (1978)

## OTHER BOOKS BY BARRY UNSWORTH
- ▶ *The Partnership* (1966)
- ▶ *The Greeks Have a Word For It* (1967)
- ▶ *Pascali's Island* (1980)

▶ *The Rage of the Vulture* (1982)
▶ *Stone Virgin* (1985)
▶ *Sugar and Rum* (1988)
▶ *Sacred Hunger* (1992)
▶ *After Hannibal* (1996)
▶ *Losing Nelson* (1999)
▶ *The Song of Kings* (2002)

# NON-FICTION

NON-FICTION

## Paula (1995)
### Isabel Allende

**ABOUT THE BOOK**

Written during snatched moments, in hospital corridors and later at Paula's bedside in California, *Paula* began as a family history for Allende's daughter to read when she woke from the coma into which she had fallen after an attack of porphyria. Interspersed with the family's story are Allende's loving reflections on Paula and the slow, sad awareness that this was not an illness from which she would recover. Allende's language and storytelling mirrors that of her novels; it is warm, vivid and moving.

Paula collapsed in her Madrid flat during her mother's visit to promote her novel *The Infinite Plan*. Over the twelve months of her illness Allende rarely left her side. Often accompanied by her mother or by Paula's husband, she remained doggedly determined that her daughter would recover until it became clear that this was impossible. Allende weaves her memories of Paula and the anguish of that year through the history of her own maternal family. Her father disappeared from her life when she was three and her early childhood was spent in Santiago de Chile with her grandparents. Her clairvoyant grandmother Meme continued to be both enormously influential and a comfort to Allende long after her death. It was to her grandfather that her first novel, *The House of Spirits*, was addressed but Meme was its inspiration.

When her mother began a lifelong involvement with a Chilean diplomat, Allende found herself moving first to Bolivia and then to the Lebanon, returning to Chile when she was fifteen. At nineteen she married Michael Frias. After hoodwinking her way into a job with the United Nations, she managed to secure work as a television presenter and later became a journalist. She cut a distinctive figure in her flamboyant clothes, both romantic and a little naïve.

In 1970 Salvador Allende, Isabel's uncle, was elected president. Thanks to the undermining activities of the right wing and an economic blockade imposed by the United States, resulting in rampant inflation and food shortages, the new government's popularity began to wane. In 1973 the president was overthrown by Augusto Pinochet's violent coup which marked the beginning of seventeen years of military rule, oppression and terror. At first Isabel was unaware of the 'disappearances' and torture that were the tools of the new regime. Almost unwittingly, she became drawn into helping those who sought asylum until the safety of her own family was at risk. They fled their beloved Chile for Venezuela. It was as if Isabel had been awakened from a cosy, if occasionally adventurous, domesticity. The strain began to tell on their marriage and eventually Isabel and Michael separated.

During this period Isabel began to write fiction. When she heard that her grandfather was dying in Chile, still in fear for her safety, she started a letter to him which became *The House of Spirits*. Her experiences of the horrors of the Pinochet regime together with the tales of other witnesses were put to good use in *Of Love and Shadows*. As *Paula* draws to its poignant conclusion, the influence of Allende's often extraordinary life on her work becomes clear and the roots of the magical realism, which forms an integral part of her fiction, can be traced.

**ABOUT THE AUTHOR**

Isabel Allende was born in Lima, Peru, in 1942. Her father, Tomás Allende, was the cousin of Salvador Allende, a Marxist who was democratically elected as leader of his country in 1970 but overthrown by a right-wing military coup in

1973. She married Miguel (anglicized to Michael in the book) Frias when she was nineteen and soon became involved in writing – first for a women's magazine then writing plays and children's stories. The couple had two children, Paula and Nicolas. Isabel and Miguel separated in 1986. Isabel Allende has since remarried and lives in California. Her daughter, Paula, died in 1992.

Isabel Allende's novels have been translated into many languages and have met with both critical and popular acclaim. *Paula* was her first venture into non-fiction.

## FOR DISCUSSION

▷ The book opens with Isabel Allende explaining to Paula that she is going to tell her a story so that when she wakes up she won't feel so lost. What other reasons do you think there might have been for writing the book? How do you think these reasons may have changed over the course of writing *Paula*?

▷ It can be argued that since memory is not only imperfect but also subjective, autobiography can be classified as fiction. Do you think *Paula* reads like fiction? Is this the style in which it is written? Do you think that Allende believes that the book is factual from start to finish?

▷ What impression do you have of Paula from the book? To what extent do you think that this book is likely to be an accurate portrait of her?

▷ What impression do you have of Isabel Allende? What sort of mother do you think she is? What effect does Paula's condition have on Isabel Allende over the year that she is ill?

▷ What do you think Isabel Allende's attitude is to feminism? How is this illustrated? What is her view of women in Chile?

▷ How do you think the military coup and the resultant régime affected Isabel Allende? How do you think her attitude to politics changed?

▷ Magic is a strong presence in all of Isabel Allende's novels. How does it manifest itself in *Paula*? What do you think of her beliefs in the spirit world?

## SUGGESTED FURTHER READING
**FICTION**
▶ *The War of Don Emmanuel's Nether Parts* by Louis de Bernières (1990)
**NON-FICTION**
▶ *Family Life* by Elizabeth Luard (1995)
▶ **And When Did You Last See Your Father? by Blake Morrison (1993)**
▶ **The Hacienda by Lisa St Aubin De Terán (1998)**
▶ *Travels in a Thin Country* by Sara Wheeler (1995)

## OTHER BOOKS BY ISABEL ALLENDE
**NOVELS**
▶ *The House of Spirits* (1985)
▶ *Of Love and Shadows* (1987)
▶ *Eva Luna* (1988)
▶ *The Infinite Plan* (1993)
▶ *Daughter of Fortune* (2000)
▶ *Portrait in Sepia* (2001)
▶ *City of Beasts* (2002)
**SHORT STORIES**
▶ *The Stories of Eva Luna* (1992)
**NON-FICTION**
▶ *Aphrodite* (1999)

# Midnight in the Garden of Good and Evil (1994)
## John Berendt

### ABOUT THE BOOK

Largely restored to its pre-Civil War architectural glory, downtown Savannah is portrayed by John Berendt as a beautiful place, inhabited by people who love to party, proud of their reputation for eccentricity and deeply resistant to change. But *Midnight in the Garden of Good and Evil* is also a murder mystery whose details are as convoluted and baroque as any novel. Over a period of eight years, Berendt developed an intimacy with many of the people who appear in his book, including Jim Williams, later accused of murdering his lover.

The book begins with a conversation with Williams. An eminently successful antiques dealer, Williams is a respected and prominent member of the Savannah elite, as knowledgeable about the scandal and foibles of his fellow Savannahians as he is about the city's architecture. His Christmas party is the most important date on the Savannah social calendar but inclusion on the invitation list is a source of anxiety as Williams is intolerant of the slightest offence. He is both an initiator and an important source of financial support for the restoration programme and lives in Mercer House, one of the Savannah's finest houses. While living like an aristocrat, Williams is open about his blue-collar origins. Such social ascent is not achieved without making enemies and for Williams these include Lee Adler, whom he had thrown off the board of a local museum committee.

During Berendt's first meeting with Williams, Danny Hansford bursts into the room and behaves in a violent and threatening manner. Berendt is astonished at this intrusion into the home of such a cultured man. Williams describes Hansford as a part-time employee in his workshop who stays with him during his hypoglycemia attacks.

Berendt introduces a set of characters that would seem highly improbable even in a novel. The Lady Chablis, a stunningly beautiful black drag queen, affectionately teases and taunts him. Luther Driggers, accompanied by a set of flies on coloured thread, reputedly carries a vial of poison in his pocket. Joe Odom, a tax lawyer who prefers to party rather than practise law, moves his piano from house to house as his landlords' tolerance runs out. A retired porter walks his dead employer's dog every morning although no dog is attached to the collar and lead.

Part one ends with the news that Jim Williams has shot Danny Hansford in the early hours of a May morning in 1991. Part two is taken up with an account of the murder trials.

Williams's friends are convinced that the case will not come to trial. Williams claims to have shot Hansford, known for his violent temperament, in self-defence. When it becomes clear that the newly elected district attorney, a protégée of Williams's old enemy, Lee Adler, intends to take the case to trial, most assume that Williams will not be found guilty. So begins a period of eight years in which Williams is tried for murder four times and launches three successful appeals. Berendt chronicles both the trials and the events surrounding them, charting the reactions of Savannah society to the revelations that attend each trial until the final verdict.

### ABOUT THE AUTHOR

John Berendt grew up in Syracuse, New York. He studied English at Harvard where he worked on the staff of *The Harvard Lampoon*. After his graduation in

1961, he moved to New York City where he worked in publishing. From 1977 to 1979, he edited *New York* magazine. He became a freelance writer and editor for a variety of magazines, including *Esquire*, for which he wrote a monthly column from 1982 to 1994. *Midnight in the Garden of Good and Evil* was his first book. It was a great success, putting Savannah firmly on the tourist map. In 1997, Clint Eastwood made the book into a film starring Kevin Spacey as Jim Williams and John Cusack as John Kelso, the character based on Berendt. John Berendt became so associated with Savannah that the city presented him with its key.

## FOR DISCUSSION

▷ *Midnight in the Garden of Good and Evil* has been described as a non-fiction novel. What do you think is meant by this description? How accurately do you think it fits the book?

▷ Berendt becomes very much involved in Savannah's social life. How objective a commentator do you think he is? What factors do you think might influence his objectivity? Do you get a sense of Berendt from his narrative? What sort of person do you think he is?

▷ Savannah society seems to be divided along several lines. How would you describe each section? How do the different sections seem to get along together?

▷ Berendt quotes Martin Luther King as describing Savannah as 'the most desegregated city in the South' in 1964. How do you think Savannah stands on race by today's standards?

▷ As a result of the shooting, Williams's homosexuality becomes evident. What kind of reaction does this provoke, if any? What attitudes to homosexuality run through Savannah society? Would you say these attitudes are fairly typical of most modern cities? What do you think of the way Chablis handles her sexuality?

▷ Williams enjoyed the trappings of aristocracy while being open about his blue-collar background. How important is class as an issue in the book? How does the importance of money compare to class?

▷ What are the different attitudes to Lee Adler's involvement with the low-income housing in the Victorian district? Why do you think the project seems to provoke a mixture of scorn and suspicion? How do these views fit in with other social opinions in the book?

▷ How would you describe Jim Williams? Does your view of him change through the book and, if so, at what point and why? Do you think he was guilty or not? What evidence do you have for your verdict?

▷ What do you think Berendt means when he says: 'Yes, I did get Minerva's point. I got her point very clearly' after the visit to the Garden of Good and Evil? Do you think Williams did get her point? What did you make of Minerva? How does Williams consulting with her fit in with the rest of his personality?

▷ What sort of role do women seem to play in Savannah society? How typical is this role in modern society?

## SUGGESTED FURTHER READING
### FICTION
▶ *Madeleine's Ghost* by Robert Girardi (1995)
### NON-FICTION
▶ *In Cold Blood* by Truman Capote (1996)

▶ *Hiding My Candy: the Autobiography of the Grand Empress of Savannah* by Lady Chablis, introduced by John Berendt (1997)
▶ *The Shark Net* by Robert Drewe (2000)

# Skating to Antarctica (1997)
## Jenny Diski

### ABOUT THE BOOK
Part travelogue, part searching autobiography, *Skating to Antarctica* is Jenny Diski's first full-length work of non-fiction. The description of her journey from London to Cabin 232, her refuge aboard the cruise ship *Akademik Vavilov,* and her experiences in Antarctica are interspersed with an examination of her deeply disturbed childhood and its effect on her adult life. The result is a raw, very personal book, infused with dry wit and a sense of adventure.

In search of oblivion, Diski decides to go to Antarctica to 'satisfy her hunger for blankness', but the only way to travel there alone is to take a cruise, something of anathema to someone who dislikes having her time organized for her. When she finally arrives at the ship after an arduous journey by way of Buenos Aires and Tierra del Fuego, she finds the simple, white-painted 'monk's cell' that she longs for, in Cabin 232.

Aboard ship, Diski attends bird-watching lectures, watches whaling videos and, far more exciting, sees a film shot on board Shackleton's *Endurance* in 1914. She strikes up acquaintances with her fellow passengers, some brief and a little awkward, some more lasting. A shore visit takes her to an old whaling station on South Georgia where she talks to a couple of British soldiers, paralysed with boredom in this bleak and lonely posting. South Georgia is the site of Ernest Shackleton's grave, whom she affectionately describes as 'a bit of a chancer' in contrast to the pukka Scott, pointing out that all members of the Shackleton expedition survived while Scott's expedition was entirely wiped out.

Woven into this travelogue are Diski's reflections on her other journey – back into a childhood for which the word dysfunctional seems wholly inadequate. Before she set out, her daughter Chloe announced that she wanted to discover whether her grandmother was still alive. After one of their many lapses in contact, Diski let things drift until she no longer wanted to know whether her mother was dead or alive. Although apparently reluctant for Chloe to follow this through, Diski had started her own investigations, tracing her old neighbours and asking them about their memories of her family. Hers was a childhood marked by the excessive emotion of both parents: suicide threats and attempts, visits from the bailiffs, histrionic quarrels and threats of eviction were commonplace events. Diski was first admitted to a mental institution when she was fourteen and spent time in hospital being treated for depression in her twenties. It is something to which she has become warily accustomed. So painful are these memories that she distances herself from them to the extent of referring to 'Jennifer' and 'me' as if they were separate people. Perhaps, she thinks, she has exaggerated all this, but a visit to her old neighbours confirms it.

When she returns from the cruise, she finds that Chloe has left a pile of birth, marriage and death certificates for her, together with notes of conversations that she and her father have had with her grandmother's last neighbours. Questions have been asked, some have been answered and, perhaps, a possibility of peace found.

## ABOUT THE AUTHOR

Jenny Diski was born in 1947 in London, where she lives and works. In addition to being a novelist, she has been the *Mail on Sunday*'s radio critic and regularly contributed to both the *Observer* and the *London Review of Books*. *Skating to Antarctica*, her first non-fiction book, met with a good deal of critical acclaim. In the second volume of her autobiography, *Stranger on a Train*, Diski picks up where *Skating to Antarctica* left off, combining a journey through America with her continuing exploration of her illness and her past.

## FOR DISCUSSION

▷ Why do you think Diski chose to call her book *Skating to Antarctica*? What do you think she means by it?

▷ Why do you think Diski is searching for oblivion? To what extent does she find what she wants in Antarctica?

▷ Why do you think that Diski is so reluctant to find out about her mother? How do you think she feels about Chloe's research and its results?

▷ When she visits her ex-neighbours at Paramount Court, Diski finds she has to reassess her father. Why do you think she has been able to see her mother fairly accurately but not her father?

▷ Diski has adopted a strategy of distancing herself from the child 'Jennifer'. Why do you think she did this? Has it helped her and, if so, in what way?

▷ Diski describes at some length her reactions to people taking photographs and using camcorders around the bull elephant seals. What did you think about this?

▷ What do you think of Diski's attitude to the rest of the people on the cruise? How do you think she feels about people in general?

▷ How did you feel about the way Diski wove her childhood experiences into her description of the journey to Antarctica?

## SUGGESTED FURTHER READING

**FICTION**

▶ *Frost in May* by Antonia White (1933)

**NON-FICTION**

▶ *The Worst Journey in the World* by Apsley Cherry-Garrard (1922)

▶ **An Unquiet Mind by Kay Redfield Jamison (1995)**

▶ *South* by Ernest Shackleton (1919)

▶ *Terra Incognita* by Sara Wheeler (1996)

## OTHER BOOKS BY JENNY DISKI

**NOVELS**

▶ *Nothing Natural* (1986)

▶ *Rainforest* (1987)

▶ *Like Mother* (1988)

▶ *Then Again* (1990)

▶ *Happily Ever After* (1991)

▶ *Monkey's Uncle* (1994)

▶ *Only Human: A Divine Comedy* (2000)

**SHORT STORIES**

▶ *The Dream Mistress* (1996)

# Hidden Lives: A Family Memoir (1995)
Margaret Forster

## ABOUT THE BOOK
*Hidden Lives* covers the Forster family history from 1869 to 1981. It begins with Margaret Forster's investigations into her grandmother's life and the mystery of Alice, her illegitimate daughter. The second part takes up the story of Forster's mother Lily, but soon becomes autobiographical, focusing on her troubled relationship with Lily. Born in 1938, Forster's opportunities differed greatly from those of both her grandmother and her mother. *Hidden Lives* is a vivid portrait of working-class women across three generations at a time when class barriers were being eroded and women were finding their own place in the world.

When a mysterious visitor arrives asking for her mother in 1936, Lily is reluctant to let her in. Margaret Ann is not well and Lily does not want her upset. Although her mother never refers to the visit, she becomes withdrawn and, within three months, she is dead. On the day of her funeral, another stranger appears, claiming to be a fourth daughter of Margaret Ann. The door is firmly closed in her face. Many years later, Forster's curiosity is aroused by this story but she feels unable to investigate until after Lily's death.

Margaret Ann had successfully concealed her illegitimacy, a terrible stigma at that time. It must have been doubly shaming when she became pregnant outside wedlock and an absolute necessity to keep the child secret. Forster can find no records of Margaret Ann's life between 1871 and 1893.

When Margaret Ann met Thomas Hind, a nine-year courtship began. As a butcher, Hind represented both respectability and financial security. The couple had three daughters, Lily, Jean and Nan. After Hind's death, times became hard but, thanks to her well-paid job with the Public Health department, Lily was able to help. Of the three sisters, she was the responsible one. Jean became pregnant, married and moved away. Nan gave up her dressmaking business to join her married lover in Glasgow.

Like her mother, Lily had a lengthy courtship, reluctant to give up her job and her independence when she finally married. As Arthur Forster's wife her time was absorbed in housework, trying to make ends meet, keeping up appearances and raising her three children, Gordon, Margaret and Pauline.

The narrative becomes autobiographical when Forster recounts her first memory, her fifth birthday party. She is precociously bright, constantly asking questions, challenging her mother's beliefs, unable to understand why Lily endures such a difficult and circumscribed life. She wins a scholarship to the local high school, something not thought worth considering for her mother, also a bright child. Her sights set on Oxbridge, she wins an Exhibition for Girton College but takes up an Open Scholarship for Somerville at Oxford.

Having long decided that marriage and children lead to poverty and a life too narrow to contemplate, Forster begins to see that a happy domestic life can be combined with a career. After graduating she marries, begins to write and eventually, like her mother, has three children, but leads a life which is very different from Lily's.

When her mother dies, there is still an awkwardness between them, a sense of not quite knowing or understanding each other.

## ABOUT THE AUTHOR

Margaret Forster was born in Carlisle in 1938. She has published both fiction and non-fiction and is the author of two award-winning biographies: *Elizabeth Barrett Browning,* which won the Royal Society of Literature's Award in 1988, and *Daphne du Maurier,* which was awarded the 1994 Fawcett Book Prize. Her first novel, *Georgy Girl,* was made into a film starring Lynn Redgrave and Charlotte Rampling. *Hidden Lives* was published in 1995 and was followed by a companion volume, *Precious Lives,* about the deaths of her father and sister-in-law. Margaret Forster is married to the writer Hunter Davies and divides her time between London and the Lake District.

## FOR DISCUSSION

▷ What was Forster's motivation in investigating her 'hidden' family history? Given that her grandmother had gone to such great pains to hide her past, do you think her secret should have died with her or do people have a right to know their history?

▷ Forster keeps herself out of the first part of the book as much as possible, but given that she is writing about her own family, how objective is she likely to be? What do you learn about Forster, besides what she writes about herself? How does the book change when Forster begins to write in the first person?

▷ How accurate a view do you have of your own family history and how important is it to you? Does the book strike any chords for you?

▷ How would you describe the relationship between Forster and her mother? What are the main differences between them? How have their lives been shaped by their different circumstances? Forster says to her mother: 'There's no real difference in what we've achieved.' What do you think of this statement?

▷ What impression do you have of Lily? Why is she so hard to please? What does her attitude to other people seem to be? Why is she so different from her sisters?

▷ The book looks at three generations of women – Margaret Ann, Lily and the author. What are the significant changes between the generations? What are the opportunities available to each of the women? What factors contribute to the broadening of opportunities between each generation? What do you think has changed since Forster was a girl?

▷ The book covers a time of great social change. What do you think were the most significant changes for the Forsters? What were Forster's parents' attitudes towards class? How important a factor was it in their lives? Were there other factors that shaped the way they lived and, if so, what were they?

▷ Forster's marriage seems very different from her parents' relationship. What expectations do the women in the book have of marriage? Are these expectations fulfilled? How different are they from present-day expectations?

## SUGGESTED FURTHER READING

▶ *Shadow Man* by Mary Gordon (1996)
▶ *Family Life* by Elizabeth Luard (1995)

▶ *Angela's Ashes* by Frank McCourt (1996)
▶ *British Society since 1945* by Arthur Marwick (1987)
▶ *Hons and Rebels* by Jessica Mitford (1960)

## OTHER BOOKS BY MARGARET FORSTER
### NOVELS

▶ *Georgy Girl* (1966)
▶ *The Seduction of Mrs Pendlebury* (1974)
▶ *Mother Can You Hear Me?* (1979)
▶ *Private Papers* (1986)
▶ *Have the Men Had Enough?* (1987)
▶ *Lady's Maid* (1990)
▶ *The Battle for Christabel* (1991)
▶ *Mother's Boys* (1994)
▶ *Shadow Baby* (1996)
▶ *The Memory Box* (1999)

### BIOGRAPHY

▶ *The Rash Adventurer: The Rise and Fall of Charles Edward Stuart* (1975)
▶ *William Makepeace Thackeray: Memoirs of a Victorian Gentleman* (1978)
▶ *Significant Sisters – The Grassroots of Active Feminism 1838–1939* (1986)
▶ *Elizabeth Barrett Browning* (1988)
▶ *Daphne du Maurier* (1993)
▶ *Rich Desserts and Captain's Thins* (biography of the Carr biscuit manufacturing family) (1987)

### AUTOBIOGRAPHY

▶ *Precious Lives* (1998)
▶ *Good Wives* (2001)

# Lost in Translation: A Life in a New Language (1989)
## Eva Hoffman

### ABOUT THE BOOK

*Lost in Translation* is divided into three parts. In 'Paradise' Hoffman writes of her childhood in Cracow, weaving bright memories of friends and family through descriptions of life in post-war Poland. 'Exile' tells of the family's arrival in Vancouver and the difficulty of fitting in to a new and very different culture. 'The New World' is about Hoffman's arrival in the United States where she finally finds a way to be at ease with herself. Her writing gives us a glimpse of how it feels to be an exile trying to navigate a path through a new and foreign world without a map.

Hoffman is the eldest daughter of Polish Jews who spent the Second World War in hiding. Both parents have lost many members of their families but Hoffman's memories of her childhood are happy, surrounded by friends, comfortably enough off to afford a maid. She is a bright child with a promising talent as a pianist.

Life in post-war Poland is not easy. Jews still suffer the old prejudices and public allegiance to communism is a necessity. Everyone does a little something on the side, including Hoffman's father who deals on the black market. In 1957, when the ban on Jewish emigration is lifted, many family friends, including Hoffman's childhood sweetheart, leave for Israel. Convinced that Canada is the land of opportunity, Hoffman's father heads for Vancouver.

When the family arrives in Canada, there is little in the way of a support system. They stay briefly with a Polish family but are soon on their own. Hoffman and her sister start school two days after their arrival. The teachers give them new names that Canadians can easily pronounce. Throughout Hoffman's school years she struggles to fit in, groping to find the right words, trying to soak up cultural references so that she can make sense of things and never quite sure that she is doing the right thing. The loss of nuance in both language and culture results in a painful dislocation. Despite her difficulties she is a prize-winning student and is offered a scholarship at a university in Houston, Texas.

Hoffman comes into herself at college. It's the 1960s, a time of social upheaval when everyone is trying to reinvent themselves. She does well in her studies, makes friends and begins to feel less of an outsider. By the time she arrives at Harvard to take up a doctorate in literature, she is confident enough to argue and question the views of her American friends. She has become a 'partial American', a 'resident alien'.

In 1977 Hoffman returns to Cracow, her first visit since her arrival in Canada. She sees her old friends, walks the streets engraved on her memory and, on her return to America, dreams in English for the first time.

In the early 1980s, a wave of Polish immigrants arrives in New York where Hoffman now lives. She finds herself acting as a cultural interpreter, trying to ease them through the difficulties of transition from one culture to another. Finally, it seems that the gap between her Polish and American selves has been bridged.

## ABOUT THE AUTHOR

Eva Hoffman was born in the city of Cracow in Poland in 1945. She and her family emigrated to Canada in 1959. She was educated at Rice University, Houston, Texas, and went on to take her doctorate in literature at Harvard. She worked for some time as an editor of the *New York Times Book Review*. *Lost in Translation*, her first book, was published in 1989.

## FOR DISCUSSION

▷ Near the beginning, after recounting several of her parents' wartime experiences in hiding, Hoffman writes that she acknowledges that 'the pain of this is where I come from, and that it's useless to try and get away'. What does she mean by this? How do her parents' experiences affect her life and the way she approaches it? How have they been affected?

▷ What difficulties do Hoffman's parents face in post-war Poland? How do they deal with these difficulties? How do things change between the end of the war and their departure for Canada? Why do they decide to leave?

▷ How does Hoffman feel about learning English? Why is language so important to her? What is the most painful thing about the loss of her first language? Hoffman's writing is both elegant and eloquent. How important do you think this is to her?

▷ Hoffman writes: 'Linguistic dispossession is a sufficient motive for violence, for it is close to dispossession of one's self.' How persuasive is this argument? Can you think of illustrations in the book or in recent history?

▷ How is Hoffman expected to change her behaviour when she gets to Vancouver? Why is this particularly difficult and painful for her?

▷ Hoffman begins to come into herself at university in Houston. Why do think this happens at this point?

▷ Hoffman writes about the quarrels she begins to have with her 'American friends' once she arrives at Harvard. Why do you think this happens? How would you describe the American point of view? How would you describe Hoffman's position? Where would you put your own views?

▷ Does the visit to Cracow help Hoffman to resolve anything and, if so, what? How much has Hoffman's view of her own cultural identity changed by 1981 when there is a surge in Polish emigration to New York?

▷ Has *Lost in Translation* helped you to understand how it feels to be an immigrant and, if so, how? If you are an immigrant yourself, how does Hoffman's experience compare with your own?

▷ Hoffman uses both past and present tenses in her descriptions of past events throughout the book. What effect does this have?

## SUGGESTED FURTHER READING
### FICTION

▶ *By the Sea* by Abdulrazak Gurnah (2001)
▶ *Fruit of the Lemon* by Andrea Levy (1999)
▶ *Accordion Crimes* by Annie Proulx (1996)
▶ *The Joy Luck Club* by Amy Tan (1989)

### NON-FICTION

▶ *The File* by Timothy Garton Ash (1998)
▶ *Café Europa* by Slavanka Drakulić (1996)
▶ *Anne Frank: The Diary of a Young Girl* by Anne Frank (1947)
▶ *Roots Schmoots* by Howard Jacobson (1995)
▶ *Konin: A Quest* by Theo Richmond (1995)
▶ *The Man Who Lost His Language* by Sheila Hale (2002)

## OTHER BOOKS BY EVA HOFFMAN
### FICTION

▶ *The Secret* (2001)

### NON FICTION

▶ *Exit into History: A Journey Through the New Eastern Europe* (1994)
▶ *Shtetl: The History of a Small Town and an Extinguished World* (1997)

# An Unquiet Mind: A Memoir of Moods and Madness (1996)
# Kay Redfield Jamison

### ABOUT THE BOOK

As a psychiatrist, Kay Redfield Jamison kept her illness under wraps for many years, afraid that she would lose her licence to practise. In *An Unquiet Mind* she lays bare what it is to be subject to episodes of extraordinary vividness followed by suicidal depressions. Her experience of manic-depressive illness, both personal and professional, enable her to provide a singular insight into an illness that is rarely discussed openly by its sufferers.

Jamison was born into an American Air Force family. Her mother took care to provide a stable home as a counterbalance to a peripatetic life and to the unpredictable enthusiasms which seized her husband. Looking back, Jamison remembers her own mercurial nature, comparing it with the steadiness of her brother who became the emotional lynchpin in her life.

When she was in high school, her father took a civilian job in California which he lost when his own manic-depressive illness became more pronounced. It was in California that Jamison struggled with her first manic episode, filled with restlessness, insomnia and marvellous insights followed by a terrible lethargic depression. Brought up not to complain, she kept her feelings to herself.

Jamison became an undergraduate at the University of Los Angeles. Subject to extreme mood swings, she recognized her symptoms in a lecture on depression and tried to seek help but backed out at the last minute. A year's break in Scotland provided a respite and on her return to UCLA she became a research assistant to a psychology professor, eventually completing a doctoral thesis in psychology. She had enjoyed a remission throughout most of her doctoral study but within three months of her appointment as an assistant professor she was seized by a severe manic attack. During this episode she experienced an hallucination so terrifying that she called a colleague for help. Recognizing her symptoms, he insisted that she see a psychiatrist.

Finally diagnosed as suffering from manic-depressive illness, Jamison began the programme of lithium and psychotherapy that eventually led her to a more stable life. She fought her reluctance to take her medication, whose side-effects affected her vision so that she was unable to read and left her nauseous. Her mood swings were now under control, but she mourned the loss of their vividness. Lapses in medication resulted in manic episodes, one of which led to a suicide attempt.

Throughout this period, Jamison succeeded in concealing her illness from the university authorities. When she set up an Affective Disorders Clinic at UCLA to treat manic-depressive illness she constructed a safety net to ensure that she would not put her patients at risk.

After a love affair that ended tragically, she took a sabbatical in Britain, dividing her time between Oxford and London. Although her grief was terrible, unlike her illness, she was able to control it. Some years later, she married and returned to Washington where she had spent much of her childhood. Finding work as a professor at Johns Hopkins University, she steeled herself to reveal her illness only to find that it had long been an open secret.

### ABOUT THE AUTHOR

As Professor of Psychiatry at the Johns Hopkins University School of Medicine in Washington D.C. Kay Redfield Jamison has won many scientific awards and was a member of the first National Advisory Council for Human Genome Research. She has also served as the clinical director for the Dana Consortium on the Genetic Basis of Manic-Depressive Illness. Her first book aimed at a general readership was *Touched with Fire: Manic-Depressive Illness and the Artistic Temperament*, published in 1993. It provided the basis of three television programmes in the United States – one on manic-depressive composers, another on Vincent van Gogh and a third on Lord Byron.

### FOR DISCUSSION

▷ Jamison writes: 'The long and important years of childhood and early adolescence . . . were to be an extremely powerful amulet, a potent and positive countervailing force against future unhappiness.' What aspects of her early life and upbringing helped her in her battle against her illness?

▷ Jamison describes manic depressive illness as 'unique in conferring advantage and pleasure, yet one that brings in its wake almost unendurable suffering'. What 'advantage and pleasure' does she find in her illness?

▷ For many years Jamison told only a few close friends and colleagues about her illness. What had made her conceal it for so long? Why did she decide to lay it bare so publicly?

▷ Given her study of psychology, why does it take Jamison so long to recognize and accept her illness?

▷ How is Jamison's life affected by lithium? The advantages of taking it are obvious; what are the disadvantages? Despite the risks involved in reducing her dosage, why does she decide to do so? How does psychotherapy complement lithium in the treatment of her illness?

▷ When Jamison uses the word madness in the title of a lecture, she is castigated by a member of the public. Where do you stand in the ensuing debate on the use of language in describing mental illness? What difference does it make?

▷ Jamison comes, almost reluctantly, to recognize the importance of emotional stability but she acknowledges that 'somewhere in my heart, however, I continued to believe that intense and lasting love was possible only in a climate of somewhat tumultuous passions'. Do you think that this idea is unusual or do many of us feel that love must be accompanied by passion to be 'real'? How important are love and friendship to Jamison? How is this illustrated in the book?

▷ When Jamison discloses her illness to the colleague and erstwhile friend she calls Mouseheart, he asks her if she really thinks that someone who is suffering from mental illness should be allowed to treat patients. How would you answer this? What light does Jamison's account of her professional experience shed on the question?

▷ When discussing the work of the Human Genome Project with which she was associated, Jamison asks whether 'we risk making the world a blander, more homogenised place if we get rid of the genes for manic-depressive illness'. What would your answer to this question be and why?

▷ How successful is Jamison in conveying how it feels to suffer from manic-depressive illness? How does she set about this?

▷ How well do we deal with mental illness in modern society? Has reading *An Unquiet Mind* changed any ideas you might have had about mental illness and the people who suffer from it? If so, how have your views changed and why?

## SUGGESTED FURTHER READING

### FICTION
▶ *One Flew Over the Cuckoo's Nest* by Ken Kesey (1962)
▶ *Last Things* by Jenny Offill (1999)
▶ *The Bell Jar* by Sylvia Plath (1963)

### NON-FICTION
▶ *Virginia Woolf: The Marriage of Heaven and Hell* by Peter Dally (1998)
▶ **Skating to Antarctica by Jenny Diski (1997)**
▶ *Girl, Interrupted* by Susanna Kaysen (1993)
▶ *Genome: The Autobiography of a Species in 23 Chapters* by Matt Ridley (1999)
▶ *Darkness Visible* by William Styron (1992)
▶ *Prozac Generation* by Elizabeth Wurtzel (1995)

## OTHER BOOKS BY KAY REDFIELD JAMISON

▶ *Touched with Fire: Manic-Depressive Illness and the Artistic Temperament* (1993)
▶ *Night Falls Fast: Understanding Suicide* (2000)

# The Drowned and the Saved (1986)
## Primo Levi

### ABOUT THE BOOK
Unlike Primo Levi's best-known book, *If This is a Man, The Drowned and the Saved* is not a straightforward autobiographical account of his experiences in Auschwitz. It is more an attempt to understand how such atrocities came to be committed and to convey the repercussions of survival as well as a necessary continuation of bearing witness. This is a slim but profound and sometimes harrowing book that requires time and a good deal of reflection.

Levi begins by explaining the difficulties of remembering for both sides. Stressing the importance of bearing witness to the horrors of the camps, he reminds us that memories become distorted by distance and they are also subjective and may be shrouded in self-justification and shame.

The 'grey zone', as Levi calls the issue of collaboration, is particularly painful and difficult to remember. Those prisoners who expected to find comfort from their fellows on arrival at the camps were shocked when they were first beaten or betrayed by their own kind. Levi explains that there were many who collaborated either in a small way or, perhaps most shockingly, as members of the Special Squads who were in charge of the crematoria. He is careful to make it clear that he does not judge collaborators and that we, who have never endured such horrors, are not qualified to do so. Even those who survived but did not collaborate experienced a sense of shame rather than joy at their liberation. They had been stripped of their humanity and were ashamed of their own survival and the small acts of selfishness or failure to help others it had required.

There were many ways in which the Nazis systematically destroyed the dignity of the prisoners, from the frequent public nakedness to the branding of their skin with an identification number. Even the language used to communicate with prisoners was a bastardized form of German. Those who did not understand stood little chance of survival unless they were able to find someone who could speak their own language. Attempts at escape were futile. Even if a prisoner was strong enough, after months of malnourishment, and succeeded in penetrating the stringent security of the camps, who would have helped him on the outside?

Levi explains that the hierarchy of the outside world was turned upon its head in the camps. The educated, with their inability to cope with manual work, were at the bottom of the pile. He compares his ideas on the advantages and disadvantages of being an intellectual with those of his friend, the philosopher Jean Améry, who later committed suicide.

In his final chapter, Levi discusses the letters that he was sent by Germans in response to the publication of *If This is a Man* in Germany in 1961.

### ABOUT THE AUTHOR
Primo Levi was born in Turin in 1919. He graduated with honours in chemistry shortly before laws were passed which prohibited Jews from taking academic

degrees. In 1943 he joined a partisan group in northern Italy. He was arrested and taken to Auschwitz where his knowledge as a chemist helped him to survive. When the Russians liberated Auschwitz in 1945, Levi and his fellow Italian inmates were sent to White Russia. On his return to Italy he found work as a chemist from which he retired in 1975. Levi's first and best-known book, *If This is a Man*, is an account of his experiences at Auschwitz and is published in a single volume together with *The Truce*, in which he tells of his long and arduous journey home to Italy. On 11 April 1987, Levi is believed to have committed suicide by throwing himself down the stairwell of the apartment building where he had been born and where he had lived for much of his life. *The Drowned and the Saved* was the last book he wrote before he died.

## FOR DISCUSSION

▷ What is the significance of the quotation from Coleridge's *The Rime of the Ancient Mariner* which prefaces the book?

▷ At the end of his introduction, Paul Bailey applies to Primo Levi's work Geoffrey Grigson's comment that W.H. Auden's poetry contained 'explicit recipes for being human'. What are Levi's 'explicit recipes'?

▷ In his preface, Levi says that he wants to try to answer the questions: 'How much of the concentration camp world is dead and will not return . . . How much is back or coming back? What can each of us do, so that in this world pregnant with threats, at least this threat will be nullified?' These are difficult questions. To what extent do you think Levi answers them? What are his answers? How would you answer them?

▷ How does Levi explain the collaboration which took place between some of the prisoners and the Nazis? How important were the collaborators to the Nazis? Who were most likely to become Kapos and why? Why does Levi call the creation of the Special Squads who tended the crematoria, the Nazis' 'most demonic crime'? How difficult do you find it to follow Levi's example in not passing judgement on these people? What does Levi mean when he states after the story of Chaim Rumkowski that 'we are all mirrored in Rumkowski'?

▷ In his introduction, Bailey states that many have interpreted the chapter in which Levi discusses the shame suffered by survivors at being alive when others are dead as evidence of Levi's intent to kill himself. Bailey disagrees with this. What are his arguments on this point? Have you formed an opinion on this since finishing the book? How does Levi explain his feelings of shame when he is released from Auschwitz?

▷ When Levi's religious friend says that Levi was chosen to survive in order to bear witness, Levi is troubled by this idea because he 'cannot see any proportion between the privilege and its outcome'. How important do you think Levi's testimony and the testimony of other camp survivors is? Do you think it can make a difference and, if so, how?

▷ Levi speculates about the possibility of a future genocide, mentioning Cambodia in passing. In more recent times there has been slaughter on an appalling scale in Rwanda. Can what happened in the camps be compared with what happened in Rwanda? What are your reasons for your answer?

▷ How does Levi define the 'useless violence' which he describes in chapter 5? Might the stripping of prisoners of their dignity have been useful to the Nazis and, if so, how?

▷ What advantages does Levi's philosopher friend, Jean Améry, see in being an intellectual in the camps? What disadvantages does he cite? To what extent does Levi agree or disagree with Améry?

▷ Levi says that he has often been faced with the questions 'Why did you not escape? Why did you not rebel? Why did you not avoid capture beforehand?' How does he proceed to answer these questions?

▷ When Levi's account of his incarceration in Auschwitz, *If This is a Man*, was published in Germany, his introduction stated that he could not understand the Germans and that he hoped the book would have an 'echo' in Germany. What kind of echo did it have? Do any of the letters that Levi received help you to understand what happened or do they simply throw up more questions?

▷ Paul Bailey begins his introduction with a quotation from *The Drowned and the Saved* – 'We, the survivors, are not the true witnesses'. He goes on to say that this 'deeply held conviction informs virtually everything Primo Levi wrote'. How do you interpret this quotation and how does it inform the book?

## SUGGESTED FURTHER READING
### FICTION
▶ *The Archivist* by Martha Cooley (1998)
▶ *The Tin Drum* by Günter Grass (1959)
▶ **Stones From the River by Ursula Hegi (1994)**
▶ *Schindler's List* by Thomas Keneally (1985)
▶ *The Time of Light* by Gunnar Kopperud (1998)
▶ **Fugitive Pieces by Anne Michaels (1997)**
▶ **The Reader by Bernhard Schlink (1997)**
▶ *Music for the Third Ear* by Susan Schwartz Senstad (1999)
▶ *One Day in the Life of Ivan Denisovitch* by Aleksandr Solzhenitsyn (1963)
▶ *A Model Childhood* by Christa Wolf (1988)

### AUTOBIOGRAPHY
▶ *The Past is Myself* by Christabel Bielenberg (1970)
▶ *All But My Life* by Gerda Weissmann Klein (1997)
▶ *Speak You Also* by Paul Steinberg (2001)
▶ *Night* by Elie Weisel (1981)

### HISTORY
▶ *Hitler's Willing Executioners* by Daniel Jonah Goldhagen (1996)
▶ *Konin: A Quest* by Theo Richmond (1995)

## OTHER BOOKS BY PRIMO LEVI
▶ *If This is a Man* (1958)/*The Truce* (1963) published in one volume.
▶ *The Periodic Table* (1975)
▶ *The Wrench* (1979)
▶ *Moments of Reprieve* (1981)
▶ *If Not Now, When?* (1982)

### PUBLISHED POSTHUMOUSLY
▶ *Survival in Auschwitz: The Nazi Assault on Humanity* (1993)
▶ *The Search for Roots* (2001)

# And When Did You Last See Your Father? (1993)

## Blake Morrison

### ABOUT THE BOOK

Knowing that he is about to lose his father, Morrison attempts to understand his relationship with the man who has exerted so much influence over his life. He blends his memories of his father through childhood, adolescence and adulthood with his impressions of the few weeks leading up to his father's death and its aftermath. The result is often painful, sometimes funny but never sentimental. *And When Did You Last See Your Father?* deals with a difficult subject in an unflinchingly honest fashion.

Morrison's memories begin with a family outing to the Oulton Park motor-racing track in September 1959. Stuck in a traffic jam, with the racetrack enticingly in earshot and only one hour left until the Gold Cup finale, Arthur Morrison can stand it no more. He attaches his stethoscope to the rearview mirror, drives along beside the seething queue and arrives at the track where he gets his family into the most expensive enclosure despite their cheap tickets.

Thirty-odd years later Arthur, now seventy-five, is in Airedale hospital where he visited so many of his patients before he retired. He has been diagnosed with terminal cancer. He cannot eat or drink and he has been reduced to using a catheter but seems cheerfully determined to ignore the imminence of his death.

Weaving the memories which seem to haunt every corner of his parents' house through his description of his father's swift decline, Morrison reconstructs the father he knew as a child, as an adolescent and as an adult, in an attempt to understand him.

Arthur Morrison and his wife were both GPs in the Yorkshire village of Earby. As Blake grew up in the 1950s they were well respected and comfortably off enough to afford a live-in maid. He recalls their family holidays – the disastrous camping trip with his father one wet half-term, the skiing trip as an undergraduate when Arthur seemed more capable of winning the attractive young tour representative's attentions than he was. He remembers his father's ability to get on with people, to tell entertaining and possibly tall stories, his constant willingness to be of use when illness struck. He also remembers his Auntie Beaty, a close friend rather than an aunt, but how close he has never been able to establish.

Morrison returns to London while Arthur is still in hospital. Called back to Yorkshire only ten days after his father's diagnosis, he finds the difference in Arthur shocking. The final summons comes early one morning and Morrison is afraid that he will not arrive in time but Arthur lives through one more difficult night.

Arrangements must be made; the funeral and the wake have to be got through. Morrison and his mother keep Arthur with them at home for one more day before the undertaker comes, finding comfort in his presence.

The rituals over, Morrison is left to ponder his unanswered questions about his father and to find some way of dealing with the yawning absence in his life. The book ends with Morrison's description of the last time he *really* saw his father.

### ABOUT THE AUTHOR

Blake Morrison was born in Yorkshire in 1950. He has taught at both London University and the Open University. He is a prominent critic of both poetry and fiction and has contributed reviews to the *Observer*, *The Times Literary Supplement*, *The Literary Review* and *The Independent* as well as publishing his own poetry. *And When Did You Last See Your Father?* was published to great acclaim in 1993 when it won the *Esquire*/Volvo/Waterstone's prize for non-fiction. His first novel, *The Justification of Johan Gutenberg*, was published in 2000. *Things My Mother Never Told Me*, a companion volume to *And When Did You Last See Your Father?* which explores Morrison's mother's life, was published in 2002.

## FOR DISCUSSION

▷ How would you describe Arthur Morrison's character? What are the traits that his son has most difficulty in accepting? What is it that he loves about his father? Are there any traits that they share? How would you describe their relationship?

▷ What impression did you gain of Arthur's relationship with his wife? They are both doctors. To what extent do you think he treats her as an equal?

▷ Morrison is very careful in his choice of words. How does he use language to convey the intimacy of his relationship with his father? How would you describe his tone?

▷ The book is unflinching, sometimes painful, in its honesty. Why do you think Morrison refuses to spare us the details of his father's illness and death, no matter how intimate? How do we cope with death and illness in society today?

▷ At several points before his father's death, Morrison describes himself as 'scared' and 'frightened'. What is it that frightens him about his father's death?

▷ At one point, when Morrison presses his father about his relationship with Beaty, Arthur says he was obsessed. Morrison also seems to be obsessed with the relationship. Why do you think this is so? To what extent is the matter resolved at the conclusion of the book?

▷ Why do you think Morrison decided to write the book? Why do you think he chose the title?

## SUGGESTED FURTHER READING
**FICTION**
▶ *One True Thing* by Anna Quindlan (1994)
**NON-FICTION**
▶ **Paula by Isabel Allende (1995)**
▶ *Iris and Her Friends* by John Bayley (1999)
▶ **Hidden Lives by Margaret Forster (1995)**
▶ *The Shadow Man* by Mary Gordon (1996)
▶ *Remind Me Who I Am, Again* by Linda Grant (1998)
▶ *The Undertaking: Life Studies from the Dismal Trade* by Thomas Lynch (1997)
▶ *On the Death of a Parent* edited by Jane McLaughlin (1994)
▶ *A Voyage Around My Father* by John Mortimer (1971)

## OTHER BOOKS BY BLAKE MORRISON
**FICTION**
▶ *The Justification of Johan Gutenberg* (2000)
▶ *The Yellow House* (children's) (1987)
**NON-FICTION**
▶ *The Cracked Pot* ((1996)
▶ *Pendle Witches*, with Paula Rego (1996)
▶ *As If* (1997)
▶ *Too True* (1998)

# The Hacienda: My Venezuelan Years (1997)

## Lisa St Aubin de Terán

### ABOUT THE BOOK

The bare bones of *The Hacienda* read like the synopsis of a florid romantic novel – beautiful, ethereal schoolgirl is pursued by South American aristocrat, marries him and travels around Europe until she returns with him to his Venezuelan estate. But the reality was far from romantic. Virtually abandoned by her unstable husband and snubbed by his contemptuous relatives, Lisa St Aubin de Terán was left to make her own way in a culture where her every action was closely monitored for social acceptability.

At sixteen St Aubin de Terán found herself pursued by Jaime Terán, twenty years her senior and unable to speak English. They married six months later. On his wedding day Jaime confessed that he was a bank robber. After two years travelling in Europe with his wife and two political refugees, Jaime heard of his pardon and seized the opportunity to return to his beloved *hacienda*.

When the couple arrive in Caracas with their two beagles, St Aubin de Terán finds herself surrounded by a legion of haughty Terán cousins. Shy and wary of her crude Spanish, she silently listens to an endless stream of insulting observations about herself.

At the *hacienda*, they learn that the main house has been rented out as a restaurant. Antonio, the foreman, finds them a dilapidated cottage. Jaime disappears for long periods, leaving his wife without food or company. It takes some time before she can establish a way of getting food. She cannot simply go to the local shop; she is now la Doña and must conform to the intricate code of behaviour expected of her or *qué dirán*, what will people say?

A routine establishes itself. She is visited daily by Antonio's daughter, takes her unruly dogs for walks, and is kept company by a tame vulture. She rarely sees her husband and although she takes comfort in writing to her mother, even this communication is restricted. Her mother is fighting a severe depression and receives an edited account of life on the *hacienda*.

When Antonio's young son is accidentally poisoned, St Aubin de Terán is shocked by the appalling conditions in the local hospital. She establishes a daily dispensary for the *hacienda* workers, sending home for medical books and supplies. She begins to make friends but is still lonely and frightened by Jaime's violent, erratic behaviour.

Much to her surprise and delight she finds that she is pregnant, despite believing herself to be infertile, but the birth is difficult and Iseult is a sickly child. During her pregnancy Antonio suggests that she take control of the *hacienda*.

Jaime can no longer be trusted to make sensible decisions and the workers need someone to respect. Between the two of them they manage to turn the estate around but in 1976 a fifteen-month drought sets in and a downturn begins that cannot be arrested. They finally cease sugar production after 150 years.

Still only twenty-three, St Aubin de Terán is unsure what to do with her future but when Jaime's behaviour becomes so unpredictable that she sleeps with a gun under her pillow, she decides it's time to leave.

## ABOUT THE AUTHOR

Lisa St Aubin de Terán was born in 1953. Her first novel, *Keepers of the House*, won the Somerset Maugham Award in 1982 and was followed by *The Slow Train to Milan*, which won the John Llewelyn Rhys Prize in 1983. She currently lives in London and Italy.

## FOR DISCUSSION

▷ What effect does the dictum '*Qué dirán* – what will people say', which seems to rule all sections of Venezuelan society, have on St Aubin de Terán's life?

▷ 'When I first arrived on the *hacienda*, I felt ashamed.' Why does St Aubin de Terán feel this way? To what extent do you think her shame is justified? How do you think you would have felt in her circumstances?

▷ Venezuelan society seems to be very rigidly structured. What factors make it difficult for St Aubin de Terán to find a niche for herself? What are the differences between English and Venezuelan culture that make life most difficult for her and how does she overcome them?

▷ How does St Aubin de Terán's narrative differ from her letters to her mother? What might account for these differences? What do you learn of her character from the letters?

▷ What are the problems faced by *la gente*? How does St Aubin de Terán try to help? How successful is she?

▷ When St Aubin de Terán is told to get the priest for Capino's burial she writes: 'I was timid, shy and absurdly passive'. To what extent do you agree with her opinion of herself. How does she change during her time at the *hacienda* and what brings about these changes?

▷ Are there particular ways in which St Aubin de Terán finds comfort? If so, what are they and how do they help?

▷ Jaime is an absence rather than a presence for the most part. His violence is rarely referred to although veiled references such as the one to '"the accident" caused by a monumental blow to the top of my head' make it clear that it must have been very frightening. Why do you think she stays for seven years at the *hacienda*? What makes her finally decide to leave and how difficult is this decision?

## SUGGESTED FURTHER READING

▶ *Paula* by Isabel Allende (1995)
▶ *Not a Hazardous Sport* by Nigel Barley (1989)
▶ *Lost in Translation* by Eva Hoffman (1989)

## OTHER BOOKS BY LISA ST AUBIN DE TERÁN
NOVELS
▶ *Keepers of the House* (1982)
▶ *The Slow Train to Milan* (1983)

- *The Tiger* (1984)
- *The Bay of Silence* (1986)
- *Black Idol* (1987)
- *Joanna* (1990)
- *Nocturne* (1992)
- *The Palace* (1997)

**SHORT STORIES**
- *Southpaw* (1999)

**TRAVEL**
- *Off the Rails* (1989)
- *Venice: The Four Seasons* (Mike Lindberg, 1992)
- *A Valley in Italy* (1994)
- *Elements of Italy* (2001)

**AUTOBIOGRAPHY**
- *Memory Map* (2002)

**EDITED**
- *The Virago Book of Wanderlust and Dreams*


## Girlitude: A Memoir of the 50s and 60s (1999)
Emma Tennant

### ABOUT THE BOOK

Following on from *Strangers*, her fictional memoir of her family, Emma Tennant recounts her experiences in the 1950s and 1960s as she finds her way from her wealthy establishment background into the literary, artistic and political circles that were in the vanguard of the 'Sixties Revolution'. Central to the book is her awareness of her seeming inability to pass from a state of 'girlitude' to woman-hood.

The book opens with Tennant's description of a photograph taken in 1955 shortly before her coming-out ball. She is seventeen, lives with her parents and has 'no visible means of support', having left school at fifteen. She belongs to a wealthy family whose import/export business is entailed to her half-brother, Colin.

On the eve of her entry into the 'marriage market', Tennant is infatuated with Rory McEwen, the first in a long string of men who for one reason or another do not return her feelings.

By 1957 she is embroiled in an affair with a man who conducts his dubious financial dealings around London's casinos. The affair ends disastrously in a terminated pregnancy. Tennant swiftly, albeit reluctantly, becomes engaged to Sebastian Yorke, son of the novelist Henry Green, whom she comes to regard as her literary idol. Within a year, she gives birth to a son.

Unable to settle into domesticity, Tennant frequently visits friends in Rome, leaving her husband and son in London. The marriage is short-lived. She continues to travel, flirting with the fantasy of playing First Lady to Gore Vidal's US President, infatuated with the impossibly attractive and unavailable Bruce Chatwin and proposing to Fred Warner, her travelling companion in Greece, who proclaims himself 'too queer' to accept.

Back in London, her finances depleted and her servants' wages unpaid, Tennant takes a job as travel editor for *Queen* magazine but soon becomes disenchanted. Still seeking an escape route she tries out New York but finds it lacking despite making the acquaintance of Andy Warhol and Norman Mailer.

In 1962 she writes her first novel, *The Colour of Rain*. Published under the pseudonym Catherine Aydy, the novel satirizes the 'young marrieds of Kensington', some of whom are sufficiently recognizable for lawyers to be consulted.

Having fallen in love with satire, Tennant becomes involved with the groundbreaking *That Was The Week That Was* team and finds herself married to Christopher Booker of *Private Eye*. Discovering after a very short time that they have little or nothing in common, she makes her escape to Greece for the summer where she meets a beautiful young man called Luc.

When she returns to London she takes a job in the features department at *Vogue* but soon retreats to Wiltshire before joining her parents in Corfu.

Back in London once again, Tennant embraces the 'real' 1960s, allies herself to the *New Left Review*, travels to Cuba and marches through the streets of Paris with Alexander Cockburn in 1968. When she discovers she is pregnant, she and Cockburn marry. Their daughter is born in February 1969.

## ABOUT THE AUTHOR

Emma Tennant was born in London in 1938. She spent much of her childhood in Scotland and was educated at St Paul's Girls' School in London. Her first novel, *The Colour of Rain*, was published in 1964. In the 1970s she founded and edited the literary review *Bananas*, whose contributors included Angela Carter and J. G. Ballard. In 1998 she published *Strangers*, a fictionalized memoir of her family. The first part of her autobiography, *Girlitude*, appeared in 1999 swiftly followed by *Burnt Diaries* which caused something of a stir in the literary world with its revelations of her affair with Ted Hughes.

## FOR DISCUSSION

▷ How does Tennant feel about her family and her background? How does she seem to fit in to the world of debutantes? What seems to be the role of women of Tennant's class background in the 1950s and early 1960s? How do you think their lives differed from other women's?

▷ What does Tennant mean by 'girlitude'? Is it a term that could be applied to young women today? The final sentence of the book reads: 'If I have given birth to a woman, I ponder afterwards, can I at last give up being a girl?' Do you think she can?

▷ How would you describe the young Tennant's character? What factors have contributed to shaping her? What impression do you form of the way Tennant feels about her younger self? She says, 'Yet again I am so unsure of who I am that I don't even know who I'm trying to look like.' Do you think she has a better idea of who she is by the end of the book and, if so, why?

▷ Tennant suggests that the novelist Henry Green, her first husband's father, is rather contemptuous of her own family. How do the two families differ in the way that they live?

▷ Tennant says: 'I shall leave "Mr Booker" – but I don't know yet for whom.' What do you think of this remark? Why is it so difficult for Tennant to contemplate life without a man? What do you make of Tennant's attitude towards men and marriage? Why do you think she is attracted to so many men who are unlikely to return her interest?

▷ How different is the young woman in the photograph Tennant describes at the beginning of the book from the thirty-one-year-old at the end? What are the most important factors in bringing about that change?

▷ Tennant's novels have been described as being written in powerful poetic prose. How would you describe her style in *Girlitude*?

▷ Tennant has described her book *Strangers: A Family Romance* as a fictional memoir of her family, while *Girlitude* is classified as autobiography. Can autobiography be considered to be completely factual?

## SUGGESTED FURTHER READING

▶ *The Ossie Clark Diaries* by Ossie Clark, edited by Lady Henrietta Rous (1998)

▶ *All Dressed Up* by Jonathon Green (1999)

▶ *Hons and Rebels* by Jessica Mitford (1960)

▶ *Hippie Hippie Shake* by Richard Neville (1995)

▶ *Promise of a Dream: Remembering the Sixties* by Sheila Rowbotham (2000)

## OTHER BOOKS BY EMMA TENNANT

### FICTION

▶ *The Colour of Rain* (1964)

▶ *Hotel De Dream* (1976)

▶ *The Bad Sister* (1978)

▶ *Wild Nights* (1979)

▶ *Alice Fell* (1980)

▶ *Woman Beware Woman* (1983)

▶ *The House of Hospitalities* (1987)

▶ *A Wedding of Curiosity* (1988)

▶ *Sisters and Strangers: A Moral Tale* (1990)

▶ *Faustine* (1992)

▶ *Tess* (1993)

▶ *Strangers: A Family Romance* (1998)

▶ *The Ballad of Sylvia and Ted* (2001)

▶ Emma Tennant has written 'sequels' to Jane Austen's *Pride and Prejudice* and *Emma*:

*Pemberley* (1993)

*An Unequal Marriage* (1994)

*Emma in Love* (1999)

### AUTOBIOGRAPHY

▶ *Burnt Diaries* (1999)

▶ *A House in Corfu* (2001)

# Resources

The resources listed below include books, magazines and websites aimed at helping you choose new books and seek out background information such as author profiles, book reviews or historical background, for your discussions. You'll also find several online reading groups listed in the Internet section, together with a directory of more online groups should you want to explore that option further.

## Books

*The Reading Groups Book* by Jenny Hartley (Oxford University Press, 2002). The result of a survey of 350 groups in the UK, Jenny Hartley's book offers an insight into the history of reading groups as well as examining their current popularity. Packed with information on the way groups work, the book includes lots of anecdotes and members' comments plus lists of favourite books.

*The Good Web Guide for Book Lovers* by Susan Osborne (The Good Web Guide, 2003). In spite of theories about the demise of the book and of reading in general after the birth of the Internet, books are thriving on the Web. The author has scoured the Internet to find the best sites for every book lover. Categories include: the best Internet bookshops; rare and specialist bookshops; book clubs; literary magazines; reading group resources; sites for budding writers; author-specific sites and publishers' own websites. www.thegoodwebguide.co.uk

*Good Reading Guide* edited by Nick Rennison (Bloomsbury, 2003).

*Opening the Book* (1996) by Rachel van Riel and Olive Fowler with a foreword by Alan Bennett, obtainable from Opening the Book, 181 Carleton Road, Pontefract, West Yorks WF8 3NH, tel: 01977 602188, fax: 01977 690621, e-mail info@openingthebook.com.

*The Good Fiction Guide*, edited by Jane Rogers, Mike Harris, Douglas Houston, Hermione Lee (Oxford University Press, 2002)

The latter three books are packed with recommendations along the 'if you like that, you'll like this' basis, with the emphasis on modern fiction.

*The Writers' and Artists' Yearbook* (published yearly by A & C Black) lists contact details for UK and Irish publishers. You should be able to find a copy in your local library.

## Magazines

*The Mail on Sunday*'s *You Magazine* hosts an immensely successful reading group. Information can also be found at the *You* Reading Group website (www.you-reading-group.co.uk) which has details of past choices as far back as the group's inception. Selections tend towards literary fiction such as Michael Frayn's *Headlong* and Barbara Kingsolver's *The Poisonwood Bible*, with the occasional foray into biography.

*newBOOKS.mag* is aimed at all readers, with a particular emphasis on reading groups, and includes book extracts, interviews and lots of recommendations contributed by reading group members. The magazine is available in bookshops and libraries or from 15 Scots Drive, Wokingham RG41 3XF, email: guypringle@waitrose.com.

*Waterstone's Books Quarterly* includes a wide selection of articles together with reviews of over 100 new books per quarter and is available at all branches of Waterstone's.

## The Internet

The Internet is an excellent place to research background information to bring to discussions, book reviews and articles about books. There are lots of online reading groups and although these haven't taken off in the UK to quite the extent that they have in the US, there's nothing to stop you engaging in a transatlantic exchange of views.

www.bbc.co.uk/arts/bigread

This site offers information and quizzes on the UK's favourite books, as well as links to a searchable database of reading groups in the UK and several resources for readers.

www.bedfordstmartins.com/litlinks

This is a useful site for readers seeking advice on developing a more critical approach to reading.

www.bloomsbury.com

As well as a reading groups section, which includes a notice board and discussion forum, Bloomsbury's website offers a reading club, online courses, author profiles and a calendar of literary events.

www.bookbrowse.com

The Bookbrowse website contains a growing bank of book extracts supplemented by press reviews, author interviews and, in some cases, readers' guides, covering a range of books by popular literary authors, from Jane Hamilton and Alice Hoffman to Nick Hornby and Michael Crichton. This is an American site but many of the books featured are available in the UK.

www.bookcouncil.org.nz

Set up by the New Zealand Book Council, this site has a special section aimed at reading groups which includes a notice board and a set of reading group guides devoted to New Zealand authors.

www.booktrust.org.uk

Founded in 1926, Booktrust is a charity set up to promote reading and literacy in the UK. As well as a wide range of information on the book world, from the latest publications to announcements of literary prize winners, the Booktrust website includes a small section devoted to reading groups called Bookmates. Booktrust can also be contacted at Book House, 45 East Hill, London SW18 2QZ, tel: 020 8516 2977, fax: 020 8516 2978.

www.britishcouncil.org/arts/literature/festivals

The British Council have set up a handy database of literature festivals throughout the UK, complete with dates and contact details.

www.guardianunlimited.co.uk/books

The books pages of *The Guardian*'s website offer an excellent source of information for readers and reading groups. Alongside the usual articles and reviews the site has a database of information on a wide range of authors, from Peter Ackroyd to Emile Zola, plus a growing selection of first chapters and book extracts to dip into. It also hosts a lively online reading group, with monthly choices ranging from Margaret Atwood's *Edible Woman* to Dostoevsky's *Crime and Punishment*.

www.harpercollins.co.uk

HarperCollins's website has lots of author interviews, a database of author information including contact details, and book extracts.

www.oprah.com

Oprah Winfrey can claim some credit for the phenomenal rise of reading groups in the US and her monthly book choices have all become instant bestsellers. Although she has announced that she will no longer be recommending monthly book choices on her show, Oprah's website still has information about past choices, ranging from Toni Morrison's *Song of Solomon* to Joyce Carol Oates's *We Were the Mulvaneys*. Lots of background material is provided for each choice and online discussions continue to be as passionate as ever.

www.penguin.co.uk

As well as articles, book extracts and author profiles, Penguin's website also has a lively readers' group section which includes a notice board plus a reading group directory to help groups get in touch with each other.

www.readinggroupguides.com

Frequently updated American website containing a wide range of readers' guides, interviews with reading group members, links to other reading groups sites and, to round it all off, a monthly recipe.

www.whichbook.net

Book Forager offers a novel way to choose your next book. Its starting point is your mood, taste or particular interest rather than titles and authors.

www.word-of-mouth.org.uk

Lots of recommendations from fellow readers with a brief description of the book and why it was chosen. You can add your own recommendations and join in the discussion forum.

http://dir.clubs.yahoo.com/Entertainment___Arts/Humanities/Books_and_Writing/Reading_Groups

A well-organized directory of online reading groups.

http://library.christchurch.org.nz/Guides/IfYouLike

Part of New Zealand's Christchurch City Libraries' website, this is an excellent site for recommendations along the 'If you like this you'll like . . .' lines.

## Radio

Radio 4 is an excellent source of information on books, from *Start the Week* to the early evening arts review *Front Row*, which includes coverage of events in the book world. Three programmes are likely to be of particular interest for reading group members.

*The Radio 4 Bookclub*, hosted by Jim Naughtie, is broadcast monthly and, where possible, features the author of the current book choice in conversation with reading group members from around the country. Details of both the current choice and previous choices can be found on the Internet at www.bbc.co.uk/education/bookcase/bookclub.

*A Good Read* is an occasional series in which the presenter plus two guests each nominate a favourite book to discuss. Choices are often a little outside the mainstream and the resulting discussions are lively, enthusiastic and often inspiring.

*Open Book* is a weekly programme featuring author interviews, discussions and a round-up of new fiction and non-fiction paperbacks.

## Readers' guides

A few publishers publish free readers' guide leaflets for a selection of their books. You may be able to find these in your local bookshop or you can contact the publisher direct.

Guides for a selection of Vintage and Arrow books can be obtained from the marketing department at Random House, 20 Vauxhall Bridge Road, London SW1V 2SA, tel: 020 7840 8400, fax: 020 7233 8791, email: readingguides@randomhouse.co.uk. Some guides are also available at the Random House website www.randomhouse.co.uk.

Transworld publishes guides for a selection of Black Swan and Corgi books. They can be obtained from the marketing department at Transworld Publishers, 61–63 Uxbridge Road, London W5 5SA, tel: 020 8579 2652, fax: 020 8579 5479. Some guides are also available at the Transworld website www.booksat transworld.co.uk.

Readers' guides for a range of books published by Bloomsbury can be obtained from their marketing department at Bloomsbury Publishing, 38 Soho Square, London W1D 3HB, tel: 020 7494 211, fax: 020 7434 0151. Printable versions of the guides are also available via www.bloomsbury.com.

## Other

Bradford Library is leading the way in providing information and resources for both reading groups and individual readers at their Readers' Days events. Panel discussions, workshops, quizzes and author events make for a lively and entertaining day with lots of group participation. For further information contact Tom Palmer at Central Library, Prince's Way, Bradford, West Yorkshire BD1 1NN, or email tom.palmer@bradford.gov.uk.

Bradford City Library also publishes a leaflet, *The Booklover's Guide to the Internet*, which can be obtained by sending a first-class SAE to Tom Palmer at the above address or viewed online at www.reader2reader.co.uk.

*The Reading Group Toolbox*, a joint development between Opening the Book and Waterstone's, contains lots of ideas for developing lively discussions and keeping a reading group going. It can be obtained from the Reading Group Toolbox Co-ordinator, Waterstone's CLS, 14 Brewery Road, King's Cross, London N7 9NH, tel: 0207 619 7500, fax: 0207 609 6635. It's also worth asking your local library whether they have one you can look at.

# Suggested Further Reading

If you've enjoyed the fifty books featured in this guide, the following fifty (in addition to the other books suggested for further reading in the readers' guides) also come highly recommended both as 'good reads' and as material for lively group discussions.

**Fiction**
- *The Anatomist* by Federico Andahazi (1997)
- *A Recipe for Bees* by Gail Anderson-Dargatz (1998)
- *The Hero's Walk* by Anita Rau Badami (2001)
- *The Kindness of Women* by J.G. Ballard (1991)
- *The Girls' Guide to Hunting and Fishing* by Melissa Bank (1999)
- *K-Pax* by Gene Brewer (1995)
- *The Swimmer* by Bill Broady (2000)
- *Audrey Hepburn's Neck* by Alan Brown (1996)
- *If I Told You Once* by Judy Budnitz (2000)
- *Girl with a Pearl Earring* by Tracy Chevalier (2000)
- *Arcadia* by Jim Crace (1992)
- *Flying to Nowhere* by John Fuller (1983)
- *The Pirate's Daughter* by Robert Girardi (1997)
- *Dogs Days, Glen Miller Nights* by Laurie Graham (2000)
- *The Cast Iron Shore* by Linda Grant (1996)
- *Plainsong* by Kent Haruf (1999)
- *The Fall of a Sparrow* by Robert Hellenga (1998)
- *The Drink and Dream Teahouse* by Justin Hill (2001)
- *Underground* by Tobias Hill (1999)
- *Amaryllis Night and Day* by Russell Hoban (2001)
- *The Prince of West End Avenue* by Alan Isler (1994)
- *The Mighty Walzer* by Howard Jacobson (1999)
- *The Underground Man* by Mick Jackson (1997)
- *Boxy an Star* by Daren King (1999)
- *Intimacy* by Hanif Kureishi (1998)
- *Mr Phillips* by John Lanchester (2000)
- *The Inn at the Lake Devine* by Elinor Lipman (1998)
- *Homestead* by Rosina Lippi (1998)
- *Heat Wave* by Penelope Lively (1996)
- *So Long, See You Tomorrow* by William Maxwell (1997)
- *Ghostwritten* by David Mitchell (1999)
- *Broke Heart Blues* by Joyce Carol Oates (1999)
- *Day of Atonement* by Jay Rayner (1998)
- *This is My Daughter* by Roxanna Robinson (1998)
- *The Fig Eater* by Jody Shields (2000)
- *The Map of Love* by Ahdaf Soueif (1999)
- *Felicia's Journey* by William Trevor (1994)
- *Bless the Thief* by Alan Wall (1997)
- *Almost Heaven* by Marianne Wiggins (1998)
- *East Bay Grease* by Eric Miles Williamson (1999)

**Non-fiction**
- *Café Europa* by Slavenka Drakulić (1996)
- *Almost Heaven* by Martin Fletcher (1998)
- *Bury Me Standing* by Isabel Fonseca (1995)
- *Younghusband* by Patrick French (1994)
- *Rodinsky's Room* by Rachel Lichenstein and Iain Sinclair (1999)
- *The Snow Leopard* by Peter Matthiessen (1979)
- *Midnight in Sicily* by Peter Robb (1996)
- *Touching the Void* by Joe Simpson (1988)
- *No Place Like Home* by Gary Yonge (1999)
- *An Intimate History of Humanity* by Theodore Zeldin (1994)

# Index

**Bold** page numbers indicate main references